WOMEN RESISTING VIOLENCE

Spirituality for Life

Edited by

**Mary John Mananzan, Mercy Amba Oduyoye, Elsa Tamez,
J. Shannon Clarkson, Mary C. Grey, Letty M. Russell**

ORBIS BOOKS

Maryknoll, New York 10545

Published by Orbis Books, Maryknoll, NY 10545-0308 in cooperation with the Institute of Women's Studies, St. Scholastica's College, P.O. Box 3153, Manila, Philippines

Published by Orbis Books, Maryknoll, NY 10545-0308
Manufactured in the United States of America

Library of Congress Cataloging-in-Publication Data

Women resisting violence : spirituality of life / edited by Mary John
    Mananzan . . . [et al.].
        p.   cm.
    Proceedings of a conference held Dec. 7-12, 1994, in San José,
Costa Rica.
    Includes bibliographical references.
    ISBN 1-57075-080-7 (alk. paper)
    1. Women—Social conditions—Congresses.   2. Women—Crimes
against—Congresses.   3. Sex discrimination against women—
Congresses.   4. Patriarchy—Congresses.   5. Feminist theology—
Congresses.   6. Liberation theology—Congresses.   I. Mananzan,
Mary John.
HQ1106.W636   1996
305.42—dc20   96-22683
                                                      CIP

To
SUN AI LEE PARK

CONTENTS

PART THREE
ECONOMIC AND MILITARY VIOLENCE

PART FOUR
WOMEN'S STRUGGLE FOR LIFE

EDITORS AND CONTRIBUTORS

Denise M. Ackermann, Professor of Practical Theology, University of the Western Cape, Cape Town, South Africa.

Elizabeth Amoah, Lecturer, Department of the Study of Religions, University of Ghana, Legon-Accra, Ghana.

María Pilar Aquino, Assistant Professor of Theological and Religious Studies, University of San Diego, San Diego, California, U.S.A.

Stella Baltazar, Teacher, Britto Convent, Sathyamangalam, Tamil Nadu, South India.

Chung Hyun Kyung, Professor of Theology, Ewha Women's University, Seoul, Korea.

J. Shannon Clarkson, Assistant Professor of Education, Quinnipiac College, Hamden, Connecticut, U.S.A.

Mary C. Grey, Professor of Contemporary Theology, University of Southampton, Southampton, United Kingdom.

Ada María Isasi-Díaz, Associate Professor of Ethics and Theology, Drew University, Madison, New Jersey, U.S.A.

Ursula King, Professor and Head of the Department of Theology and Religious Studies, University of Bristol, Bristol, United Kingdom.

Mary John Mananzan, Director, Institute of Women's Studies, St. Scholastica's College, Manila, Philippines; International Coordinator, EATWOT Women's Commission.

Mercy Amba Oduyoye, Former Deputy General Secretary of the World Council of Churches; Former Faculty Staff of University of Ibadan, Nigeria.

Marlene Perera, Asian Coordinator of EATWOT, Colombo, Sri Lanka.

Rosemary Radford Ruether, Georgia Harkness Professor of Applied Theology, Garrett-Evangelical Theological Seminary, Evanston, Illinois, U.S.A.

Letty M. Russell, Professor of Theology, Yale University Divinity School, New Haven, Connecticut, U.S.A.

Elisabeth Schüssler Fiorenza, Krister Stendahl Professor of Divinity, Harvard University Divinity School, Cambridge, Massachusetts, U.S.A.

Elsa Tamez, President, Professor of Theology, Seminario Biblico Latino-americano, San Jose, Costa Rica.

Susan Brooks Thistlethwaite, Professor of Theology and Culture, Director, Center for Theology, Ethics, and the Human Sciences, Chicago Theological School, Chicago, Illinois, U.S.A.

Reinhild Traitler-Espiritu, Director, Protestant Academy, Boldern, Zurich, Switzerland.

PROLOGUE

Mary John Mananzan

It was a historic event when forty-five women theologians from fourteen countries convened in San Jose, Costa Rica, on December 7-12,1994, to have a dialogue on the theme *Spirituality for Life: Women Struggling against Violence*. This was the culmination of a process which started in Geneva in 1983, when the Women's Commission of the Ecumenical Association of Third World Theologians (EATWOT) was established.[1]

EATWOT had been established in 1976, but it was only at the General Assembly in New Delhi in 1981 that the gender issue came to the forefront of the discussion. This was occasioned by the opening prayer of Jaquelyn Grant calling on God as Father and Mother, which provoked heated discussions. Moreover, the plea of Marianne Katoppo for inclusive language met with trivializing jokes and comments. It became clear to the women members of the Association that the gender issue must be addressed in the organization and that a theologizing from the perspective of women must be developed. The surfacing of this issue was called by Mercy Oduyoye an "irruption within an irruption."[2]

It was not until the International Dialogue between EATWOT theologians and First World theologians in Geneva in 1983 that this aspiration could be realized.[3] The women participants in that Dialogue met and established the Women's Commission, with the task of developing liberation theology from the perspective of Third World women. Regional coordinators were named who were to work with the then General Secretary, Virginia Fabella. The Asian coordinator was the pioneering Asian feminist theologian, the Rev. Sun Ai Lee Park. As founder and editor of *In God's Image* from 1982 until 1995, Sun Ai Lee Park has worked tirelessly for the development of the women's network in Asia and in EATWOT. Although failing health made it impossible for her to be with us in Costa Rica, her tireless energy and strong spirit was very much among us and we wish to dedicate this volume to her.

It was decided that the process would consist of the following phases: national consultations, regional consultations, intercontinental consultations, and international dialogue with First World feminist theologians. The first three phases were realized with the Intercontinental Meeting held at Oaxtepec, Mexico, in 1986. In this meeting, the Women's Commission was decentralized, and

1

each region did its own projects independently of the others. Having no central coordination, it was difficult to implement the fourth phase of the process.

In the General Assembly of EATWOT in Nairobi in January 1992 it was a unanimous decision to re-activate the international coordination of the Women's Commission. It was therefore re-organized with an international coordinator as well as regional coordinators. Even before the Nairobi assembly, a preparatory team had met to plan the international dialogue. The Nairobi assembly finalized the theme of the dialogue and assigned the Women's Commission to launch the same process of national, regional, and intercontinental consultations on the theme and then finally to bring about the international dialogue with the First World feminist theologians.

The Women's Commission met in Brussels, Belgium, in April 1992 to draw out the program for the intercontinental meeting of EATWOT women theologians as well as the International Dialogue that would be held in San Jose, Costa Rica. A team composed of the international coordinator, a European coordinator, and a North American coordinator was formed. They met in Miami in February 1993 to plan the agenda and to form the local organizing committee in Costa Rica. In the course of the preparation, the participation in the dialogue was expanded to include women theologians from Eastern Europe, Japan, South Africa, the Pacific, and Palestine.

After two years' preparation, the long-awaited dialogue finally took place in December 1994, and this book is the documentation of that memorable event. We were not able to include all the papers and the proceedings of the group discussions. Therefore, the book is limited to the keynote addresses and the papers on the different forms of violence against women. Violence against women must be viewed in the context of the atmosphere of violence in society. The many forms of violence were thus elucidated in panel discussions that were stimulated by a topic paper on a particular form of violence and a theological reflection on it.

In Part One on cultural and ecological violence Elsa Tamez discusses cultural violence in the Latin American context. According to her, the liberation theologians did not treat culture with sufficient depth until the 1990s. The interaction with Asian and African theologians has contributed to the realization of the importance of culture. Elsa tackles the question of cultural violence against women on three levels, namely: the basis of violence against women in one's own culture; the elements in one's own culture that have to be safeguarded or reclaimed in order to keep one's identity; and the imposition of foreign patriarchal culture on one's own culture. She supports the proposal of Musimbi Kanyoro to develop a "cultural hermeneutic" that would distinguish what is liberating and what is oppressive in one's own culture [17].[4] She suggests strategies for struggle against cultural violence which include: cultural critique of our own traditions; international dialogue with mutual respect; international alliances among women against the imposition of patriarchal foreign culture; the development of a non-discriminatory Christian theological discourse, and of a theological praxis of transformed relationship between women and men.

In response to Elsa's article, Letty Russell treats the theme of cultural violence in the context of the international dialogue itself, where the women felt what Letty describes as "a tense truce between women of different colors, cultures, and political realities"[20]. However, the very same gathering showed the possibility of intercultural dialogue despite differences, especially on the global phenomenon of violence against women, which cuts across class, race, creed, and nationality. The struggle against violence, according to Letty, is not just one topic of feminist liberation theology. It belongs to its core topic. A spirituality for life is imperative in the resistance against cultural violence. The cultivation of such a spirituality calls for a cultural hermeneutic, cultural sharing, and cultural transformation. The work of feminist liberation theologians contributes to the task of transformation, which can come only from resistance, interpretation, and shared action, which should result in the reshaping of culture that affirms life-giving values and spirituality.

Ecological violence is a relatively new issue in the agenda of social activists. As a counter-movement to ecological violence, Rosemary Radford Ruether advocates ecofeminism. She discusses the different levels of the ecofeminist analysis—the cultural-symbolic level, the socio-economic level—and then relates to these the impact of religion, particularly of the Hebrew-Christian tradition. She issues a very important warning: "An ecofeminism which is not primarily a mystical (mystified) and recreational escapism for a privileged western female elite must make concrete connections with women at the bottom of the socio-economic system"[31]. She considers the feminist theologian as the artisan of a new ecofeminist culture and spirituality, and for this important task, she suggests two patterns of biblical thought as resources: covenantal ethics, which emphasizes the interwovenness of all creation, and sacramental cosmology, which recognizes the sacredness of the cosmos. In the creation of the new culture, all traditions of East and West as well as the indigenous heritage have to be harnessed.

Part Two opens its discussion of domestic and physical violence with a formidable array of statistical citations of cases of violence against women, presented by Elisabeth Schüssler Fiorenza's article on domestic violence. Then follows a penetrating and comprehensive analysis of the root causes of this phenomenon. Patriarchal *kyriarchy* is the term Elisabeth uses to describe the overarching system of elite male domination that prevails in society and that gives rise to this phenomenon: "Violence against women constitutes the heart of kyriarchal oppression"[45]. She points to four disciplinary practices of kyriarchal culture and religion that perpetuate women's victimization: the prescription of the "ideal feminine body," the conditioning of a "docile female body," "the display of the feminine body as an ornamental surface," and the erotization and sexualization of male domination and female submission [46]. In spite of its avowed condemnation of violence against women, mainline theological and religious discourse, in its advocacy of the kyriarchal politics of submission and its glorification of suffering, reinforces rather than puts an end to the victimization of women and children. To stop its collusion with kyriarchal violence, Christian theologies must help to formulate an ethos and politics of meaning that "can engender resistance to all forms of victimization and foster responsibility for changing structures and discourses that produce suffering, violence, and murder"[51].

Stella Baltazar, in her response, draws deeply from her Christian as well as Hindu heritage. She picks up Fiorenza's term, "patri-kyriarchy," and shows its concrete manifestations in the Bible and in Hindu practices. She recognizes, however, that the very same sources provide liberating elements. She re-reads the story of Martha and Mary to heal the dichotomy between contemplation and action and cites the examples of Indian women who have redefined their roles in a liberating way—for example, the women of Chittoor area who prevented a bloody war; Mallika Sarabai, an Indian classical dancer who challenged the figure of Rama; the Chipko women who defended the forests by embracing the trees doomed to be felled. In a sentence which shows the integration of her Christian faith and her Indian experience, Stella states: "The question for us is not how to make Jesus become a woman. Rather, the transcended Christ can be the embodiment of the feminine principle, the Shakti, the energizer and vitalizer"[64]. These reinterpretations of the Scripture as well as the reclaiming of one's cultural roots could be potent forces in breaking through the patri-kyriarchal culture that perpetuates violence against women.

From domestic violence, the discussion was further focused on violence against woman's body. Reinhild Traitler cites poignant, sometimes shocking, testimonies of women who have suffered violence coming from different races, nationalities, and cultures. Common to these stories are the facts that the perpetrators are often people the women know and trust; the violence is supported by cultural customs; and the violence results in a physical and psychological subjugation which places the control of the woman's body more firmly in the hand of the aggressor. Reinhild points out the close connection between violence on woman's body and male control of her sexuality: "Since patriarchy has constructed woman's body as a sexual body, violence against women's bodies is almost always violence against women's sexuality"[69]. In the struggle against this violence, women need to deconstruct the "body" that is the product of male fantasy and then reconstruct it on their own terms, taking into account not only sexual differences, but also social, economic, and cultural differences that have shaped women's bodies. A new paradigm of power has to be established where women claim authority over their lives and bodies, proclaiming their bodies as intrinsically good and beautiful and claiming their right to bodily integrity, health, and well-being.

The African culture is the context of Elizabeth Amoah's discussion of violence against woman's body. She describes male control of woman's body in different forms: female circumcision, dress code, marital practices, physical and psychological battering, reproductive laws and customs, prostitution, use of women's bodies in the smuggling of drugs, sexist advertisements, violent subjugation of so-called witches, etc. Amidst these multiple forms of violence to women's bodies, Elizabeth cites as signs of hope the growing number of women who are "challenging the dominant stereotypes and are breaking new ground in expressing options that emphasize and enhance their dignity, self-respect, and autonomy"[85].

In Part Three on economic and military violence Ada María Isasi-Díaz and María Pilar Aquino tackle the question of economic violence from their respective contexts; the former from the perspective of a cultural minority group in the United States (in the belly of the beast, so to speak), and the latter from a Latin American perspective. Both show the exploitative and oppressive effects of the neo-liberal capitalist economy, patriarchal social relations, and present-day colonialism. In the elaboration of a theological discourse which seeks to contribute to the elimination of economic violence against women, María Pilar discusses several factors. First of all, the self-understanding of the theological agenda by women of the South calls for the reappropriation of one's own power and self-esteem and the conscious intervention in women's social movements that seek justice and integrity for all. Second, considering the complexity of the current social phenomena, there must also be an acceptance of the diverse social strategies and practices for change. Third, there is the urgency to criticize rigorously today's neo-liberal capitalism, its civilization model, its predatory logic, and the consequences of all these in the growing sexual, racial, and social inequalities[105]. There is a resonance of these ideas in Third World women living in First World societies because as Ada María expresses it, "most of the strategies of exploitation and domination that the USA uses in Third World countries are first 'practiced' on us, the minority groups in the USA"[89].

From the ethnic violence that is going on in Sri Lanka, Marlene Perera shows how women are caught up in war situations and become prey to rape, sexual slavery, torture, genocide, and other forms of gender-specific violence. She shows the relationship of militarization and the globalization of the economy. Military force and repressive laws are used to promote foreign industries and investments. She calls for a mobilization of world opinion towards a lasting and constructive peace that is based on fundamental, constructive, and comprehensive actions that address the root causes of the problem.

In her article Susan Thistlethwaite shows how militarism constructs an understanding of body and sexuality, economics, race/ethnicity, and culture in a way that gives rise to the sex industry, commodification of woman's body, violent racism, and genocide. She denounces a "culture of double speak" where the reversal of values leads to a culture of death. It is imperative to delegitimize militarism and its construction of these realities. It is equally important to reconstruct the human person as "destined for community with God and with one another"[125].

In Part IV the writers turn to women's resources in the struggle for life. Chung Hyun Kyung, the keynote speaker from the Third World, takes the story of Soo-Bock, a Korean "comfort woman," as a starting point for her powerful feminist reflections on victimization of women. With deep empathy she traces the harrowing experiences of the "comfort women" obliged by the Japanese military to serve as sexual slaves during World War II. She then discusses the four factors which made the cruel system possible: the emperor state of Japan, colonialism, capitalism, and patriarchy. The fate of the "comfort women" of the past is continued in the prostituted women in many countries of Asia today in the context of tourism. Indeed, after the series of wars in Asia, Asia has become the "brothel of the world"[136].

She expresses impatience and even despair at seeing the futility of the women's movement in stopping violence against women. She marvels at how women who have been so degraded and humiliated have in them the power and strength to survive and to live meaningful lives afterwards. She feels that beyond theoretical analysis and organized mass movement, there is need for the "more" that is expressed in the words Ki, Chi, Shakti, prana, Tao. This mysterious female power, which she is still seeking to understand, already feels like something "growing in my womb"[139].

In response to Hyun Kyung's article, Denise Ackermann calls attention to the feelings of Japanese women about the matter. This is a hitherto unreflected side of the "comfort woman" issue. This reflection was occasioned by the presence of Hisako Kinukawa, a Japanese feminist theologian, who, as Hyun Kyung described the interminable sufferings of the comfort women, dropped her head into her hands and wept. Denise describes the encounter of these two women: "Two women from very different contexts: the one speaking for the oppressed and violated, the other wrestling with belonging to the oppressors; one speaking, the other listening and then responding in vulnerability"[142]. In Soo-Bock's story, Denise highlights the intermingling forces of risk, hope, and struggle that constitute a spirituality for life in the face of overwhelming odds.

Ursula King was the keynote speaker from the First World. She takes the European context as the grounding of her reflection on violence against women and her own personal story of being born in a country at war, the experience of material and cultural deprivation, the unsettling experiences of an immigrant in a foreign country, and later on, the experience of discrimination as a woman in a theological seminary. She asks whether the discourse about violence and resistance truly empowers, or whether it is more often a debilitating discourse. She expresses preference for a focus on the positive resources and possibilities for change to enable women to go from "victimization and violence to a vision of strength and empowerment"[148]. She defines a spirituality of life not only as merely struggling to survive, for "it is also the tremendous effort to live a fuller, more abundant, richer and more meaningful human life"[154].

In response to Ursula, Mercy Amba Oduyoye affirms many statements that apply to the situation of African women, such as spirituality taken as the struggle for life, its effort and pain to produce and bring life into the world, and its being a force for survival and transformation. Mercy provides concrete examples of how African women's spirituality of resistance has helped them in the context of the violence suffered by Africa as a whole because of racism and economic exploitation. She expresses the solidarity that African women seek from global sisterhood, claiming their "rightful space to say our own word"[170]. Although she agrees with Ursula to avoid militaristic violent language, she asserts that often the language of struggle and resistance "is the only language that penetrates the barricades of the powers of domination"[170]. She believes that the work of transformation and renewing the face of the earth calls for working with men who also seek life and justice for all.

These chapters contain much of the rich and thought-provoking input that stimulated animated discussions at our meeting. What cannot be documented here is the communion achieved by creative, innovative, and colorful women's celebrations where differences were acknowledged but transcended in the sincere and intense longing for sisterhood in the face of a common suffering. One can also not capture the atmosphere of gaiety of planned and unplanned "happy hours" where the theologians shed their academic dignity and became like little children just frolicking and having fun discovering the holiness of spontaneity and the sanctity of a sense of humor.

The International Dialogue was a breakthrough. Although it was the culmination of a process, it was likewise the beginning of a new phase of global networking as women work together in creating liberating theologies. The process of editing the book was itself part of this networking. The editors met in person and by fax and phone to further the work of resisting violence. The publication work itself was made possible by the able assistance of Salli Clarke and Maria Malkiewicz at the computer and in the library. Our thanks to them is multiplied as we remember the many ways that Sue Perry, our editor at Orbis Books, accompanied us as we carried out our halting plan for global editing.

NOTES

[1] Virginia Fabella and Sergio Torres, eds., *Doing Theology in a Divided World* (Maryknoll: Orbis Books, 1985). Unless otherwise indicated, Scripture quotations are from the New Revised Standard Version of the Bible, copyright 1989 by the Division of Christian Education of the National Council of Churches of Christ in the U.S.A.

[2] Virginia Fabella, *Beyond Bonding: A Third World Women's Theological Journey* (Manila, Philippines: Ecumenical Association of Third World Theologians and the Institute of Women's Studies, 1993), 93. This book is a description of the history of women's participation in EATWOT.

[3] Fabella provides a description of the use of the term "Third World" in EATWOT. "The Third World is marked by economic, political, cultural, racial, gender and/or other forms of oppression; it is the underside of affluence and dominance." The countries of the "North," or First World, have been associated with this affluence and dominance and were formerly joined by the Second World countries belonging to the former Soviet Bloc. "Third World" is used in EATWOT to refer to oppressed persons regardless of their geographical location. (Ibid., 3-4.)

[4] Musimbi Kanyoro, "Cultural Hermeneutics: An African Contribution" in *Women's Visions: Theological Reflection, Celebration, Action*, ed. Ofelia Ortega (Geneva: WCC, 1995), 18-28. Brackets in the text indicate cross-references to other articles in the present volume.

Part One

CULTURAL AND ECOLOGICAL VIOLENCE

CULTURAL VIOLENCE AGAINST WOMEN IN LATIN AMERICA

Elsa Tamez

Feminist liberation theology in Latin America appeared only at the end of the decade of the 1970s and was consolidated in the 1980s. It is a feminist liberation theology because it was born from and with liberation theology and embraced its method. That is to say, it reflects about faith from the standpoint of the reality of oppression, and it aims towards the transformation of that reality. This theology starts its reflection from the double or triple oppression of women (because of gender, poverty, and/or race), and it tries to gather and recognize women's aspirations as those of persons of dignity and worth. Latin American feminist theology rejects the patriarchal model in society and in the church, and advocates the construction of new relationships between men and women in their common reality. At present, it is seeking feminist theories, reconstructing its identity, renewing inter-human relationships, and reading the Bible and theological formulations in an inclusive way.

Until the decade of the 1990s, this theology responded to the Latin American women by focusing its attention on the suffering and struggles of marginalized women: their poverty and resistance against the blows of an exploitative, oppressive, and repressive society. The revolutionary movements, the grassroots organizations, and the struggle against the dictatorships made the recognition of women as beings capable of being actors and subjects of history possible. This led, in many cases, to women becoming aware of the injustices brought by a patriarchal society and not just by a capitalistic one. From the late 1970s to the beginning of the 1980s, a two-fold struggle was launched against a social situation of economic and political oppression and against a machistic, sexist ideology which imposed degrading identities on women. The ideological polarization and the anti-imperialist struggle did not allow for a dialogue between feminists of the rich and poor countries. The Latin American feminists who did not struggle against imperialism but centered their efforts on the vindication of women were generally isolated from the grassroots movements and the popular women's movements.

On the domestic scene, women were abused, beaten, and violated. This violence could be found within the people's movements as well, movements which were seeking societal changes. Regrettably, this situation of violence was continually relativized by the urgent political, economic, and global struggles. Violence against women was criticized only within the close circles of the home, friends, and political groups.

Up until the 1990s the dimensions of culture were generally not treated in depth at any level. That was considered the specific task of anthropologists. Perhaps this was because the grassroots movement was composed mainly of mestizos, whose culture was a mixture of the values of the whites and of ancient traditions. There was also the influence of certain social sciences, coming especially from Europe, which were limited with respect to cultural and anthropological interpretations. At any rate, culture was not viewed as important by most of the ideologists of the struggle.

The interaction of our theologians with Africa and Asia, encouraged by EATWOT, has helped us in a significant way to recognize the importance of culture. We must admit, though, that this was viewed as a problem in our continent. Already in 1985 in Latin America, the blacks had posed the problem of the racist culture, and that same year women began to question more radically those cultural values which are patriarchal.[1]

In this essay I will begin with my understanding of culture, its positive and negative values, what is implied by pluralism of cultures and the attitudes we should take with respect to them. After discussing myths as a basis for cultural violence against women, I will end with some proposals for developing a cultural hermeneutic.

DISTINGUISHING LEVELS OF LATIN AMERICAN CULTURES

By *culture* I mean the customs, attitudes, and worldviews practiced consciously or unconsciously by a society. Generally, the customs proceed from traditions and, by force of habit, they become normal and part of the natural order. Whoever steps outside of tradition is censured and punished for breaking the rules. But there are other habits or attitudes which do not come from one's own tradition. Rather, they proceed from other cultures which in some historical moment were generally imposed by force. When two cultures become mixed, a greater value is placed on the one with more prestige.

Enough studies have already been made on this "culture of oppression" of culture. Many women, especially mestizos and white, have denounced the communications media, the educational system, discrimination in the workplace, and domestic violence. They reject the false identity imposed on them by society and all the diffusion media. These women live the process of breaking down and building up the identity of woman as a person of dignity and worth. I am not going to spend any time on the "culture of oppression," promoted especially by advertisements; I am going to refer, first of all, to our own customs in the different cultures of Latin America.

There are also other attitudes which become cultural, but which proceed neither from ancient tradition nor from another culture. Instead, they are constructed externally by economic interests in order to strengthen these interests. Since the 1950s, the economic development of Latin America, manipulated by and dependent on the international economic order, has been creating a culture of despair.[2] Perhaps, at this level, it should not be called "culture," but instead, the "anticulture" of despair. This has already been denounced sufficiently by the women's movement. Then there is the patriarchal capitalistic level which constructs gender identities prejudicial to women. I am going to refer above all to the first two levels mentioned above.

The first level is made up of indigenous and black cultures, and the second and third levels are made up of the mestizo-white culture.[3] This last imposes itself as a hegemony over the indigenous and black cultures, and at the same time it is permeated with and dominated by the cultural values of the rich countries (third level).

If we are going to talk about cultural violence against women, we have to do it on at least three levels. We have already said that generally we talk about safeguarding our cultural values in order to keep our identity in the face of the invasion of other cultures whose interests are domination and exploitation. But, up to now, we have not talked about the values inherent in our own culture which form the basis for violence against women. As women we cannot deceive ourselves by saying that everything that comes from outside is bad, and everything that belongs to our own culture is good. We know that in all cultures there are ambiguities and that there are negative and positive elements in the same culture. A struggle against violence toward women has to place its analysis within its own culture and in relation to the foreign patriarchal imposition of other cultures. If this is not done, we deceive ourselves, because all cultures, in one form or another, to a greater or lesser degree, have legitimized the power of men over women, and this has generated the violence of the superior against the subordinate, who is considered inferior. This violence is, in turn, doubled when one culture dominates another.

MYTHS AS THE BASIS FOR CULTURAL VIOLENCE AGAINST WOMEN

One way of beginning a critique of the cultural violence within one's own culture would be an analysis of the myths which form the basis of society, and this without ignoring the fact that the evolution of the means of production, through various modes of exploitation, has conditioned the oppression of women.[4] Milagros Palma, in her book, *La Mujer es uno cuento, simbolica mitico-religiosa de la feminidad aborigen y mestizo* (Woman is a unique story, the mythical religious symbolism of aboriginal and mestizo femininity), brings to light the unconscious contents of the values of society with respect to women.

For this author, violence is the basis of the creation of woman.[5] She proves this with an analysis of several myths of the aborigines of the Amazon which shows a struggle between man and woman (when a sexualized human being did not yet exist) and the triumph of man over the sexuality of woman. In several myths, there appears the image of a vagina with teeth which man destroys to assure his supremacy (p.12). To subdue the original woman, who rejected her maternal vocation,[6] man has to use subterfuge. Various myths relate different deceptions: some in order to cut the teeth of the vulva, others to rob her of the design of her vagina, which is the seat of her power; others detail flute-making, which fulfills the same function as fertilizing the woman (p.13). Another deception is to make her pregnant and to tame her in this way. Let us look at two myths, one which belongs to the Letuamas and Macunas of the Amazonas, and the other to the Suna natives.[7]

The first myth recounts that in the beginning women were stronger than men. The men deceived "the woman of the world," frightening her by changing themselves into an anaconda. Frightened, she fell unconscious into the river; the men took her out and examined her body thoroughly to find out where her power resided. Finally, they found her vulva, which they had never seen before; they drew on it, carving flutes[8] with the same form as the bamboo, and in this way they took to themselves the power of the woman. The myth continues: The four men were in the woods, wondering how they could make the woman conceive. Then, while in the woods eating *caimos,* they got the idea of emptying one that was especially beautiful in order to fill it later with their own semen and offer it to her. They gave it to her and at the first bite, the dark fruit with its milky juices broke, and a thick drop slid between the breasts of the woman, went down to her navel, and kept going down till it penetrated deep into her womb. When she felt the dampness, she hurried to clean herself with leaves, but it was already too late. Her disgrace could not be remedied. At the end of five moons, the woman with her swollen abdomen grumbled at the men, but when nine months had passed, tormented by terrible pains, she gave birth to a son which the men took and painted black, and whom they brought up themselves.[9] This myth reveals much about the belief of the superiority of man over woman and about the daily practices of sexual violence. The men dominate the body of the woman, they possess the sacred instruments, and they control the education of the children.

The following myth of the Suna also shows how man imposes himself after dominating the woman sexually. The moon man was disgruntled because his older sister didn't love him. On one of his trips, when he found the *cumare* tree, from which they take fibers to make hammocks, the thought occurred to him to use the tree as a trap to gain the favor of the young woman. So he brought her under the tree, which was heavily laden with fruit, and he climbed it to bring her some. The moon man shook the branches of the tree, and the ripe fruits rained down, sweet as the honey of the *juansocoll.* They fell on the head of the girl who ate them with relish until she became drunk. When he came down from the tree, the moon man saw that his sister was in a deep sleep. He spread her legs and when he smelled the odor of her vulva, he went to get a fragrant cane of the *flor de viuda* (widow's flower) to rub her with and to be able to examine her more closely. As he opened the thick lips, he discovered some teeth, sharp as those of a piranha, which had been well hidden, and immediately he broke them with a stone. Then, the little bird which was watching him began to sing, "Ivitii, abu . . . ivitii. I took them out, I took them out." The moon man climbed up the tree again. The girl awakened and realized that the moon man had violated her. Furious, she began to kick the trunk of the tree, and with each kick the tree grew higher so that the moon man was trapped very high at the top. There he stayed for several days, until a little animal arrived and began to eat the ripe fruit. It ate so much that it became drunk, and its saliva ran out and changed itself into a thick cane break. The moon man was saved by coming down through the cane . . . The myth ends with the moon man doing evil using thorns against the father of the girl. In pain, the father-in-law was changed into a bird with a rose-colored breast. According to Milagros Palma, from the act of the man's violation of the woman, the man also becomes a dominator of another man to perpetuate the logic of dominator and dominated.[10]

In Latin America and the Caribbean, we women of different cultures cannot but help recognizing that there are myths in our traditions which reflect the violent ways in which women are perceived simply because they are women, and which are used to legitimize the practice of unequal relationships. Violence against women has universal roots; it is not just the product of Western capitalistic society. It is true that there are myths which serve a liberating function for the community by preserving the life and spirituality of the cultures. There are also myths in several cultures which reveal a binary perception of society in which feminine and masculine form a whole. These myths should be salvaged, re-read, and shared with other cultures which are highly androcentric. But there are other myths which should be questioned by women.

In the culture of the mestizo-white world, machismo is imposed with violence. Much of the time it is accepted as part of the tradition. The old popular songs, as well as the new ones, reflect it very crudely. We dance the salsa, *cumbia*, and merengue ignoring or not noticing the fact that the words are often obviously "machistic."

These lyrics include, for example, the song which talks about the "stick, stick, stick with which the husband hits his wife on the head to teach her to obey."[11] Or the Mexican *corridos* which speak of the macho man in terms describing a king: "With money or without, I always do what I want, and my word is law; I have neither a throne nor a queen, or anyone who understands me, but I'm still a king." This is a song which reflects the daily life of the poor, downtrodden, and exploited male; humiliated by his boss, he arrives at his house drunken and beats his wife. Because he is macho, he is the king. There are liberating *ballenatos* and *cumbias*, and there are *corridos* which sing of the Mexican revolution, but there are also songs, many songs, which picture the evil of the domination of a patriarchal culture. Just because it is "our own," women should not ignore the machistic elements in the mestizo culture which reflect negatively against and degrade women.

In a rural society, there are legends and myths which form part of the masculine sexual fantasy about women. Women in Latin America who have been out on the farm have heard, from the time we were children, the stories of the Candeleja, the *llorona*, the *patasola*, and the *sombrerona*. These are legends about women who frighten solitary travellers at midnight. They are beautiful, elegant women with long, black hair who attract men. Afterwards, they turn out to be evil spirits who terrorize them. Some, like the "patasola," eat them alive and they steal children, etc.

"The Candeleja" is one of these stories about a woman who changes herself into a ball of fire. According to legend, many men in their solitary travels have seen the Candeleja in person with their own eyes, and because of this indelible fright they affirm that it is an evil spirit. The Candeleja is a very pretty woman who follows the cowboy late at night and mounts his horse. When he turns his head, the rider is met by the vision of long, straight hair floating in the wind that blows furiously the length and breadth of the plains. After this lovely image, it changes itself into a ball of fire which attacks the horse from all sides, making it jump and neigh madly. The rider's whip and obscenities scare it off. This is the only remedy. Neither Christ, nor scapulars, nor medals, nor holy water can help. The more you pray, the closer she comes; that's why men who are prepared use the machete on her without even thinking about it. Violence is the remedy for this beautiful woman who threatens the cowboys. The legend says: "The men who are alerted to this vision shout obscenities while at the same time swing the blades of their machetes and scrape the ground to scare off the Candeleja with the hum of their furious machetes."[12]

People say that the Candeleja is the grieving soul of a woman who was burned alive on her own ranch, when no one came to help her.[13] Milagros Palma takes up the version of an old woman who completes the story. She tells about a rural woman who lived alone on her farm. She planted rice, yucca, and bananas, and raised hens and hogs. She did not want to have lovers, having been warned by her mother of the evils of men. She never accepted promises or gallantries of those who were in love with her. One day some men arrived at her ranch and raped her. She resisted with all her might, but the men with "bestial fury" rent her to pieces while she was alive and then killed her. Therefore, she persecutes the men to avenge her martyrdom. "Those cursed swine violated her, then they killed her. That's why she scares them . . . That's her vengeance. God gave her that power."[14]

The legend is ambiguous. It shows the ferocity of man against woman. It also shows the desire for vengeance on the part of the woman for the violence done against her. In daily life, the legend teaches that a woman should not live alone, because this could make her vulnerable to violence from men. The man is afraid that the woman will tell on him, and therefore he threatens her with his machete and with obscenities.

When Christianity arrived in our lands with the conquest, it entered with violence against our culture by imposing itself by force. Alternative theological discourse throughout the five hundred years since the invasion has achieved the recovery of the original meaning of the God of Jesus Christ, who acted as Liberator and in solidarity with us. We know, however, that myths and histories which form the basis of the Judaeo-Greco-Roman tradition are patriarchal and androcentric, and so have been accomplices to the violence against women.[15] The patriarchal myths of our own culture and the myths of Christianity have reinforced and aggravated the violence against women.

TOWARDS A CULTURAL HERMENEUTIC

What I have presented here is only an example of the violence that resides within our culture and which is generated by it. Women of different cultures should organize themselves against these intrinsic principles of their culture and, at the same time, re-evaluate those elements of culture which give dignity to their people and preserve it from damaging external influences.

Today we feel the necessity of a "cultural hermeneutic" as it is proposed by Musimbi Kanyoro, an African woman from Kenya.[16] Out of her concern for cultural practices against women, she proposes that women stop what they are doing unconsciously and begin to analyze their culture and traditions. For her, culture is frequently used as a euphemism to justify actions which require analysis. Kanyoro suggests a serious, honest dialogue with one's own culture about the concerns of women. For this, mutual trust and openness to change are necessary. We must know the right moment, the who, how, and when to make the feminist critique of culture.

I welcome Kanyoro's proposal because, as I pointed out above, in our Latin American context, we have centered our criticism on the patriarchal Western society which was imposed on us during the colonial period. It was correct that we did this, because this imposition has been fatal not only for women but for all peoples in general. Nevertheless, when we analyze cultural violence against women, we must pause and look into our own culture, whether it be aboriginal, black, mestizo or white, in order to pinpoint and question those values which legitimize violence against women.

A feminist critique of Latin American culture requires us to distinguish the different cultural levels as well as to recognize cultural diversities. We have mentioned three cultural levels—the aboriginal, the black, the mestizo-white—as well as that of the Western society spreading through the ideology of capitalism.

Women who are aboriginal, black, mestizo, and white should unite against the imposition of violent patriarchal values which proceed from Western society. The feminist critique of mestizo-white culture should respect the differing indigenous and black cultural values and should not impose its own values. Indigenous people have complained that groups of mestizo-white women feminists have come and disrespectfully characterized as patriarchal the authority of their indigenous leaders. This attitude is the same as that of the Spanish conquerors.

Women should seek an intercultural dialogue between women in the framework of mutual respect and recognition. It is women who are both the victims and the protagonists within every culture who can make a critical evaluation of their own culture. Dialogue enriches one's outlook. Otherwise, the arrogant position of the Christian missionary, who criticizes the new culture from the perspective of the white Western culture, will be repeated.

I had an example of an enriching dialogue while conversing with a Mayan woman. To her, it seemed interesting that we Christian women speak of the feminine side of theology and on this basis criticize certain practices of our culture. For her, this was not legitimate, according to her sacred tradition. She said, "I have noticed that our colleagues do not speak of God as mother and father but as father and mother. In the Popol Vuh, it is not this way; rather, our God is mother and father, and mother comes first." Perhaps some of her friends had been influenced by the Christian image of God as Father. This is not a secondary matter. If we Christian women would begin the "Father and Mother who is in heaven" with "our Mother and Father who is in heaven" this would attract much more attention.[17]

As I have said, it is necessary to differentiate cultural critique from within with that from without. From within, the women of a particular culture analyze the practices of violence against women which proceed from tradition. From without, women seek dialogue with women of other cultures in order to overcome violence against women. Also from without, they defend those cultural values which help them resist with dignity the attacks of a hegemonic cultural imposition which only seeks its own economic and political interests and which is sustained by the "kyriarchal" pyramid.[18]

In conclusion, I want to summarize some points which serve as strategies for the struggle against cultural violence.

1. Given the fact that cultural violence exists in the majority of cultures, it is important that we, who are women, belonging to different cultures, *question our own traditions that legitimize violence against women*. Likewise, we should try to reconstruct new myths or reinterpret existing ones in order to transform the relationships between women and men in their common reality.

2. Given that the dominant cultures in Latin America seek to impose themselves on others, women must reject this attitude. *We must seek intercultural dialogue with mutual respect.* The objective would be to help each other in solidarity as women to plan defense strategies which stop violent practices in our culture, both from within and from without, and to share theological insights which are liberating and dignifying to women.

3. With respect to the patriarchal Western culture, which is supported by the present economic system, and through which all women in the world become victims, *we must make an international alliance of women from all cultures and races* to do battle against it. It is no longer possible to accept the marginalization to which thousands of women and men are subject, nor the erosion of the planet due to the regulations of the neo-liberal market system.

4. With respect to Christian women theologians, we must continue to seek

new gender theories which help us break down the Christian theological discourse which discriminates against women. As Ivone Gebara proposes, *we must rebuild Christian theology with new paradigms which are neither sexist nor patriarchal*, and whose basis, symbolism, and language respect profoundly the integral creation of the human being as woman and man. A new anthropological and theological praxis will generate a different type of society with transformed relationships between women and men.[19]

NOTES

[1] Cf. Elsa Tamez, *Through Her Eyes: Women's Theology from Latin America* (Maryknoll, NY: Orbis Books, 1989).

[2] Franz J. Hinkeiammert, "Changes in the Relationships between Third World Countries and First World Countries," in *Spirituality of the Third World: Ecumenical Association of Third World Theologians (EATWOT) 1992 Assembly, Nairobi, Kenya,* ed. by K. C. Abraham and Bernadette Mbuy-Beya (Maryknoll, NY: Orbis Books, 1994), 9-19.

[3] Here I include the Latin American whites, because they usually assume and breathe the same mestizo culture.

[4] This is discussed by the ethnologist Marcela Lagarde, "La participacion social de las mujeres" (The social participation of women), unpublished article.

[5] Milagros Palma, ed., *La Mujer es un cuento: simbolica mitico-religiosa.* (Bogota, Colombia: Ediciones Tercer Mundo, 1986), 11.

[6] For the Macunas, the woman was untamed and did not have a vocation as a mother, and to inculcate in her this painful vocation, he tries to penetrate her by force (ibid., 13).

[7] I do not dare to mention stories of Afro-Latin American cultures, because I do not know them well. I prefer to follow the analysis of Milagros Palma, who has studied a great quantity of indigenous and mestizo myths closely.

[8] The flute is a sacred instrument in these cultures.

[9] Palma, ibid., 14. Painting the boy black signifies baptism.

[10] Ibid., 16.

[11] Ibid.

[12] Ibid., 33.

[13] Ibid., 34.

[14] Ibid.

[15] Cf. Joanne Carlson Brown and Carol Bohn, eds., *Christianity, Patriarchy, and Abuse: Feminist Critique* (New York: Pilgrim Press, 1989).

[16] Musimbi Kanyoro, "Cultural Hermeneutics," study paper for the "Consultation of Women in Dialogue: Wholeness of Vision towards the 21st Century," Bossey Ecumenical Institute, May 1994.

[17] This fact was made clear to me by a group of Argentinean women called "Gucumatz."

[18] A term coined by Elisabeth Schüssler Fiorenza. "Introduction," in *Violence against Women (Concilium, 1991*), ed. by Elisabeth Schüssler Fiorenza and M. Shawn Copeland (Maryknoll, NY: Orbis Books, 1994), xii-xvii.

[19] Ivone Gebara, *Incomodas filhas de Eva na Igreja da America Latina* (The Uneasy Daughters of Eve in the Church of Latin America) (Sao Paulo: Edicoes Paulinas, 1989).

2

SPIRITUALITY, STRUGGLE, AND CULTURAL VIOLENCE

Letty M. Russell

When you gather forty-five women from twenty-four countries in the same place for nearly a week you are likely to get a lot more than dialogue! Hisako Kinukawa called it "multi-logue," but it was frequently a tense truce between women of different colors, cultures, and political realities.[1] The struggle to oppose cultural violence was not somewhere else. It was in our midst. The cultural violence of white, Western, European culture was ever present in the resources, English language, and academic status of many of those from the North. We were always on the edge of what Elsa Tamez calls "foreign patriarchal imposition of other cultures" [13].

Nor were the other two dimensions of cultural violence described by Elsa Tamez missing. Women from many countries experienced tensions among themselves in their embodiment of indigenous cultures as well as cultures that had been imposed on their people in generations past [12]. It was painful for mestizo or white women to recognize the ways their work still tended to dominate that of indigenous and black cultures, or for all of the women to be self-critical of their own traditional cultures. For instance, among the North American groups the interracial tension was even more difficult than with other groups because we knew each other so well and had a long history of working with each other in many different contexts.

Yet, as Elsa Tamez points out in her conclusion, there is the possibility of "intercultural dialogue between women" when we are willing to critique the ways that "our own traditions legitimize violence against women" and when we work together with "mutual respect" to rebuild Christian theology [18]. This solidarity is made possible as women in all nations work together to oppose the domination of the neo-liberal economic system. This system perpetuates domination of countless women, men, and children, and the fragile eco-system which supports life for all. We came together around the suffering of women, shared that suffering, and made many links at the points of our pain.[2]

There were at least three common elements that we discovered about women and violence. The first was that *violence is very local, but also global*. It is part of the lives of women in all parts of the world and is constantly increasing as international economic and political violence continues to escalate. The second was that *spirituality for life is a way of life* for women in their resistance to the continuing violence. Women talked of spirituality as life itself, for it was the way they integrated their search for integrity and meaning into their constant struggle to resist dehumanization. Lastly, we discovered that this *struggle against violence is a core topic of feminist liberation theologies* because women on the margin, and all women in a patriarchal society, suffer violence of many kinds that is legitimized both by religions and by the societies of which we are a part.

The working group on cultural violence elaborated on Elsa Tamez' description of culture, calling it *a way of life of a people* which is shaped by its language, collective memory, history, social and religious practices, art, symbols, laws, and values.[3] Cultural violence is both destruction and alienation of a culture by external domination of political, economic, familial, military, and religious forces, and internal reinforcement and legitimization of the domination of one group over another within a society. Like economic, military, ecological, domestic, and bodily violence, cultural violence is a coercive attempt to "restrict, to limit, to thwart the exercise and realization of a human person's essential and effective freedom."[4]

Elsa Tamez helps us to understand these many layers by saying that women need to resist violence that proceeds from tradition within their cultures, and resist violence that seeks to destroy their cultures from without [18]. In this response to Elsa Tamez and to the discussion of our working group on cultural violence I want to draw out the insights that we discovered into the ways in which this violence works. Then I will turn to the clues we discovered for the practice of spirituality for life as we sought to describe women's ongoing resistance to violence in their lives. "No mas violencia contra las mujeres."

FEMINIST INSIGHTS INTO CULTURAL VIOLENCE

Many feminist insights into cultural violence against women can be discovered in the way that Elsa Tamez combines careful analysis with a recounting of myths underlying the cultural violence against women in Latin America. Such myths can be found in almost every culture, as the working group on cultural violence discovered. It is important, however, to hear them told out of one culture in order to make direct connections with our own myths and to appreciate the violence done to women in traditions that reinforce myths of women's power and evil, and of men's need to resort to sexual violence and domination in order to subdue them [13]. In this section of my response, I want to discuss three of these feminist insights into cultural violence.

The first insight is that *culture is a tool of domination* within the culture through social reinforcement of dominant patterns of behavior and social structures. It is also a tool of domination from outside: a culture is subjected to the "hegemonic cultural imposition [of multi-national capitalism,] which only seeks its own economic and political interests" [18]. As long as the cultures are patriarchal, the traditions of those cultures will reinforce the right of men to dominate and oppress women, and legitimate sexual violence against women. Elisabeth Schüssler Fiorenza makes this abundantly clear in her description of patriarchy, or what she calls "kyriarchy," in her article, "Ties That Bind: Domestic Violence against Women."

> Kyriarchy [the rule of the master or lord] as a pyramid of interstructured oppression specifies women's status in terms of the class, race, country, or religion of the men to whom they "belong" [43].

In all layers of culture this domination prevails: "the aboriginal, the black, the mestizo-white—as well as that of the Western society spreading through the ideology of capitalism" [17].

We began the first day of the Costa Rica meeting with an exposure trip to three women's centers in San Jose that deal with different issues of violence against women. At the shelter for young women, victims of domestic and incest abuse and teenage pregnancy, we were struck by the multi-national aspect of patriarchal violence as we heard the same statistics about incest in San Jose as we might have heard in Seattle. Teenage pregnancy is most often caused by incest or by a close family member. The patriarchal structures are the same, although the particular cultural manifestation is different. For instance, in a machismo culture such as that of Costa Rica it is considered the father's "right" to engage in incest and in domestic violence. As Tamez says, "In the culture of the mestizo-white world, machismo is imposed with violence. Much of the time it is accepted as part of the tradition" [15]. The religious reinforcement of this violence is seen in the fact that, for these young women, abortion is illegal due to opposition of the Roman Catholic Church and conservative Protestant churches. These churches also condemn the young women who have now committed sin and have lost their virginity.

This religious dimension of the cultural reinforcement of sexual violence against women leads us to the second feminist insight, that *double culture leads to double oppression*. In Latin America the indigenous myths make very clear that women are to be dominated, although, as with all cultures, there are life-affirming myths as well. These indigenous cultures have been overlaid with the cultures of Euro-American imperialism and with the Christianity associated with it. In this way both the cultures and their religious practices combine to oppress women with double patriarchal force [11-12]. Both need to be resisted, and both need to be carefully studied in order to discover the truths and falsehoods they carry in regard to women's dignity and full humanity.

In feminist liberation theologies they are approached with a perspective that there is no one absolute truth. Truth depends on one's social location and on the particular mental and social structures that set the parameters of what is being called truth. Cultural and religious monopolies and domination are based on the myth that there is only one truth and that the others are false, inferior, and heretical. As Lisa Meo said in our cultural violence working group, in Fiji she had spent years trying to learn in her theological education "that there was only one truth," and what that truth was. Now in this gathering of women she was discovering that the idea of one truth was often a justification of cultural domination.

A third feminist insight is that *cultural violence is a barrier to forming networks.* As I mentioned at the beginning of this article, the cultural differences were very important in our struggle to work as a community of women committed to ending violence against women and affirming the full humanity of all women, beginning with those who are the most disadvantaged. The differences themselves are not the problem, as Audre Lorde has long since made clear in her essay, "Age, Race, Class, and Sex: Women Redefining Difference."[5] It is that the differences are used as an excuse for domination by white Western culture and justification of economic and racial imperialism. In her chapter on women's "Spirituality of Resistance and Reconstruction," Mercy Amba Oduyoye describes this barrier:

> The violence that Africa suffers because of racism and exploitation that are built into her relation with the Euro-American world moves African women to cultivate and to feed on a spirituality of resistance that avoids the smooth talk which hides the violence among women. In any global dialogue of justice-loving women the violence arising out of class, education, and race cannot be overlooked [163].

Even our determined efforts to face our differences still did not prepare us for the pain in the presentation of Chung Hyun Kyung, "Your Comfort vs. My Death." This pain came from the pain of the "comfort women," the pain of the Korean nation, the pain of Chung Hyun Kyung. A pain that needed to be faced, claimed, and shared in order for women to find a way to a spirituality of resistance. It also came from our Japanese participant, Hisako Kinukawa, who could not change the imperialist history of her nation. She was prepared, however, not only to apologize on behalf of her nation but also to make clear in her own report to the group how women in Japan had joined in solidarity with Korean women. Together they were struggling to force the Japanese government to apologize for their abuse of the so-called "comfort women" and to make a just restitution to the women who were forced into sexual slavery.

CLUES TO SPIRITUALITY FOR LIFE

Out of such common action of resistance to violence against women comes the basis of spirituality for life. Women are constantly faced with painful and contradictory situations of violence, so they must constantly develop their spiritual resources for *cultural resistance.* As our working group on cultural violence pointed out:

> Spirituality can be a chief source of resistance against cultural violence as it draws on all that is just and life giving in people's traditions, and critiques those parts of the tradition that are death dealing in women's lives and the lives of their communities and their lands.[6]

This spirituality must be holistic and cosmic, connecting our bodies, our spirits, and our communities in the search for meaning, direction, and value for our lives. It is a "passionate, and a compassionate" spirituality.[7] In the face of cultural appropriation by dominant cultures, the cultivation of the spirituality of a community is key to its survival, as Mercy Amba Oduyoye points out in her article in this volume [163].[8]

A second clue to this cultivation is the need for careful *cultural hermeneutics* in which women interpret their own culture and traditions, recognizing that culture is frequently a euphemism to justify actions that require analysis and exposure [17]. Musimbi Kanyoro, the Kenyan theologian whom Elsa Tamez cites in this respect, has given us all a good beginning at unraveling the layers of culture. She looks at the African context to examine the violence perpetuated in both indigenous and biblical traditions, and where it is reinforced and globalized by destructive white, Western imperialism.[9]

The danger here is that white, Western feminists try to critique the cultural practices of an African, Asian, or Latin American culture without considering the ways in which that culture is important to the preservation of a particular community. On the other hand, the men of that community will reject feminist views of woman's equality and the integrity of her body, saying that the traditional practices must be upheld as a form of resistance to post-colonialism. Women from the South find themselves critiqued from all sides, and need to have the space to sort out their own cultural hermeneutic of what is and is not violence to women. One particularly painful example of this need to sort things out carefully and slowly is the continuing conversation in Africa about the cultural practice of female circumcision. Both Musimbi Kanyoro and Mercy Amba Oduyoye call for an intense cultural hermeneutic to be carried out by those *directly involved*, and support from those women who share their concern.

This leads to a third clue about spirituality for life. This spirituality can be cultivated across barriers of difference in social location, language, and history through *cultural sharing*. This sharing needs to be mutual because cultural dialogue requires "a space and safe environment of mutual trust and mutual vulnerability."[10] There is no way to address such complex structures of violence without a willingness to learn from one another and to stand in solidarity with one another.

This cultural sharing is not to be another form of cultural appropriation in which we all steal one another's "stuff," but rather a practice of cultural reciprocity.[11] It is a careful dialogue in which all persons and groups identify their own cultural location and the realities of colonialism and structural racism and sexism that are involved. The first step is the willingness of those from dominant groups to join in the struggle against oppression and in the reciprocal sharing of resources. A second step is for all persons and groups to do their own spiritual work to find the sources of life in the traditions of their own communities.[12] The final step is the reciprocity that comes with the sharing of what has been learned about possible transformation of our cultures and religious traditions so that they reinforce spirituality for life.

Only by working together in this way can we even begin the *cultural transformation* that is needed if we are to practice a spirituality for life in the face of violence against women. Transformation only comes through resistance, interpretation, and shared action. It comes partially and slowly as small pieces of our cultures are lifted up and reshaped to affirm life-giving values and spirituality. The work of feminist liberation theologians is part of this work as we join Elsa Tamez and Ivone Gebara in rebuilding Christian theology "*with new paradigms which are neither sexist nor patriarchal,* and whose basis, symbolism, and language respect profoundly the integral creation of the human being as man and woman" [19].

Elsa Tamez has not only spoken and written about the possibility of "intercultural dialogue between women, in the framework of mutual respect and recognition" [18]. She herself is modeling this in her work as the only woman president in the seventy-four-year history of Seminario Biblico Latinoamerico in Costa Rica. The seminary seeks to respond to the cultural, socio-economic, and ecclesial realities of Latin America and the Caribbean. It offers new models of education including a specialty in Women and Theology. In its work to build up educational structures that can transform and inform the church and society this seminary is about to become a university and to move into a new building as Universidad Biblica Latinoamericana.

She has invited all women together around the globe, rich and poor, North and South, to share in this exciting venture by joining the One Million Women fund-raising effort for the new building. Elsa Tamez writes,

> I have a dream: *that one million women from all over the world will build the new home* of the Latin American University. To make this dream a reality, we are asking *one million women to send their name accompanied by one dollar.* The symbol of one dollar each is to allow all women—poor and rich, black and white, indigenous and mestiza—to participate equally in building our dream.[13]

This is only one of many joint-action projects evolving out of the Costa Rica meeting, but it shows again that cultural transformation can begin to draw women together in a new network of sharing. Through their struggle against cultural violence, and all types of violence, women become ever more firmly rooted in spirituality as life itself.

NOTES

[1] Hisako Kinukawa, "A Milestone of Feminist Theology in Japan," *Journal of Women and Religion* 13 (1995): 39-44. Center for Women and Religion, Graduate Theological Union, Berkeley, CA.

[2] Cf. my discussion of the Geneva EATWOT meeting in 1983: "I discovered, however, that there was a point at which we all could come together to hear one another into speech and action, and that was at the *point of pain*" (*Household of Freedom: Authority in Feminist Theology* [Philadelphia: The Westminster Press, 1987]).

[3] Unpublished report.

[4] M. Shawn Copeland, "Editorial Reflections," *Violence against Women: Concilium, 1994/1,* ed. Elisabeth Schüssler Fiorenza and M. Shawn Copeland, (Maryknoll: Orbis Books, 1994), 119.

[5] Audre Lorde, *Sister Outsider: Essays and Speeches* (Trumansburg, NY: The Crossing Press, 1984), 114-123.

[6] Unpublished report.

[7] Virginia Fabella and Mercy Amba Oduyoye, eds., *With Passion and Compassion: Third World Women Doing Theology* (Maryknoll, NY: Orbis Books, 1988).

[8] Cf. Myke Johnson, "Wanting to Be Indian: When Spiritual Searching Turns into Cultural Theft," *The Brown Papers* 1 (Boston: Women's Theological Center, April 1995), 1-15.

[9] Musimbi Kanyoro, "Cultural Hermeneutics: An African Contribution," *Women's Visions: Theological Reflection, Celebration, Action,* ed. Ofelia Ortega (Geneva: WCC, 1995), 18-28.

[10] Ibid.

[11] Toinette M. Eugene et. al., "Appropriation and Reciprocity in Womanist/Mujerista/Feminist Work," *Feminist Theological Ethics: A Reader,* ed. Lois K. Daly (Louisville: Westminster John Knox Press, 1984), 88-117.

[12] Myke Johnson, "Wanting to Be Indian," 8-9.

[13] Elsa Tamez, "Circular Letter to One Million Women" (San Jose: Seminario Biblico Latinoamericano, March 8, 1995), 1.

3

ECOFEMINISM: FIRST AND THIRD WORLD WOMEN

Rosemary Radford Ruether

What is Ecofeminism? Ecofeminism represents a union of two concerns: ecology and feminism. The word "ecology" emerges from the biological science of natural environmental systems. Ecology examines how these natural communities function to sustain a healthy web of life and how they become disrupted, causing death of plant and animal life. Human intervention is the main cause of such disruption as it occurs today. Thus ecology was popularized as a combined socioeconomic and biological study in the sixties to examine how the human use of nature is causing pollution of soil, air, and water, the destruction of the natural life systems of plants and animals, and threatening the base of life upon which the human community depends.

Deep ecologists have insisted that it is not enough to analyze this devastation of the earth in terms of human social and technological use. We have to examine the symbolic, psychological, and cultural patterns by which humans have distanced themselves from nature, denied their reality as a part of nature, and claimed to rule over it from outside. Ecological healing demands a psychocultural conversion from this anthropocentric stance of separation and domination. We have to recover the experience of communion in nature and rebuild a new culture based on the affirmation of being one interconnected community of life.[1]

Feminism is also a complex movement with many layers. It can be defined as a movement within liberal democratic societies for full inclusion of women in political rights and access to equal employment. It can be defined more radically in socialist and liberationist feminism as a transformation of the patriarchal socioeconomic system in which male domination of women is the foundation of all social hierarchies. Feminism can also be studied in terms of culture and consciousness, charting the symbolic, psychological, and cultural connection between the definition of women as inferior mentally, morally, and physically, and male monopolization of knowledge and power.

This third type of feminist analysis has affinities with deep ecology, although many ecofeminists have faulted deep ecologists for their lack of gender analysis and their failure to see the relations between anthropocentrism and androcentrism.[2] Ecofeminism is founded on the basic intuition that there is a fundamental connection in Western culture, and in patriarchal cultures generally, between the domination of women and the domination of nature. What does this mean?

Among Western ecofeminists this connection between domination of women and domination of nature is generally made, first, on the cultural-symbolic level. One charts the way in which patriarchal culture has defined women as being "closer to nature," or as being on the nature side of the nature-culture split. This is shown in the way in which women have been identified with the body, earth, sex, the flesh in its mortality and weakness, vis à vis a construction of masculinity identified with spirit, mind, and sovereign power over both women and nature.[3]

A second level of ecofeminist analysis goes beneath the cultural-symbolic level and explores the socioeconomic underpinnings of how the domination of women's bodies and women's work interconnects with the exploitation of land, water, and animals. How have women as a gender group been colonized by patriarchy as a legal, economic, social, and political system? How does this colonization of women's bodies and work function as the invisible substructure for the extraction of natural resources? How does the positioning of women as the caretakers of children, the gardeners, weavers, cookers, cleaners, and waste managers for men in the family both inferiorize this work and identify women with a subhuman world likewise inferiorized?

This socioeconomic form of ecofeminist analysis then sees the cultural-symbolic patterns by which both women and nature are inferiorized and identified with each other as an ideological superstructure by which the system of economic and legal domination of women, land, and animals is justified and made to appear "natural" and inevitable within a total patriarchal cosmo-vision. Ecofeminists who stress this socioeconomic analysis underlying the patriarchal ideology of subordination of women and nature also wish to include race and class hierarchy as well.

It is not enough simply to talk of domination of women as if women were a homogenous group. We have to look at the total class structure of the society, fused with racial hierarchy, and see how gender hierarchy falls within race-class hierarchy. This means that women within the ruling class have vastly different privileges and comforts than women in the lowest class, even though both may be defined in a general sense as mothers, child raisers, and sex objects. It also means that there are different ideologies about upper-class and lower-class women, exacerbated when racial ideologies are also present. Thus in American society, the images of the white woman as sheltered leisure-class Lady, and the Black woman as strong Mammy or sexually available tart, shaped by slavery, still informs cultural patterns, despite the much greater complexity of actual class-race patterns affecting real African-American and Euro-American women today.

How does religion come into this mix of ecofeminist cultural-symbolic and socioeconomic analysis? Religion, specifically the Christian tradition with its roots in the Hebrew and Greco-Roman worlds, has been faulted as a prime source of the cultural-symbolic patterns which have inferiorized women and nature. The patriarchal God of the Hebrew Bible, outside and over against the material world as its Creator and Lord, fused with Greek philosophical dualism of spirit and matter, is seen as the prime identity myth of the Western ruling-class male. He has made this God in the image of his own aspiration to be both separate from and ruling over the material world, such as land and animals or non-human "resources" and subjugated groups of humans.

The denunciation of Christianity and scientific ideology as the main sources and enforcers of the domination of women and nature is often connected with what might be called an ecofeminist "fall from paradise" story. In this story, humans in the hunter-gatherer and hunter-gardener stages lived in egalitarian classless societies in a benign nurturing relation to the rest of nature. The social system of war, violence, and male domination came in with a series of invasions by patriarchal pastoralists from the northern steppes sometime in the sixth to third millennia B.C.E, reshaping earlier egalitarian societies into societies of militarized domination. This view has been popularized in Riane Eisler's book, *The Chalice and the Blade*.[4]

Key to this shift is a religious revolution from the worship of a Goddess, who represents the immanent life force within nature, to a patriarchal sun God positioned outside and ruling over nature as warrior Lord. The implication of this ecofeminist "fall from paradise" story is that recovery of a partnership relation between men and women and a life-sustaining relation with nature demands a rejection of all forms of patriarchal religion and the return to, or re-invention in some way of, the worship of the ancient nature Goddess. This viewpoint is expressed by groups of women and some men, not simply as a theory, but as a practice of creating worship groups that have developed ritual practices that they see as reviving the ancient worship of the Goddess. Perhaps the best-known theologian and liturgist of this neo-pagan or Wiccan movement is Starhawk, author of books such as *The Spiral Dance: A Rebirth of the Ancient Religion of the Great Goddess*.[5]

My own view is that this "fall from paradise" story is a myth, a powerful contemporary myth. By myth, I do not mean that it is "untrue," but that it is a vastly simplified and selective story that contains elements of truth about the actual shaping of Western history in the last 6000-8000 years. It charts a process that led from the invention of agriculture and the domestication of animals to the shaping of early urban cultures and empires in the ancient Middle East in the third millennium, with their patterns of patriarchy, slavery, temple and palace aristocracies controlling the land and labor of peasants and slaves, and the subjugation of women. It re-imagines a lost alternative that lay behind and was covered over by this process of shaping the system of domination.

This story, as told by its contemporary myth-makers, however, also tends to take for granted certain gender stereotypes about masculinity and femininity and the connection of women and nature with nurture that have more to do with certain lines of American Victorian culture than with ancient Anatolia or Crete. This is why the story "rings true" to many contemporary American women and some men. Like all good myths, this story should be taken seriously, but not literally. We should ask what it tells us about ourselves and our histories, but also how it may mislead us about ourselves and our histories and particularly about what is to be done to heal ourselves, our relations to each other and to the earth.

Here I see a sharp distinction between two lines of thought among ecofeminists, even though they may share many common values. One line of thought sees the woman-nature connection as a social ideology constructed by patriarchal culture to justify the ownership of and use of both women and the natural world as property. In reality women are no more like nature than men, or, to put it another way, men are as much like nature as women.

This critique of the woman-nature connection as a patriarchal cultural construction can be used to separate both men and women as humans, who are much like each other, from the rest of nature. Or it can be used to insist that men as much as women need to overcome the myth of separation and learn to commune with nature as our common biotic community, while respecting trees, lakes, wolves, birds, and insects as beings with their own distinct modes of life and raison d'etre apart from our use of them. Ecofeminists see the separation of women from men by patterns of cultural dualism of mind-body, dominant-subordinant, and thinking-feeling—and by the identification of the lower half of these dualisms with both women and nature—as a victimology. These dualisms falsify who women and men (and also nature) really are in their wholeness and complexity, and justify the treatment of both women and nature as property of men, to be used as they wish. Ecofeminism is about deconstructing these dualisms, both in regard to women and in regard to nature.

A second line of ecofeminism agrees that this patriarchal woman-nature connection justifies their domination and abuse, but also believes that there is a deeper truth that has been distorted by it. There is some deep positive connection between women and nature. Women are the life-givers, the nurturers, the ones in whom the seed of life grows. Women were the primary food gatherers, the inventors of agriculture. Their bodies are in mysterious tune with the cycles of the moon and the tides of the sea. It was by experiencing women as life-givers, both food providers and birthers of children, that early humans made the female the first image of worship, the Goddess, source of all life. Women need to reclaim this affinity between the sacrality of nature and the sacrality of their own sexuality and life-powers. To return to worship the Goddess as the sacred female is to reconnect with our own deep powers.[6]

I find this exaltation of woman and nature as Great Goddess exciting, but also potentially dangerous and misleading. First of all, this religion either excludes men altogether or else allows them in as "sons" of the great Mother, which means not only that men can't be dominators, but also that they cannot be adult peers of women. Some men will be content in this role (i.e. to be taken care of all their lives), but most men will be turned off. Some will be filled with vehement outrage that demands retaliatory vengeance.[7]

We have seen such outrage and self-righteous retaliatory backlash in much of the anti-feminist New Right today. Such backlash also tells us something about where we are and have come from, but in a way that reduplicates the old patterns that have long underlain and reproduced patriarchy. We are still far from the kind of transformed story that will break the cycle of both female maternalism and submission, of both male insecurity and retaliatory dominance, and find real partnership.

Much of Western essentialist or matricentric ecofeminism (as distinct from social ecofeminism) fails to make real connections between the domination of women and classism, racism, and poverty. Relation with nature is thought of in psycho-cultural terms; rituals of self-blessing of the body, dancing on the beach, chanting to the moon, etc. I do not disvalue such ceremonial reconnecting with our bodies and nature. I think they have a place in our healing of our consciousness from patterns of alienation.

But I believe they become recreational self-indulgence for a privileged counter-cultural elite, if our cultural expressions of healing of our bodies and our imaginations as white Americans are not connected concretely with the realities of over-consumerism and waste by which the top 20% of the world enjoys 82% of the wealth while the other 80% of the world scrapes along with 18%, and the lowest 80% of the world's population, disproportionately female and young, starves and dies early from poisoned waters, soil, and air.

An ecofeminism which is not primarily a mystical (mystified) and recreational escapism for a privileged Western female elite must make concrete connections with women at the bottom of the socioeconomic system. It must recognize the devastation of the earth as an integral part of the appropriation of the goods of the earth by a wealthy minority who can enjoy strawberries in winter winged to their glittering supermarkets by a global food procurement system while those who pick and pack the strawberries lack the money for bread and are dying from pesticide poisoning.

I remember standing in a market in Mexico in December looking hungrily at boxes of beautiful strawberries and wondering how I might sneak some back on the airplane through customs into the United States on an airplane. A friend of mine, Gary McEoin, a longtime Latin American journalist standing next to me, said softly, "Beautiful, aren't they, . . . and they are covered with blood." To be an ecofeminist in my social context is to cultivate that kind of awareness about all the goods and services readily available to me.

I look for an important corrective to the myopias of the white affluent context from dialogue with ecofeminists from Asian, Africa, and Latin America, as well as from the struggles of racial-ethnic peoples against environmental racism in the United States and other industrialized countries. I find that ecofeminism sounds very different when it comes from women in these class, racial, and cultural contexts. Ecofeminists in the United States could profit from reading how these women see the women-nature connection.

While there are also many differences among women of these many non-white and non-affluent contexts, what seems to me basic is that women in Latin America, Asia, and Africa never forget that the baseline of domination of women and of nature is poverty—the impoverishment of the majority of local people, particularly women and children, and the impoverishment of the land. This connection of women and nature in impoverishment is present in everyday concrete realities. Deforestation means women walk twice and three times as long each day gathering wood; it means drought, which means women walk twice and three times farther each day to find and carry water back to their huts.

When these women talk about how to heal their people and their land from this impoverishment and poisoning, they talk about how to take back control over their resources from the World Bank and the wealthy nations. They critique the global system of economic power. They also envision ways of reclaiming some traditional patterns of care for the earth and indigenous forms of spirituality, but in a flexible, pragmatic way. For example, women from Zimbabwe and Malawi point to local territorial cults in their traditions where women were the spirit mediums and guardians of the land. Women led ceremonies calling for rain and giving thanks for harvests, kept sacred forests from being cut down, and guarded sacred pools.[8]

But these traditions are not romanticized. These African women also know how women were limited by pollution taboos that forbade them access to forests and kept them from growing their own trees. They want to combine pragmatically some of the old customs that cared for the water, trees, and animals with modern understandings—of conservation and the legal right of women to own land and have equal access to agricultural credit—that have come to them from Western liberalism. If they are Christians, they don't mind citing some good stories from the Bible, side by side with good stories from their indigenous traditions. In short, they are practical ecumenists who know how to cross cultures, to speak Shona and also English, to use whatever comes from these many cultures to enhance life for all, particularly for women at the bottom of the society.

I believe Western feminists of Christian background need to be similarly ecumenical and similarly clear-sighted about the economic system in which we stand. I don't believe there is a readymade feminist ecological culture that can be resurrected from prehistoric cultures, although we can catch glimpses of alternatives in ancient pasts that might help midwife new futures. We also need to mine our Greek, Hebrew, and Christian heritages, as well as modern emancipatory traditions, for useable insights.

Catherine Keller has suggested that feminist theologians are the great recyclers of culture, just as women have always been the recyclers of the waste products of human productions.[9] In constructing an ecofeminist culture and spirituality, we are the cultural equivalent of the many marginalized people around the world who pick through garbage heaps seeking for useable bits and pieces from which to construct a new habitation. While this is a grim picture of our relation to the past, it does highlight two important aspects of our task. First, that there is much of our Christian and Western past which is useable, but only by being reconstructed in new forms, as material reorganized by a new vision, as compost for a new organism. Second, it is we who must be artisans of this new culture. It will not come to us readymade, either from Christianity or science, or from Asian or Indigenous peoples.

We are facing a new situation which humans have never faced before—namely, that the human species' power, actualized by a dominant class, has grown so great that it may destroy the planetary basis of life for all other humans, as well as the non-human biosphere. Past cultures, whether they sought to harmonize humans with each other and with nature in the name of immanent deities or to subdue nature in the name of a transcendent God, did not imagine that such power was ours to possess. Most accessible cultures, including indigenous ones, had some patterns of subordination of women, and many tied this to serf, slave, or worker populations. Their cosmologies and ethical codes reflect and justify these social patterns.

But religious cultures have not only mandated the social patterns of their societies. They have also, in various ways, sought harmony and justice, overcoming enmity and alienation, reconciling humans and humans, humans and animals, humans and the ultimate Source of life. It is these many quests for harmony, reconciliation, and justice which we can assemble as the gold in the trash heaps of past cultures. Our legacy will doubtless need to be reconstructed by our children and grandchildren. At best we may construct a new foundation that is more sustainable as the base for their rebuilding.

Many cultures can provide us with clues to a healing culture. The great Asian spiritualites of Taoism and Buddhism, Hinduism and Confucianism have possibilities to be explored, particularly in their vision of letting go of overweening individualism, which releases an outflowing compassion for all sentient beings, the harmonization of the dialectical forces at work in society and the cosmos.[10]

The many cultures of indigenous peoples of the Americas, Asia, Africa, and the Pacific islands, long scorned as "pagans," have begun to be accorded more respect as we recognize how each of these peoples created its own bio-regional culture that sustained the local human group as part of a community of animals and plants, earth and sky, past ancestors and future descendants. Euro-Americans can also look for hints of such indigenous spiritualities in our pre-Christian pasts in the Celtic, Germanic, and Slavic worlds, careful to separate these roots from their misuse by fascist racist ideologies.

But we Western Christians also need to free ourselves from both our chauvinism and our escapism to be able to play with the insightful aspects of our

Jewish, Greek, and Christian legacies, as well as critically appraising their problems, letting go of both the need to inflate them as the one true way, or repudiate them as total toxic waste. In my book *Gaia and God* I suggest two patterns of biblical thought that are important resources for ecological theology and ethics: convenantal ethics and sacramental cosmology.[11]

Covenantal ethics gives us a vision of an integrated community of humans, animals, and land that seeks to live by a spirituality and code of continual rest, renewal, and the restoration of just, sustainable relations between humans and other humans, and between humans and the land, in one covenant under a caretaking God. We need to reject the patriarchal aspects of this covenantal tradition, while reclaiming the vision of community sustained by processes which continually righted the distorted relationships created by unjust domination and exploitation: the fertility of the land renewed by letting it lie fallow, the human and animal workers given rest, the debts forgiven, those in servitude emancipated, and land restored to those who had become landless.

Covenant ethics can be complemented by the Jewish and Christian heritages of sacramental cosmology. Here we have a sense of the whole cosmos come alive, as the bodying forth of the Holy Spirit, the Word and Wisdom of God, which is its source and renewal of life. In God we live and move and have our being, not as some detached male ego beyond the universe, but as the Holy One who is in and through and under the whole life process.

Covenantal ethics and sacramental cosmology are profound resources from our biblical and Christian heritage, but we Christians also have to let go of the illusion that there is one right way to create the new ecological world culture and that we can and should do it all. We need to see ourselves as part of a converging dialogue, as ecofeminists in many regions make their distinctive cultural syntheses: as Zimbabwe ecofeminists interconnect spirit mediums and kinship with animals with themes of just self-government that came to them from the British; as Indian ecofeminists, such as Vandana Shiva, connect the pre-Hindu understanding of Shakti, the feminine cosmic life principle, with the critique of Western science and development;[12] and as Korean ecofeminists, such as Chung Hyun Kyung, integrate a Buddhist woman Bottisatva and shaman dance with Christian emancipatory visions.[13]

But white affluent Western Christian feminists must not only shape cultural syntheses from the best of their traditions, in dialogue with those of others; we also need to know who we are. We are those who profit from the most rapacious system of colonial and neo-colonial appropriation of the land and labor of the earth ever created. We need to repudiate this system and its benefits to ourselves in order truly to stand in solidarity with poor women.

We need to keep their reality firmly in our mind's eye, as they hold the child dying of dehydration from polluted water and trek long hours to fetch basic necessities, and also as they continue to struggle to defend life with a tenacity that refuses to be defeated. Only as we learn to connect both our stories and also our struggles in a concrete and authentic way can we begin to glimpse what an ecofeminist theology and ethic might really be all about.

NOTES

[1] Cf. Bill Devall and George Sessions, *Deep Ecology: Living as if Nature Mattered* (Salt Lake City: Peregine Smith Books, 1985).

[2] Cf. Marti Kheel, "Ecofeminism and Deep Ecology: Reflections on Identity and Difference," in Irene Diamond and Gloria F. Orenstein, eds., *Reweaving the World: The Emergence of Ecofeminism* (San Francisco, CA: Sierra Club Books, 1990), 128-137.

[3] Cf. Ynestra King, "Healing the Wounds: Feminism, Ecology, and the Nature/Culture Dualism," in Diamond and Orenstein, *Reweaving the World,* 106-121.

[4] Riane Eisler, *The Chalice and the Blade* (San Francisco, CA: Harper and Row, 1987).

[5] Starhawk, *The Spiral Dance: The Rebirth of the Ancient Religion of the Great Goddess* (New York: Harper and Row, 1979).

[6] Charlene Spretnak, "Ecofeminism: Our Roots and Flowering," in Diamond and Orenstein, *Reweaving the World,* 1-14.

[7] Cf., for example, the column by Jon Margolis, "Gyno-supremacism Engenders a Political Revolt," *Chicago Tribune,* editorial page, January 30, 1995, and reply by Rosemary Ruether, "Letters to the Editor," February 18, 1995.

[8] These essays from African, Asian, and Latin American women appear in Rosemary Ruether, ed., *Women Healing Earth: Third World Women on Ecology, Feminism, and Religion* (Maryknoll, NY: Orbis Books, 1996).

[9] Oral remarks by Catherine Keller in a workshop on Buddhist-Christian Dialogue, Berkeley, CA, August 1991. Cf. her article, "Talk about the Weather: The Greening of Eschatology," in Carol J. Adams, ed., *Ecofeminism and the Sacred* (New York: Continuum, 1993), 43.

[10] Cf. Mary E. Tucker and John A. Grim, eds. *World Views and Ecology: Religion, Philosophy, and the Environment* (Maryknoll, NY: Orbis Books, 1994).

[11] Rosemary Ruether, *Gaia and God: An Ecofeminist Theology of Earth Healing* (San Francisco: Harper, 1992), chapters 8 and 9.

[12] Vandana Shiva, *Staying Alive: Women, Ecology, and Development in India* (New Delhi: Kali for Women, 1989).

[13] Chung Hyun Kyung, "Come Holy Spirit: Renew the Whole Creation," address at the World Council of Churches conference in Canberra, Australia, February 1991. Published in Michael Kinnamon, ed., *Signs of the Spirit,* Geneva: WCC Publications, 1991, pp. 37-47.

Part Two

DOMESTIC AND PHYSICAL VIOLENCE

4

TIES THAT BIND: DOMESTIC VIOLENCE
AGAINST WOMEN

Elisabeth Schüssler Fiorenza

Domestic violence[1] is at the heart of patri-kyriarchal[2] relations of oppression. Violence against women and their children remains all-pervasive. It is not limited to one specific class, geographical area, or type of person. Rather it cuts across social differences and status lines: white and black, rich and poor, Asian and European, Hispanic and Anglo-Saxon, urban and rural, religious and secular, professional and illiterate, heterosexual and lesbian, able-bodied and differently abled, young and old, women face violence daily in North America because they are women.[3]

SITUATIONAL ANALYSIS[4]

Such violence can take many forms and the list of abuse is endless: sexual and domestic abuse,[5] child pornography, sexual harassment in schools and jobs, lesbian bashing, right-wing neo-Nazi terror against women,[6] eating disorders, psychiatric hospitalization, battered women and children, incest, homelessness, poverty, intellectual colonization, spiritual exploitation, refusal of women's equal rights, H.I.V. infection, impoverishment of widows and older women, emotional violence in all forms, cosmetic surgery, strip search and prison rape, sex clinics, forced sterilization, welfare harassment, surrogacy, incarceration of pregnant women with substance abuse, witch burning, stranger rape, rape in marriage, acquaintance rape, date rape, food deprivation, serial murder, sadomasochism, soft and hard pornography, sexual objectification, psychiatric dehumanization, femicide, sexual abuse of the mentally ill, illegal aliens, imprisoned and disabled. Such violence is not always forced upon women, but also can be self-inflicted in the interest of feminine self-esteem, love, and marriage. For instance, in the U.S. more than two million women have "freely elected" breast implants. The number of women who have "chosen" cosmetic surgery has increased more than 60 percent in the past decade.[7] When women tell me that they are not feminist or are post-feminist because they do not experience any discrimination but are equal and even privileged, I point to this endless list of abuse.

In the U.S. a woman is beaten in her home every fifteen seconds.[8] Every month more than 50,000 women seek restraining or protection orders. Police are more likely to sign a formal report if the offender was a stranger rather than an intimate. In 1993 the American Association of University Women reported that 66 percent of high school boys admitted to being sexual harassers. Only 7.8 percent of women in the U.S. claim that they have not been assaulted or sexually harassed during their lifetime.[9] If all women victimized by domestic violence in 1993 joined hands, the line would stretch from New York City to Los Angeles and beyond.[10] Domestic violence is the leading cause of injury to women, producing more injuries than muggings, stranger rapes, and car accidents combined. Children of abused mothers are six times more likely to attempt suicide, and 50 percent more likely to abuse drugs and alcohol. More than half of abused mothers beat their children. At least 25 percent of the victims of domestic violence are beaten while pregnant. Fifty percent of all homeless women and children are fugitives from domestic violence. Rural women must travel often more than 100 miles to get to a battered women's shelter. For every two women with children admitted in 1990 to a shelter in Boston, five were turned away.

Femicide,[11] the murder of women, is the deadly outcome of domestic violence. Most women in the U.S. are murdered in their homes by men with whom they have shared daily life. Nine out of ten women murdered are killed by men known to them; four out of five are murdered at home.[12] For example, a study of 73 women who were murdered between 1975 and 1979 in Dayton, Ohio, showed that 80 percent knew their killers intimately as husbands, friends, family members, prior sex partners, or acquaintances. Fully 72 percent of the women were killed in their homes.[13] In the U.S., battering is the single greatest cause of deadly injury to women. According to the National Coalition against Domestic Violence, at least four women are murdered by their partners every day.[14] In Massachusetts, a woman is killed by her husband or lover every nine days. The majority of women and children who were killed in the metropolitan area of Boston in the first quarter of 1993 had asked the police for help and even had obtained restraining orders.

The media almost always report domestic violence and femicide from the perspective of the batterer. They sensationalize such incidents but do not bring to public consciousness that statistically a woman is more likely to be raped, battered, or killed at night in her own house than on the most crime-infested streets. At least one-third and probably one-half of all femicide victims are murdered by their husbands and lovers, who almost never have any criminal record or a known psychiatric history. Nevertheless, the public perception still prevails that such murders are rare and are committed by hardened criminals or psychiatric cases. Headlines such as "Woman Shot by Jealous Lover" or "Woman

Stabbed by Cuckolded Husband" make femicide not only anecdotal but also "deserved." Although the man wages an assault, the woman is portrayed as retaliating by deliberately trying to provoke his jealousy or anger. In many cases the battered woman is held responsible for the problem. Her uppity demeanor, her sloppy dressing, her withholding sex or other marital services, her nagging and accusations, her low self-esteem, her indirect expression of needs, her love for her children, her whining, or, worst of all, her sexual promiscuity—all these and more are construed as "provocative" and hence as a valid excuse for battering or murder.

Radio talk show hosts such as Rush Limbaugh have generated a near fascist climate that makes violence against women common sense and labels women who fight against it "femi-Nazis." "Serious" newspaper and TV coverage provide a public platform to so-called post-feminists or "new feminists" who decry the victim mentality of women and discredit the statistics on domestic violence or sexual abuse as exaggerated and a figment of feminist propaganda. In December 1989, Marc Lepine killed 14 college engineering students at the University of Montreal in Canada. He gave as reason for his action that they were "fucking feminists." Press reports speculated that he harbored such hatred for feminists probably because he had experienced intense humiliation by women, especially at the hands of a domineering mother. However, such practices of overt physical and sexual violence are not isolated incidents or perverse behavior but must be explored as structurally normative practices.

The increased violence against women and the backlash against the limited feminist gains which have been made in the past two decades are spearheaded by very vocal and well-financed political New Right organizations which are often championed by conservative women. In the U.S. the Moral Majority of the Reagan era has been replaced by the Christian Coalition, which was founded by Pat Robinson after his unsuccessful bid for the presidency in 1988. This coalition has overcome centuries of religious divisions and has unified old religious enemies by bringing together not only conservative Evangelicals and Roman Catholics but also orthodox Jews and Greek Orthodox Christians. By being pro-family and pro-censorship while at the same time insisting on their own religious freedom the religious right seeks to restore America to its greatness as a Christian nation and society that maintains biblical values. Today the Christian Coalition claims to control the Republican Party Committees in at least 18 states and to be able to deliver 15 - 40 percent of the vote depending on voter turnout. All across the country the Christian Coalition has taken over local school boards and set out to enforce traditional family values in public education.

The common ground and denominator of the political right is not just the defense of the "traditional family" but also that of traditional biblical religion that excludes women from its leadership ranks and relegates them to second-class citizenship while at the same time extolling their special natural gifts of nurture and self-sacrifice. Women themselves are often among the most fervent spokespersons of the Christian Coalition. They utilize the methods of protest developed by emancipatory movements in the 1960s for asserting fetal rights, prayer, and creationism in public schools, for advocating workfare for women on welfare, and for fighting against sex education, gay and lesbian rights, abortion, teenage mothers, birth control, and illegitimacy as destroying the American family. While the New Right overtly advocates "traditional family values," its real interest is to uphold the patriarchal form of the middle-class nuclear heterosexual family. In the name of love, this patri-kyriarchal family ethos legitimizes the chastising and battering of women and children in the home, the silence about incest and child abuse, the attack on shared parenting, child care programs, and reproductive rights, and the rejection of affirmative action programs that would guarantee economic justice for women.

Just as the religious right has done, so also feminists have identified the central role of the traditional family in social organization. But whereas political conservatives and liberals view the family as the basis of social cohesion and societal order that transmits accepted values, shapes national identities, and engenders basic loyalties, feminists have seen it as reproducing patriarchal social relations and hence as the primary site for the production and continuation of such violence not only in the private but also in the public realm. Although women's political and economic roles have changed, the ethos of the patriarchal heterosexual family has throughout history declared women's place to be the home, to be supported by and subordinated to their husbands and to maintain the well-being of the family by socializing children to their proper adult roles, caring for the sick and aged, and overseeing the household. Although this bourgeois ethos of the family is no longer livable today even for middle-class women, it still determines the status of women in the welfare system and in the marketplace.[15] Whereas 24 percent of families living in poverty in 1960 were headed by a woman, 51 percent of such families were impoverished in 1986. Older women are twice as likely to live in poverty than male senior citizens.

SYSTEMIC ANALYSIS

Verbal, emotional, economic, political, physical, or sexual violence against women must not be reduced either to abstract statistics or to episodic evidence and isolated incidents. Rather, such violence must be understood in systemic terms and placed on a continuum of elite male power and control over women and children that encompasses not only incidents of physical violence but also dehumanizing impoverishment. Most analyses of domestic violence and femicide point out that such male violence against women and children is motivated by proprietary control and jealousy which are deeply ingrained in Western cultural, political, and religious traditions and self-understandings.

Both proprietary control and lovesick jealousy are engendered by patri-kyriarchal understandings of family. However, I argue that they belong to two different historical formations of the family[16] that operate simultaneously in sustaining relations of domination and the ethos of submission and inferiority. This ethos and regime of the traditional family is maintained not only by the power and control of male heads of household but also sustained by the cultural and religious construction of docile feminine bodies and subservient feminine selves. This simultaneity of patri-kyriarchal rule is overlooked when it is argued that in preindustrial society patriarchal rule was exercised in the private sphere by the male head of household, who controlled the labor, property, and lives of all members of the household, whereas with the arrival of industrial capitalism patriarchal authority shifted from the male head of household to the marketplace and the state.

As familial patriarchy gave way to social or public patriarchy, the state assumed regulatory functions previously confined to the family, including greater regulation of marriage, inheritance, child custody, and employment. The transition signaled by an attack on public aid (outdoor relief) and the rise of institutional care (indoor relief) made public aid very harsh and punitive. The Marxist explanation of these "reforms" suggests that state-regulated deterrence became necessary to discipline the newly industrialized labor force. The feminist analysis adds that social welfare changes also operated to enforce new ideas about family life. Punitive relief programs assured that women chose any quality of family life over public aid.[17]

However, such a socialist feminist analysis conceptualizes patriarchal social relations within a dual-systems theory of productive and reproductive labor that seeks to integrate the radical feminist social analysis of patriarchy as fundamental gender domination with a Marxist analysis of capitalist class and property relations. The weakness of such a conceptualization is its inability to adequately theorize racial and colonial oppression as essential to sustaining patriarchal relations. In my own work I have therefore sought to articulate a different systemic analysis and to theorize "patriarchy" differently, by exploring the classical notion of patriarchal kyriarchy that has developed in interaction with notions of democratic equality.

Western society and family are not simply male dominated. Rather they are patriarchal (rule of the father) or, more accurately, kyriarchal (rule of the master/ lord/husband), because elite propertied men have power and control over those subordinated to and dependent on them. Kyriarchy as a pyramid of interstructured oppression specifies women's status in terms of the class, race, country, or religion of the men to whom they "belong." Yet such a mapping of patriarchal kyriarchy as an overarching system of elite male domination must not be misconstrued as a universal historical "master paradigm" but be seen as constantly adapting to new situations.

Feminist political theorists[18] have shown that in response to the emergence of democratic notions both classical and modern political philosophy has articulated a theory of kyriarchal democracy in order to justify why certain groups of people are not capable of participating in democratic government. Classical philosophy argues that whole groups of people, such as freeborn women or slave women and men, were not fit to rule or to govern, on grounds of their deficient natural powers of reasoning. Such an explicit ideological justification of patri-kyriarchal relations is necessary at a point in history when it becomes obvious that those who are excluded from the political life of the polis (the city-state), such as free women, educated slaves, wealthy metics (alien residents), and mercenaries, are actually indispensable to it.

A similar contradiction between democratic vision and socio-political kyriarchal reality becomes evident again in the West with the emergence of modern democratic politics, which has articulated itself as fraternal capitalist kyriarchy.[19] At first, modern democracy excluded propertied and all other free women, as well as immigrant, poor, and slave men and women from democratic rights and full citizenship. "Property" and elite male status by birth and education, not simply biological-cultural masculinity, entitled one to participate in the government of the few over the many. Susan Moller Okin has argued convincingly that substantive inequalities between the sexes continue to exist because conservative and liberal politicians have tacitly assumed that "the individual" or "the citizen" is the male head of the traditional household. Hence contemporary theories of justice assume, but do not discuss, that the social relations of the gender-structured family are just. Consequently they are not able to recognize the family as a political institution of primary importance for a democratic society. "To a large extent, contemporary theories of justice, like those of the past, are about men and wives at home."[20] Whereas the political-religious right seeks to restore today classical patri-kyriarchal family structures, liberal policies seek to reform the traditional family in such a way that women are better able to manage their work responsibilities without having to give up their household and family responsibilities at home. Yet such liberal policies have served women poorly and hence are threatening to many middle-class women.

Moller Okin argues that a genderless democratic family would be more just than the patri-kyriarchal family because it would result in greater justice for women understood as free moral agents and citizens, it would be more conducive to equal opportunity for both women and children of both sexes, and it would be more conducive to the rearing of citizens of a just society. A just family, she concludes, would not only increase justice for women and children but also result in just social institutions and a genderless society that is truly democratic.[21] A just family as the primary institution of society, however, would need to be conceptualized not only as genderless but also as free from structures of race, class, and colonialist exploitation if it is to benefit all women and children.

Most importantly, the argument for a just society and family would need to reconceptualize masculinity in terms of equality and responsibility and thereby undo men's need for control and their socialization to violence. Whereas in classical kyriarchal democracy elite men exercised the power of life and death over freeborn women, children, slaves, and servants of their household, in modern kyriarchal democracy every man is believed to be entitled to exercise physical control and legal power over the women and children belonging to "his" family, race, class, or nation. Personal and national power is expressed through control and violence against women, who signify all who are weak and subordinate. Hence, violence against women is not just generated by heterosexist patriarchal power but also by colonialist kyriarchal power.[22] Only if feminist discourses focus on the struggles of women at the bottom of the kyriarchal "new world order," I have consistently argued, will we be able to explore and comprehend the full complexity of domestic violence. Violence against women constitutes the heart of kyriarchal oppression. It is sustained by multiplicative structures of control, exploitation, and dehumanization: the oppressive powers of hetero-sexism are multiplied by racism, poverty, cultural imperialism, war, militarist colonialism, homophobia, and religious fundamentalism.

THE KYRIARCHAL LOVE ETHIC AND ITS DISCIPLINING PRACTICES

Since in modern times women are no longer forced to marry, one could argue that they are free to choose their husbands and to determine the number of their children. Why then do women continue to choose marriage and family after they have achieved citizenship in their own right and are on the way to gaining economic independence and sexual and reproductive freedom? That even educated and privileged women remain in violent and abusive relationships shows that it is not just important to change political and domestic institutions in order to achieve a just family and society. It also is crucial to fashion a cultural-religious ethos that is truly just and democratic. Feminist studies have pointed out over and over again that women continue to put themselves in harm's way because culture and religion tell them that they are nothing without a man or without children. Women's self-worth and self-esteem is defined by their being attached to a man and/or by becoming a mother. Yet, rather than speak of women's perduring "false consciousness" that keeps them in such violent social situations, it is important to trace the cultural and religious disciplining practices that play a decisive role in securing women's continuing collaboration in and their acquiescence to domestic and sexual violence.

Feminist analyses have amply documented how the disciplining practices of culture and religion enact and reenact received gender norms. The Western kyriarchal family ethos and its educational practices continue to socialize girls and women into self-effacing love and feminine submissive service. This kyriarchal ethos produces the cultural-religious understanding that a woman is nothing without a man and that she has to do everything possible to attain or to keep "wedded status." Such cultural socializing practices are on the one hand the genderization of people and on the other hand the production of the "feminine" body.[23] Sandra Lee Bartky has pointed out that three disciplining sociocultural practices produce the docile, subjected, and made-up body as the ideal body of "femininity."[24] However, I suggest that a fourth type of socio-cultural and religious discursive practice motivates all three of them. My contention is that the first three practices serve to reinforce a fourth one in sustaining and legitimating domestic and sexual violence. A systemic analysis of patriarchal or fraternal kyriarchy, I argue, can lay open that like race, class, or colonialism, gender is not about bipolar difference or complementarity but about the inequality of power. As Catharine MacKinnon has pointed out, such kyriarchal gender relations appear to be natural and consensual because they are sustained and perpetrated in and through the eroticization and sexualization of relations of dominance and submission. This four-pronged strategy of bodily discipline in the interest of a kyriarchal family ethic is not "forced" upon women. Rather it is perceived to be "freely chosen" for the sake of beauty and love. Yet, the overt aim of beauty and love is far removed and indeed contrary to the covert aim of such disciplining practices, which seek to produce the feminine body as a "subjected," docile, sexualized body, on which an inferior status has been inscribed.

The first assemblage of disciplining practices seeks to produce the ideal feminine body as a body of a certain size and general configuration. Its regimes are obsessive dieting in order to produce the slender, boyish body, as well as forms of exercise that shape the "ideal" feminine body form. Seventy-five percent of U. S. women aged 18-35 believe they are fat and 95 percent of enrollees in weight loss programs are women. Eighty to ninety percent of all persons with eating disorders are women. Only one in forty thousand women meets the requirements of size and shape for a model, who today weighs 23 percent less than the average woman. A California study shows that 80 percent of fourth grade girls are already dieting, 53 percent of high school girls are unhappy with their body by age 13, and 78 percent by age 18. Such a negative body image leads to erosion in the self-affirmation and self-confidence of girls as well as to the tendency of women to renounce and devalue their own perceptions, beliefs, thoughts, and feelings.[25] Even highly accomplished professional women exhibit such negative self-appraisal and self-worth: they tend to feel "illegitimate, apologetic, undeserving, anxious, tenuous, out-of-place, misread, phony, uncomfortable, incompetent, dishonest, guilty."[26]

The *second* type of disciplining practices seeks to control women's self-understanding and movement. It seeks to fashion women as passive containers and selfless signifiers of kyriarchal values. It seeks to produce the "docile" female body by enforcing a specific repertoire of gestures, postures, and mannerisms as well as by constricting women's spatiality and movement. Women are taught that when sitting, walking, and speaking, they must constrict their gestures and should not "let themselves go" in public so as not to give the impression of being a "loose woman." Such a restriction of movement in the name of "graceful" behavior is reinforced through clothing, e.g., high-heeled shoes, which are again in fashion, and certain forms of etiquette, e.g., not to spread one's legs when sitting. Through their clothing, movements, gestures, and smiles women must communicate that they are "nice," unthreatening, and subservient—in short, that they are "feminine." Their body language must be deferential, timid, and subservient. Women who are "loud," uppity, or "nagging" bring punishment and violence on themselves. They do not deserve protection and respect. By stressing subordination, refinement, and helplessness, such bodily feminine inscriptions aim to produce the character of the "White Lady." By construing countries, cities, and churches as "feminine," such discourses also create a distinct cultural, national, and religious identity in "feminine" terms. Such a feminine symbolization socializes men into becoming warriors in order to protect the "feminine" body of their own people and to ravish that of the enemy country.

The *third* type of practices is directed toward the display of the feminine body as an ornamental surface. Women's faces and bodies must be made up and made over according to normative standards of beauty. No wonder that cosmetics are a $20 billion industry worldwide. In the U.S. the cosmetic-surgery industry grosses $300 million a year and has increased 61 percent over the last decade. These normative standards of beauty are Eurocentric and racially biased. The blond, blue-eyed white Barbie doll communicates such a racist standard of "femininity." Hair must be straightened or curled, facial and bodily hair must be excised. Early on, women have to become skilled in numerous techniques of hair care and skin care; they learn to practice the narrowly circumscribed "art" of cosmetics, and even to suffer corrective surgery so that the "properly" made up woman can appear in public. Conformity to the prevalent standards of "feminine" dress and makeup is a prerequisite for well-paying jobs and social mobility.

Such inscriptions of the body seek to produce the submissive feminine by inculcating the desirability of the hegemonic feminine, the White Lady. Again and again womanist scholars have pointed out that beauty standards are not just sexist but also racist. The American ideal of beauty glamorizes elite, young white women's features and bodies. The self-esteem of African American women is undermined by colorism or pigmentocracy which highly prizes light skin and "good hair," i.e., not "kinky hair."[27] Moreover, this racist "politics of beauty" compensates the low self-esteem of white women who do not measure up to the ideal standard of beauty with the ideology that they are "better" by the mere fact of being white. Women of color in turn are stereotyped as "dirty, ugly, stupid, lazy, uppity, devious, and promiscuous" in colonialist-racist discourses. Such colonialist-racist stereotypes of femininity also serve in courts for labeling white women victims of violence such as rape or wife-beating as uppity, nagging, overbearing, or promiscuous.[28]

A *fourth* assemblage of disciplining practices presupposes and works in conjunction with the first three. It is directed toward producing kyriarchal heterosexual gender relations not only as natural sex but also as personal desire, pleasure, and love. It not only articulates the gender of women as the sexualized ideal of cultural-religious submission by inflecting the first three types of disciplinary practices in terms of its overarching goal. It also organizes the social relations between the sexes so that for men domination and for women submission become sexualized. Eroticized submission defines femininity whereas eroticized dominance constitutes masculinity. Not only gender but also sexuality and desire are socially constructed. While I do not agree with Catharine MacKinnon that the kyriarchal sex-gender system is the primary source of oppression, I agree with her that it eroticizes and sexualizes relations of dominance not only between men and women but also between elite and subordinated men.

Sexuality, in feminist light, is not a discrete sphere of interaction or feeling or sensation or behavior in which preexisting social divisions may or may not be played out. It is a pervasive dimension of social life, one that permeates the whole, a dimension along which gender occurs and through which gender is socially constituted; it is a dimension along which other social divisions, such as race and class, partly play themselves out. So many distinct features of women's status as second class—the restriction and constraint and contortion, the servility and the display, the self-mutilation and requisite presentation of self as a beautiful thing, the enforced passivity, the humiliation—are made into the content of sex for women. Being a thing for sexual use is fundamental to it.[29]

In short, in order to earn the love of a man and to fulfill their supposedly natural drive to motherhood, women must make themselves not only objects and prey for the sexual consumption of men but also define their identity in terms of romantic love defined as the emotional fulfillment of men's erotic desires and sexual needs. To question these disciplining practices of "femininity" threatens women not only with loss of jobs, family, and livelihood but also with loss of self-identity, status, and disciplining power over other women. This heterosexist kyriarchal regime is not only sanctioned by loss of patriarchal "patronage" and maintained through women's self-surveillance and collusion in the disciplining of other women, but also perpetrated in and through the construction of religious meaning and spirituality.

THE RELIGIOUS POLITICS OF MEANING

The new religious right seeks to recreate the kyriarchial Eurocentric society and world that existed before the changes brought about by the civil-rights, the women's liberation, and the gay- and lesbian-rights movements. By co-opting the politics of meaning engendered by civil-rights and liberationist discourses the religious right casts itself as an oppressed and silenced minority fighting for their cultural and political rights, which are believed to be threatened by left-wing "political correctness."[30] Christian American-style religious fundamentalism admonishes women to display their "femininity" and to utilize makeup, cosmetic surgery, diets, and fashion for seducing their husbands and maintaining their marriages. They insist on the headship of men in the Christian family as either natural or as god-given and teach sexual abstinence in place of reproductive rights, all this in defense of the "Christian family."

Still, not only the religious right but also liberal churches and theologies reproduce the socio-cultural discourses of femininity and subordination. As long as Christian faith and self-identity remain intertwined with the socio-cultural regime of subordination and its politics of meaning, it cannot but reinscribe physical and ideological violence against women and the weak. Theological and religious discourses reinscribe the inferior-object status of women and reinforce rather than interrupt the victimization of women and children if they do not question but reproduce the socio-cultural inscriptions of "femininity." True, Christian theology overtly condemns oppressive forms of exploitation and victimization such as incest, sexual abuse, femicide, or rape. Nevertheless, the Christian proclamation of the kyriarchal politics of submission and its attendant virtues of self-sacrifice, docility, subservience, obedience, suffering, unconditional forgiveness, male authority, and unquestioning surrender to God's will covertly advocates in the name of God patriarchal practices of victimization as Christian. In so doing, both types of religious regimes, the conservative and the liberal, theologically reinscribe the socio-cultural kyriarchal construction of femininity and subordination in order to maintain heterosexist kyriarchal structures of subordination.

Liberal and liberationist theologies will not be able to overcome their own violence-producing socio-cultural and religious discourses of subordination, economic exploitation, and political objectification as long as they do not publicly condemn the institutionalized structures of heterosexist kyriarchal "Christian" family and church that jeopardize the survival of the women who struggle at the bottom of the socio-cultural and economic-political pyramid of domination. As long as such structural change does not take place, Christian theologies will continue to collude in practices of physical and spiritual violence against women. Feminist theological work on violence against women and child abuse[31] has pointed to *four key traditional theological discourses* that are major roadblocks in the way of abused women and children who seek to change their violent situations.

First, the Western socio-cultural politics of subordination has its roots in Greek philosophy, and Roman law and is mediated through Jewish, Islamic, and Christian Scriptures. Especially, the so-called household code-texts trajectory inscribed in the Christian Testament has mediated these kyriarchal discourses of subordination that demand submission and obedience not only from freeborn women, wives, and children but also from servants, slaves, and barbarians, both women and men. This scriptural ethos of the patriarchal politics of subordination is compounded if it is used to provide the interpretive framework for reading originally anti-kyriarchal biblical texts that prohibit divorce as upholding patriarchal marriage relationships. It also has disastrous effects when it provides the contextual framework of meaning for the Christian theological and liturgical language about God and God's relation to the world. A Christian symbolic universe that proclaims an Almighty Father God whose will and command is revealed in the patri-kyriarchal texts of Scripture legitimizes and reinscribes religiously not only misogyny but also racism, status inferiority, homophobia, and xenophobia.[32]

Second, Paul's second letter to Corinth already refers to the image of marriage between Christ and the church and associates it with the deception of Eve (2 Cor 11:2-3). The pseudo-Pauline Pastoral Epistles explicitly link the kyriarchal theology of submission with the teaching on woman's sinfulness. They prescribe the silence of women and prohibit women's authority over men by claiming that not Adam but the woman was deceived and became a transgressor (1 Tim 2:11-15). Hence, the cultural pattern of making the victims of rape, incest, or battering feel guilty and responsible for their victimization has its religious roots in the scriptural teaching that sin came into the world through Eve and that women gain salvation primarily through bearing children when they continue in "faith and love and holiness with modesty." This religious re-inscription of the cultural politics of "femininity" and patri-kyriarchal submission has been amplified by theologians throughout the centuries.

Third, both Christian scriptural texts and traditional christological discourses theologize kyriarchal suffering and victimization.[33] For instance, the Epistle to the Hebrews admonishes Christians to resist sin to the point of shedding their blood. It points to the example of Jesus, "who for the joy that was set before him endured the cross, despising the shame" (Heb 12:2). Because they are "sons," they have to expect suffering as disciplining chastisement from God. Just as they respect their earthly fathers for having punished them at their pleasure, so they should subject themselves to "the Father of spirits and live," who "disciplines us for our good, in order that we may share his holiness" (Heb 12:9-10). Such admonitions are not isolated aberrations, but go to the heart of the Christian faith: trust in God, the Father, and belief in redemption through the suffering and death of Christ.

Feminist theology has underscored the pernicious impact of such theological and christological discourses, which stress that God sacrificed his son for our sins. If one extols the silent and freely chosen suffering of Christ, who was "obedient to death" (Phil 2:8), as an example to be imitated by all those victimized by patriarchal oppression, especially by those suffering from domestic and sexual abuse, one does not just legitimate but also facilitates violence against women and children. The work of Rita Nakashima Brock has shown that christological discourses which are articulated within the paradigm of kyriarchal submission "reflect views of divine power that sanction child abuse on a cosmic scale."[34] Moreover, Christine Gudorf[35] has pointed out that contrary to Rene Girard's[36] thesis the sacrifice of surrogate victims does not contain and interrupt the cycle of violence. Rather, by re-channelling violence, it serves to protect those in power from the violent protest of those whom they oppress. By ritualizing the suffering and death of Jesus and by calling the powerless in society and church to imitate his perfect obedience and self-sacrifice, Christian ministry and theology do not interrupt but continue to foster the cycle of violence engendered by kyriarchal social and ecclesial structures as well as by cultural and political disciplining practices.

Fourth, when preached to women and subordinated men, central Christian values such as love and forgiveness help to sustain relations of domination and to accept domestic and sexual violence. Hence scriptural texts and Christian ethics often continue the cycle of violence by preventing resistance to it. For instance, rape victims who believe obedience to God's will requires that they preserve their virginity and sexual purity at any cost not only endanger their lives but also suffer from loss of self-esteem. Hence, rape survivors feel not only that they are "used goods" but also that they are responsible for their own rape. Battered wives, in turn, who believe that divorce is against God's will cannot but remain in violent marriage relationships for "better and for worse."

Children who are taught to trust and obey adults as the representatives of God, particularly parents and priests, are especially prone to become victimized. Because of such Christian teachings incest victims do not have the spiritual means to resist the traumatic sexualization, stigmatization, betrayal, and powerlessness that lead to damaged self-image and loss of self-esteem. If such victims are taught that it is essential for a Christian to suffer, to forgive unconditionally, to remain sexually inexperienced and pure, to believe that their sinful nature is in need of redemption, and to be obedient to authority figures,[37] it becomes virtually impossible for them, particularly for little girls, either to remember and speak about sexual abuse by a beloved father, priest, relative, or teacher or to recover their damaged self-image and self-worth.

Although their original intention might have been quite different, scriptural texts such as "blessed are the peacemakers . . ."; "those who are persecuted for righteousness' sake"; "but I say to you that if you are angry with a brother or sister, you will be liable to judgment"; "it is better for you to lose one of your members than for your whole body to go into hell"; "love your enemies and pray for those who persecute you"; or "do not resist evil" (Mt 5-6) construct a sacred canopy that compels victims to accept their sufferings without resistance. Injunctions of Jesus (such as to forgive the one "who sins against me . . . Not seven times, but, I tell you, seventy-seven times" [Mt 18:21-22]) and Paul's praise of love ("love is patient and kind; love is not envious or boastful or arrogant or rude. It does not insist on its own way; it is not irritable or resentful . . . bears all things, believes all things, hopes all things, endures all things. Love never ends" [1 Cor 13:4-8]) make those who do not patiently and lovingly submit to domestic violence, sexual abuse, or ecclesial control feel guilty for resisting such violence and for having failed their Christian calling. No wonder that those women and children who take their faith seriously are convinced that resistance against violence is unchristian and that their suffering is willed by God.

It must not be overlooked, however, that such patri-kyriarchal readings of those scriptural texts and Christian traditions which might have originally had an anti-kyriarchal aim are unavoidable in a discursive and institutional politics of meaning that seeks to sustain and reproduce patri-kyriarchal cultural relations of submission. Hence, if Christian theologies and churches should not continue their collusion in kyriarchal violence, they must help to fashion an "ethics and politics of meaning" that can engender resistance to all forms of victimization and foster responsibility for changing structures and discourses that produce suffering, violence, and murder.

As long as Christian theology and pastoral practice do not publicly repent their collusion in sexual, domestic, and political violence against women and children, the victims of such violence are forced to choose between remaining a victim and remaining a Christian. However, such an alternative deprives religious women not just of their communal support but also of the belief systems that give meaning to their life. It overlooks that religious systems of meaning collude in but do not produce and sustain the socio-cultural practices of "feminine discipline." When confronted with this either/or choice, victimized religious women are likely to intensify their search for meaning rather than resort to religious and cultural nihilism. Instead of rejecting their Christian faith and moving out of their violent marriage relationship, they tend to engage in a desperate search for Christian values that could govern and make meaningful the culturally sanctioned relationship of heterosexual marriage. Autobiographical narratives indicate that a high socio-cultural valuation of marriage and family is the driving force behind women's search for religious meaning.

Hence, Susan Brooks Thistlethwaite is right in arguing that the feminist alternative, either remain Christian or leave an abusive situation, confronts Christian women with all impossible choices,[38] insofar as it encourages them to abandon their religious affiliation without having the power to disrupt the cultural-political inscriptions of the "feminine" politics of meaning. This challenge often deepens the disempowerment of religious women who refuse to accept its solution. Therefore, Brooks Thistlethwaite advocates a feminist theological strategy that underscores the alternative "liberating" traditions inscribed in Christian Scriptures and theologies. She lifts up, for instance, texts such as Lk 4:18-20; Gal 3:28 and Mt 20:25-26 and *theologoumena* such as the incarnation of Christ, God's identification with human suffering, or God's being on the side of the oppressed, for countering the negative impact of texts such as Eph 5:22 and traditions such as sacrificial Christology. Survivors of sexual, domestic, and political violence seem to confirm the validity of her argument when they point to religious experiences and Christian traditions, texts, and values that have allowed them to resist such abuse.[39]

However, battered women's experience also points to an alternative feminist theological strategy for transforming the impossible either/or choice which confronts religious women who suffer from abuse and violence. I suggest that such a critical feminist strategy of liberation must focus on women's religious agency and theological subjectivity. It must foster resistance and change by exploring the contradictions between the religious-cultural kyriarchal politics of "femininity," on the one hand, and the religious-cultural emancipatory radical democratic politics of meaning and self-worth in the eyes of God which is inscribed in Christian texts and traditions, on the other. Such a strategy attempts to shift the cultural and theological discourses on violence against women and children by focusing on the contradiction between the lived experience of survivors' agency and the discursive theological meanings that negate such agency.

Speaking from within religious and cultural communities, discourses, and traditions of meaning, such a critical feminist theology of liberation contests the authority of the practices and discourses that advocate the politics of subordination and violence on theological grounds. By surfacing the contradiction between the overt and covert aims of cultural and religious practices of "feminine" inscription as well as by providing contesting religious discourses as resources of meaning, it aims to empower those victimized by kyriarchal oppression and the whole Christian community to believe in a God who is with us in our struggles to eradicate violence and to foster self-determination, dignity, and well-being for all.

NOTES

[1] Ann Jones, *Next Time She Will Be Dead* (Boston: Beacon Press, 1993), problematizes the expression "domestic violence" as insinuating "domesticated violence." However, I would argue that the concept of domestic violence underscores that the patri-kyriarchal household (the paradigm of society, religion, and state) produces, sustains, and legitimizes violence against women.

[2] Since feminist discourses tend to conceptualize "patriarchy" (lit. reign or rule of the father) primarily in terms of gender oppression, I have coined the neologism "kyriarchy" (lit. the reign of the lord/master; in German *Herrschaft)* in order to underscore that Western patriarchy always has been and still is kyriarchy that gives ruling power to elite, propertied, educated, freeborn men of a national or religious group.

[3] Cf. Jaina Hanmer and Mary Maynard, eds., *Women, Violence, and Social Control* (London: Macmillan Press, 1987); Kate Young, Carol Wolkowitz, and Roslyn McGullagh, *Of Marriage and the Market: Women's Subordination in International Perspective* (London: CSE Books, 1981): Roxanna Carillo, *Battered Dreams: Violence against Women as an Obstacle to Development* (New York: United Nations Development Fund for Women, 1992); Margaret Schuler, ed., *Freedom from Violence: Women's Strategies from around the World* (New York: United Nations Development Fund for Women, 1992); Jessie Tellis Nayak, "Institutional Violence against Women in Different Cultures," *In God's Image,* 8 (September 1989), 4-14.

[4] An earlier version of this article can be found in my "Introduction," in *Violence against Women: Concilium, 1994/1,* ed. Elisabeth Schüssler Fiorenza and M. Shawn Copeland (Maryknoll: Orbis Books, 1994), vii-xxiv.

[5] Yvonne Yayori and Chandana, eds., "Prostitution in Asia," *In God's Image,* June 1990, 1-59; Elizabeth Bounds, "Sexuality and Economic Reality: A First and Third World Comparison," *In God's Image* (December 1990), 12-18; Mary Ann Millhone, "Prostitution in Bangkok and Chicago—A Theological Reflection on Women's Reality," *In God's Image* (December 1990), 19-26.

[6] Charlotte Bunch, *Gender Violence: A Development and Human Rights Issue* (New Brunswick, NJ: Center for Women's Global Leadership, 1991).

[7] *The Women's Action Coalition Stats: The Facts about Women* (New York: New Press, 1993), 18.

[8] *National Coalition against Domestic Violence Fact Sheet, 1991.*

[9] Catharine A. MacKinnon, *Feminism Unmodified: Discourses on Life and Law* (Cambridge: Harvard University Press, 1987), 6.

[10] For statistical facts see the issue of *Ms. Magazine* entitled "No More! Stopping Domestic Violence," 5/2 (September/October 1994).

[11] Jill Radford and Diana E. H. Russell, *Femicide: The Politics of Woman Killing* (New York: Twayne Publishers, 1992).

[12] *The Women's Action Coalition Stats,* 56.

[13] Jacquelyn C. Campbell, "If I Can't Have You, No One Can: Power and Control in Homicide of Female Partners," in Radford and Russell, *Femicide: The Politics of Woman Killing,* 99-113.

[14] Constance A. Bean, *Women Murdered by the Men They Loved* (New York: Haworth Press, 1992), 6.

[15] Cf. E. Schüssler Fiorenza and A. Carr, eds., *Women, Work, and Poverty. Concilium* (Edinburgh: T.& T. Clark, 1987).

[16] My classification is different, however, from the division into private and public family forms. Cf., e.g., Sylvia Walby, *Theorizing Patriarchy* (Oxford: Basil Blackwell, 1990).

[17] Mimi Abramovitz, *Regulating the Lives of Women: Social Welfare Policy from Colonial Times to the Present* (Boston: South End Press, 1988), 33.

[18] Susan Moller Okin, *Women in Western Political Thought* (Princeton: Princeton University Press, 1979); Page DuBois, *Centaurs and Amazons: Women and the Pre-History of the Great Chain of Being* (Ann Arbor: University of Michigan Press, 1982); Page Du Bois, *Torture and Truth* (New York: Routledge, 1990); M. E. Hawkesworth, *Beyond Oppression: Feminist Theory and Political Strategy* (New York: Continuum, 1990); E. C. Keuls, *The Reign of the Phallus: Sexual Politics in Ancient Athens* (New York: Harper & Row, 1985); A. Rouselle, Trans. by Felicia Pheasant, *Porneia: On Desire and the Body in Antiquity* (New York: Basil Blackwell, 1988).

[19] Cf. Christine Faure, *Democracy without Women* (Bloomington: Indiana University Press, 1991).

[20] Susan Moller Okin, *Justice: Gender and the Family* (New York; Basic Books, 1989), 13.

[21] See her closing chapter, ibid., 170-186.

[22] For such a distinction see my books *Discipleship of Equals: A Feminist Ecclesiology of Liberation* (New York: Crossroad, 1993) and *But She Said: Feminist Practices of Interpretation* (Boston: Beacon Press, 1992).

[23] Cf., e.g., Andrea Dworkin, *Woman Hating* (New York: E.P. Dutton, 1974); Mary Daly, *Gyn/Ecology: The Metaethics of Radical Feminism* (Boston: Beacon Press, 1978); Naomi Wolf, *The Beauty Myth* (New York: William Morrow, 1991).

[24] Sandra Lee Bartky, "Foucault, Femininity, and the Modernization of Patriarchal Power," in Irene Diamond and Lee Quinbee, eds., *Feminism & Foucault: Reflections on Resistance* (Boston: Northeastern University Press, 1988), 61-86.

[25] Lori Stem, "Disavowing the Self in Female Adolescents," in Carol Gilligan, Annie G. Rogers, and Deborah L. Tolman, eds., *Women, Girls, and Psychotherapy: Reframing Resistance* (New York: Harrington Park Press, 1992), 105-118.

[26] Peggy McIntosh, "Feeling Like a Fraud," *Work in Progress, No 18* (Wellesley, MA: Stone Center Working Paper Series, 1984), 1.

[27] For these terms see Katie G. Cannon, "Womanist Perspectival Discourse and Canon Formation," *Journal of Feminist Studies in Religion,* 9 (1993), 29-38. Cf. Katie Russell, Midge Wilson, and Ronald Hall, *The Color Complex* (New York: Harcourt, Brace, Jovanovich, 1992); and Chandra Taylor Smith, "Wonderfully Made: Preaching Physical Self-Affirmation," in Annie Lally Milhaven, ed., *Sermons Seldom Heard: Women Proclaim Their Lives* (New York: Crossroad, 1991), 243-251.

[28] Cf. Martha Mamozai, *Herren-Menschen, Frauen im deutschen Kolonialismus* (Reinbeck: Rowohlt Taschenbuchverlag, 1982), 160; May Opitz, Katharina Oguntoye, and Dagmar Schultz, eds., *Showing Our Colors: Afro-German Women Speak Out* (Amherst: University of Massachusetts Press, 1992).

[29] Catharine A. MacKinnon, *Toward a Feminist Theory of the State* (Cambridge: Harvard University Press, 1989), 130.

[30] Cf. the analysis of Heather Rhoads, "'Racist, Sexist, Anti-Gay: How the Religious Right Helped Defeat Iowa's ERA," *On the Issues* (Fall 1993), 38-42.

[31] Cf., e.g., Regula Strobel, "Der Beihilfe beschuldigt: Christliche Theologie auf der Anklagebank," *Fama, Feministisch Theologische Zeitschrift,* 9 (1993), 3-6, for a review of the discussion.

[32] For historical documentation and theo-ethical evaluation of the politics and theology of submission, see my books *Bread Not Stone: The Challenge of Feminist Biblical Interpretation* (Boston: Beacon Press, 1984), 65-92; and *In Memory of Her: A Feminist Historical Reconstruction of Christian Origins* (New York: Crossroad, 1983), 243-314.

[33] For a critical discussion of Christological discourses, see my book *Jesus: Miriam's Child, Sophia's Prophet, Critical Issues in Feminist Christology* (New York: Continuum, 1994).

[34] Rita Nakashima Brock, "And a Little Child Will Lead Us: Christology and Child Abuse," in Joanne Carlson Brown and Carol R. Bohn, eds., *Christianity, Patriarchy, and Abuse: A Feminist Critique* (New York: Pilgrim Press, 1989), 42-43. Cf. her book *Journeys by Heart: A Christology of Erotic Power* (New York: Crossroad, 1988).

[35] Christine E. Gudorf, *Victimization: Examining Christian Complicity* (Philadelphia: Trinity Press, 1992), 14-15.

[36] Cf. Rene Girard, *Job: Victim of His People* (Stanford: Stanford University Press, 1977) and *Violence and the Sacred* (Stanford: Stanford University Press, 1977).

[37] Sheila Redmond, "Christian 'Virtues' and Recovery from Child Sexual Abuse," in Brown and Bohn, *Christianity, Patriarchy, and Abuse,* 70-88.

[38] Susan Brooks Thistlethwaite, "Religious Faith: Help or Hindrance," *In God's Image* (December 1990), 7-11.

[39] Susan Hagood Lee, "Witness to Christ, Witness to Pain: One Woman's Journey Through Wife-Battering," in Annie Lally Milhaven (ed.), *Sermons Seldom Heard. Women Proclaim Their Lives* (New York: Crossroad, 1991), 15.

5

DOMESTIC VIOLENCE IN INDIAN PERSPECTIVE

Stella Baltazar

Domestic violence is the most dehumanizing form of unhappiness heaped upon women. It seems that women are meant to suffer in silence till the end of their lives. When they are given in marriage, they enter the home of the husband with a trust that from henceforth their entire life will be built around husband, children, and family matters. When violence erupts in this zone, it pushes women to a corner of impasse; they have no other escape route. Therefore, women can never develop any retaliatory measures. Violence must be tolerated and borne in silence. For most women this is the only solution. There are an exceptional few who dare to fight back.

Violence has its roots in the domestic sphere, extending to the religio-cultural and socio-political spheres, and extending still further to multinational dimensions of the domination-subordination relationship. The personal is political in the sense that every battered woman is a product of a patriarchal system. In this systemic sin patri-kyriarchy is the main agent of domination, lording over the rest of the household and extending this lordship into the public sphere in politics as well as religious practice.

Patri-kyriarchy defends and protects the traditional family and religion, since it is based on the privatizing of the lives of women. In this mode of family organization, legitimating male domination becomes the chief function of culture, religion, and ideology. I have always been intrigued by a common phenomenon among the Indian family system which motivates women to remain with their husbands even in the worst of situations. Violence in this context assumes an alarmingly great significance, for women are expected to bear all expressions of violence, both physical and mental, as a corrective measure, rather than challenge male arrogance.

The myth of women's deficiency in natural powers of reasoning found in

Greek and Roman culture, as Elisabeth Schüssler Fiorenza says, is manifested in other cultures as well. Male perception of the woman in the family rests on the male bias that men are active in the exterior world while women ought to be homebound. If all women resisted this unjust, unequal division of labor, there would be a new release of energy among women to rethink their position and role in the family and society. Barathi Thasan, a well-known Tamil poet, images women's disparity in society in this saying: "Aalai Itta Karumbakki." This means that women have been reduced to the status of sugarcane: squeezed between the heels by a society which does not care about women's personhood but only about extracting work from her. Given the situation of domestic violence, what response does it evoke from us? Anger? Sadness? Surprise? Revenge? Surrender? Or indifference?

ARE WE NOT PASSIVELY CONFORMING?

Most women know that violence is their lot. Through socialization they have learned to accept violence as something naturally bestowed on them. Fatalism thus holds women in a state of magical consciousness. Illiteracy feeds the flame of fatalism, and women learn to adjust and live in a variety of ways while trying to cope with violent situations. This type of endurance makes women look at life as drudgery and to accept violence as a necessary component of a woman's life in society, thus continuing their victimized existence. Often men promote such attitudes of fatalism in women by reinforcing women's status of inferiority and cursed existence. Proverbs abound perpetuating such attitudes in Indian society: "Women, you should not weep when you are beaten," and "Never trust a woman who raises an alarm."

Some women protest and resist violence in their family but are faced with the serious consequences of being ostracized or faced with cruel treatment. Others do get the help of other women to overcome the crisis. Many, however, remain indifferent and cold to domestic violence as a taken-for-granted affair and assume a "not my business" attitude.

This article focuses attention first on the distortions in the traditional theology of family and marriage, which are believed to be divinely ordained institutions. This is followed by women's need to unearth the hidden treasures in the Bible as well as the need to re-interpret their resources according to their context. Then we look at the way women need to re-define their place and role in the family, society, and church. In conclusion, a Third World perspective on feminist theologizing becomes an important element in this contextual theological endeavor.

Women's experience over the globe proves the convictions presented by Elisabeth Schüssler Fiorenza and confirms the fact that domestic violence is a worldwide phenomenon cutting across the barriers of caste, race, ethnicity, language, and religious affiliation. It is an expression of arrogance by a society conditioned by circumstances that make men the rulers and women the ruled.

DISTORTIONS IN TRADITIONAL PERCEPTIONS

In the Bible we see the God who walks with the marginalized and subordinated sections of society. However, by and large, women have been forced by circumstances to accept their condition as fate. Victimization and labelling have been the experience of women. For instance, in the case of Sarah and Hagar, we see this experience of hatred between woman, arising from their competition in protecting their sons in the patriarchal system. Hagar goes through the agony of being rejected by the family, facing society with no status, and being pushed to the level of seeing her own child's misery: a woman stripped of status in the family and society.

Some of the sayings in the Book of Proverbs further reduce the status of women, such as the following: "It is better to live in a corner of the housetop than in a house shared with a contentious wife" (Prov. 25:24); "A continual dripping on a rainy day and a contentious wife are alike; to restrain her is to restrain the wind or to grasp oil in the right hand" (Prov. 27:15-16). Often these sayings are quoted to women in order to make them comply with the demands of the status quo. This legitimizes the fact that good wives are those who do not count the cost of their sacrifice but continue to go on working like a wheel in a machine. And the reward for such an ardent action of "giving life" and "nurturing life," at the cost of her own self, is just praise and respect. So in order to be respected in the family by husband and children, a woman has to be proven a hardworking woman; otherwise she has no respect. She is a *nothing* by birth. All that she could acquire is by the sweat of her brow.

When religion gives such a teaching to a group of people, it eliminates the possibility of making the victim appeal to any court of justice for clemency. The victim is conscientized through socialization that it is the divine expectation for her to behave in such a manner. In the case of women, this experience oppresses them severely, since they already live as if they are the private property of their husbands. The elements of oppression found in Prov. 31:10-31 are: (1) women must keep themselves busy weaving clothing not only for the entire family but also for sale to merchants; (2) women must bring food by whatever means, since the reference is to merchants who normally earn by cheating; (3) women must wake up early and go to sleep late at night because they must be engaged in hard work throughout the day; (4) women must work in the field to produce; and (5) women must look after the family's needs. A man can earn credit and respect by his very birth, but a woman must earn it by hard work. She is worthless by her very being. Other forms of violence also follow from such lack of worth.

Ephesians 5:22-24, 29 gives us another example of the kind of victimization women might have experienced, leading the writer to exhort men to love their wives as their own flesh. What disrespect could women have shown which was the cause of not being loved by their husbands (Eph. 5:33)? If Ephesians could give such an exhortation, it is a serious matter of concern. It seems to have been a common practice that husbands took their wives for granted and treated them as outsiders or outcasts, or marginalized ones, deserving no respect and little love.

Invariably, in all cultures, women have to become victims of hard work and/ or self-negating persons in order to be recognized and respected. This attitude is reinforced by such biblical texts as that of I Timothy 2:11, which instructs wives to be submissive to their husbands. This pattern reflects the monarchical structure and reinforces the patriarchal practice of power. The victims remain voiceless and subservient.

In the Indian practice of sati (whereby the wife falls into the funeral pyre of her husband and dies), Indian culture glorified the woman after her death as a goddess. The root of this practice lies in the fact that if the woman is alive, she is eligible for the husband's property. Therefore, this is the best way to get rid of an unwanted element in the family. Deification is achieved at the cost of women's lives. The victimized woman who suffers endlessly and silently till death is the one who is praised as a saint.

POVERTY OF TRADITIONAL THEOLOGY

Traditional theology has given an understanding of suffering as a God-sent blessing for personal sanctification and for atonement of others' sins. Thus the victim's mentality was focused on personal betterment (in the future) and the sanctification of others. A misrepresentation of God sending his only Son to suffer and die has been used to justify any unjust suffering as permissible, since this was the reward given to the Son of God. Such a theology has for centuries silenced the victim of domestic violence, a condition which was seen as something to be endured.

Women were mentally conditioned to accept their agony as fate or God's will. Innocent suffering was necessary to expiate the sins of others, to bring well-being to the rest of the family members, and to achieve the long life of the woman's own husband. In Hinduism women are expected to fast for the long life of their husbands. Jat, a North Indian festival, confirms this; the victim herself was not the subject matter. The patriarchal mind-set could produce and maintain attitudes that were conducive to the perpetuation of patriarchal privileges. Women perceived themselves as totally meant for the patriarchal structure.

Our idea of God needs a radical reconstruction. The patriarchal God is in no way the God whom we call Father/Mother. This exclusively male God reflects the unjust socio-cultural system of patriarchal societies, with the image of God becoming a projection of the male image. Looked at the other way, the male attains the stature of God himself.

According to the dominant misinterpretation, this God demands the sacrifice of the innocent blood of the Son. God bestows wealth as a sign of favor, and poverty as a sign of curse, and gives rewards and punishments according to deeds. God delights in sacrifices and fasting but does not care about human beings. God demands obedience to the letter of the law. Human initiatives are frowned upon and only tradition can dictate human behavior. Under pressure of law, one does what one is told, but not with a willing heart. This awakens resentment, frustration, and eventually hatred.

Christianity should be a religion of love. It is a way of life that makes love alive in the hearts of people. Love should be the ultimate aim of Christianity. The God in whom we believe is the one who is troubled by human misery and suffering and, therefore, was in the cloud by day and fire by night, for forty years accompanying the people of Israel in the desert. This God can neither be indifferent nor look for self-glory, but delights to be in our midst. How can this God demand, allow, or permit human violence?

Many types of violence to women and children find patriarchal religious sanction when God is seen as one who dominates and legitimizes male-dominated patriarchal society. Sexuality in traditional perception is viewed with discomfort, even as being sinful. Outside marriage it is totally shameful. In marriage, the social services of a woman to her husband are seen as a duty. Her own person is not counted. The familiar platitude "Marriages are made in heaven" leaves no room for the woman to seek an alternative experience in marriage.

Regarding abortion and contraception, there is a blind eye being turned. To women's untold suffering, the topic is not even taken up for discussion with fair participation by women. Women are left in the lurch to decide for themselves, since the expectations of the family, secular society, and the church are so contradictory to one another. Women are like ants caught on a stick which is burning on both ends with no route to safety. The difficulty in getting a divorce forces women to put up with violent situations.

The poverty of traditional theology on these issues evokes a radical question: would women not make a vital contribution to the existing understanding of family and marriage? The incarnational approach surely demands such a contribution from women's perspective.

WOMEN AND RADICAL REINTERPRETATION OF THE BIBLE

God's word is a liberating experience, and for women it ought to be good news in their exploitative and violent situation. As a community committed to liberation from sexism, women must give up all meaningless exercises and engage in liberative praxis. Liberating the Scripture is one such meaningful experience. The Scripture ought to be liberated from its colonized existence of patriarchy. Women's liberation from domestic violence rests on the self-determination of women to overcome this evil. Women must free their minds from patriarchal bondage and breathe fresh air in order to look at the Scriptures from women's liberative perspective.

Theological reflection on domestic violence calls for a re-interpretation of biblical passages such as Luke 10:38-42. Jesus at the house of Martha and Mary lends himself to the domestic situation, trying to free Martha in a way, yet within a struggle of a patriarchal mind-set. When we look at this text, we feel the need of a truly human Jesus who has been lost in this text because of the seeming harshness of Jesus' words.

Traditionally the interpretation of this text has left women wondering what on earth Jesus was talking about. The admonition given to Martha seems to have had no compassion for her and for the work she was engaged in. How could Jesus look upon domestic work with such sternness? There is no family without domestic duties. It has been the vocation of mothers throughout their lives to cook food in order to feed the children and family members. The stand of Jesus seems to go against this practice.

When we try to lift the patriarchal veil from this passage, we see a dynamism different from where Jesus usually emerges. The dichotomizing of action and contemplation, that contemplation is the better position, that Martha seems to stand condemned before Mary: all of these are assumptions arising from this domination model of scriptural interpretation. It is the task of women to free Jesus from the patriarchal hold and allow him to be an ordinary man who was involved with Mary and Martha as friends. From this angle, Jesus emerges a totally different person. He tries to grasp the magnitude of Martha's love.

Women's interpretation calls for reclaiming the hidden treasures. The fact is that Jesus is in a human situation conversing with two women who are in the house. There are neither brother nor parents around. It is a moment when Jesus is totally at ease with women. Therefore we reclaim the fact that Jesus was not merely pontificating judgment over the situation of Martha. We can make an imaginative reconstruction of the incident in the following manner:

Jesus is concerned about Martha and goes out of his way to help her in the kitchen. Martha, Mary, and Jesus are all involved in the process of food preparation, and while everything is getting ready, Lazarus returns from the fields. When Martha, Mary, and Lazarus sit at table with Jesus, they are found to share his table fellowship. And Jesus, knowing well that it was Martha who took the entire trouble of food preparation, calls upon her: "Martha, Martha; you have been troubled over many things in order to prepare this food. Therefore it is your privilege now to bless this meal and share bread with us." Martha, though reluctant, seizes the opportunity to bless and break bread.

This action of voicing the consciousness of Martha witnesses to the fact that she has accomplished a noble task and, therefore, needs to be given recognition also at the table, and not only bear the burden of food preparation in the kitchen. Martha is a symbol of all mothers who have, day after day, spent time in food preparation. They have a right to be recognized at table. Table fellowship is the consequence of kitchen work. These two dimensions cannot be separated from one another. When the hard work of food preparation is over, then it is the task of mothers to relax and learn at the table. Therefore, contemplation is the consequence of being involved in kitchen work. It is in the healthy interaction between these two aspects of reality that women need to fashion their own lives.

Manual work and intellectual activity must be held in a healthy combination. Domestic duties are a necessity in order to build up healthy families. No one can escape the responsibility. Nor can it be relegated as unwanted work, since it is part of our existential situation. But, on the contrary, domestic duties should not be seen as burdensome work, nor can they be imposed upon a few, allowing the rest to enjoy only the privilege of escaping such responsibility.

The new society of partnership and equality we envision necessitates a healthy sharing of domestic duties. Both men and women are called upon to share the burden of food preparation for the well-being of the family. Women participate in equal measure as men, since both are engaged in economic pursuit as well. The notion that domestic duties belong only to women because of their biological destiny, must be dispelled. A healthy understanding of domestic duties and sharing by both partners will enable them to develop a new sense of responsibility between the husband and the wife.

CLAIMING OUR CULTURAL ROOTS

Self-definition is a sign that a person has identified his or her place and role in society and has set definite goals in life. By and large, women in our society are emerging to re-define their role, which is a sign of women coming of age in the technological and modernized society. Even such reclamation ought to be based on the cultural roots that energize us.

In Indian history *kongar padai* is a typical example of the similar experiences of Indian women who have stood for the cause of life. The ninth-century women of the Chittoor area, along the borders of the Karnataka and Tamil Nadu, had the courage to withstand the warriors who were threatening their village. Knowing their men would be defeated in the war, the women tied cradles along the battleground, placing their babies in them and stood behind them. The advancing warring Kongars were taken by surprise. According to the dharma (law) of war, women, children, and any defenseless person cannot be attacked. Thus the Kongars retreated, putting an end to the war, which would have cost the lives of many men.

Mallika Sarabai, an Indian classical dancer, has begun to challenge the mythical figure Rama by taking the role of the daughter of Sita, a position which challenges and questions the role of the traditional Sita figure, and bringing to life the real valiant woman Sita, who stood for the cause of right. She questions Rama as a coward who did not have the courage to protect his own life in spite of knowing Sita's fidelity and loyalty to her husband. Ultimately, she refuses to join her husband and takes refuge in the bosom of Mother Earth. Our Hindu sisters in this way offer a new hermeneutic of a traditionally venerated Indian myth as an attempt to re-interpret Hinduism and re-read Indian tradition from the perspective of women.

Today the veteran woman writer Medha Patkar has a powerful message for the oppressed and marginalized Tribals and Dalits of Central India, particularly the women who are badly hit by the huge dam projects proposed by the International Monetary Fund and the World Bank. What the Chipko women achieved, in preventing violence to nature and violence to women in their society, is today a far-spreading phenomenon where women take an active part in determining what has to happen to their surroundings and their society. The Indian psyche has long expressed its desire for a status of equality and mutual respect between man and woman. The woman is seen as the light of the home, as the treasure of the family and as one in whom the rest of the family relations converge. There are parents who long to have a girl baby in the family, and they repeat pregnancies specifically for this purpose.

The concept of Ardhanarishwars is another example of how women were accorded their status of equality with men. The deity with half-female and half-male parts is a symbol of the indispensable nature of the partnership, showing mutuality and the inclusive nature of the man-woman relationship. Such a relationship must be viewed from the perspective of Indian philosophical and popular traditions, where symbolisms abound expressing the relationship of inclusiveness. It is born of the experience of wholeness within oneself which is extended to other human beings and nature. The eternal conjunction of *prakriti* (nature) and *purusha* (person) is the cause of all creation and life on earth. Therefore the interrelationship between humanity and creation in a way reflects the interrelatedness between man and woman. Such an experience promotes the view of deep respect and mutual recognition. Vandana Shiva confirms this view:

> In Indian cosmology . . . person and nature (Purusha and Prakriti) are a duality in unity. They are inseparable complements of one another in nature, in woman, and in man. Every form of creation bears the sign of this dialectical unity, of diversity within a unifying principle, and this dialectical harmony between the male and female principles and between nature and man becomes the basis of ecological thought and action in India.[1]

EMERGENCE OF WOMEN

Reclaiming the word of life from our cultural context, particularly from the indigenous religious traditions and primal stories, will enable us to reinterpret the Christian faith, particularly for us women, who become

a) *life-affirming* by opting to stand for life as did our foremothers, even at the cost of our own lives

b) *life-sustaining* by drawing energy and vitality from the feminine principle

c) *life-transforming* by our collective participation in the process of assuring equality and justice to people who have been deprived and marginalized for centuries

d) *life-creating* by recreating with God our mother, the fountain and source of all life, the dynamic energy Shakti, whose presence and vital contribution has been almost forgotten and neglected, or rather ignored, in the Christian tradition

The word of God must be addressed to women as word of life. From a tradition of interpreting it often as a word of domination and a patriarchal ideological tool, the living word must be liberated and made to come alive as a double-edged sword, as a liberating essence. For those of us in India, the critical question is whether we can re-interpret Christian faith through our experience and religious heritage.

The question for us is not how to make Jesus become a woman. Rather, the transcended Christ can be the embodiment of the feminine principle, the Shakti, the energizer and vitalizer. It is a serious limitation to express the resurrected Christ in purely male or patriarchal terms. Only women can liberate him from this gross limitation. With his bodily death the maleness of Christ, too, dies. The risen Christ must be liberated from the violent male language, and this only women can do. Drawing from indigenous and primal religions, we need to make the resurrection of Christ become actual in our culture. In this way Indian culture, too, will experience a transformation by making alive an Indian cosmology of wholeness and interconnectedness which is truly the liberative potential of the cosmic Christ. The women of the Third World will begin to portray a new dimension of the face of God which has been hidden by traditional theology. Third World women will liberate the hidden face of God our Mother as Annapurani (God as the nourisher of fullness), as Ashtalaxmi (the one who fills the eight directions of the universe), as Mahisasura Mardini (the one who kills the demon), and as Vishuvarupini (cosmic vision). These images have powerful cultural influence for religious and socio-political liberation. As Indian and as Third World Christian women, we are challenged to re-root ourselves and draw from these traditional sources of God's revelation.

RE-IMAGING GOD AND RE-IMAGING THE MAN-WOMAN RELATIONSHIP

The prayer Jesus taught is a plea for wholeness and holiness. It is a prayer against violence and an appeal to recover the original identity of the human, the lost image of the children of God. In it we find cosmic harmony, community fellowship, and personal integrity. The first part of the prayer takes us to the realm of the divine, transcending all human limitation. "Holy be your name" is an echo of "Tat Tvam Asi" (Thou art that). It is a call to commune with the great, a challenge to recognize our creatureliness and realize what we could truly become, to rise above the limitedness of the human into excellence. It is an opportunity for fulfillment, for ensuring the values of justice and equality, for sharing and partnership, for developing a sense of stewardship and interconnectedness with all creation.

Jesus addresses this prayer to his father the teacher of his disciples. The persons involved are all men. Therefore, no wonder Jesus did not hesitate in repeating the Jewish category of God as male. However, the relationship of closeness with a parent is the newness Jesus brought. If today Jesus were to teach the men and women of our society to pray, what would be his prayer? This is a call to re-image God, a call to liberate God from the traditional Christian imagery. Can God be contained in a particular? God is beyond all these names and forms and transcends all such human limitation. Yet God is one who is with us in the here and now, historically journeying with people in their struggle for true humanity. Let none limit God to a particular mold and impose it on others as universal.

God is multiple in communion.

God is unity in diversity.

God is universally local.

God is transcendentally immanent.

As women we need to discover the God who supports the cause of women, the God who journeys with us in our struggle for dignity and freedom. Our concern to re-image God ought to liberate God from the dominant images of Ruler, Victor, King controlling the weak humans. The rediscovery of the feminine face of God ought to depict God as compassionate, life-giving, and life-sustaining potential, as the divine mother and father.

As Christians, it is not easy for us to image the feminine face of God. But as Indian, as Asian, and as indigenous people, we can enrich the Christian understanding of God from our perspective. Could we pray the prayer of Jesus in this way today?

O God, source and fountain of life, you are the Mother and Father of all living beings. It is your essence within us we desire to touch as we seek to receive blessings from your will and plan for humanity and creation. May we fulfill it with a relentless quest. This day let food be shared with all people of all nations. Let justice and equality be lived by us. Forgive us the times we have hoarded wealth and refused to share with others. In moments of indifference to poverty, shake us. In moments of temptation to dominate or to be sluggish, alert us. Free us from selfishness and fear; make us grow in compassionate love and build a violence-free world in the communion of all persons and creation. Amen.

NOTES

[1] Vandana Shiva, *Staying Alive: Women, Ecology, and Development* (New Delhi: Kali for Women, 1988), 40.

6

VIOLENCE AGAINST WOMEN'S BODIES

Reinhild Traitler-Espiritu

Gender-based violence is a profound health problem for women across the globe suffering from rape, domestic violence, mutilation, murder, sexual abuse, and much more. Estimates of the global burden of this "disease" indicate that in established market economies gender-based victimization is responsible for the loss of one out of every five healthy days of life for women of productive age. By sapping women's energy, undermining their confidence, and compromising their health, gender violence deprives society of women's full participation.[1]

Let us join some of these women as they cry "out of the depths of their despair" (Ps. 130:1). Consider the following testimonies about such violence reported in *Testimonies of the Global Tribunal on Violations of Women's Human Rights*.[2]

For five years, from age twelve to sixteen, New Jersey resident *Gabrielle Wilders* was sexually abused by her stepfather. When Gabrielle's mother died of a rare brain tumor, her stepfather, an ex-priest, prescribed sexual intercourse as a therapy to strengthen Gabrielle's immune system, threatening that she would die if she did not comply. When Gabrielle finally spoke up, her ordeal was by no means over. While she had to spend her time moving in and out of police stations, courtrooms, lawyers' offices, judges' chambers, and medical doctors' and psychologists' offices, her stepfather was free on bail, maintained his innocence, and refused financial support, even withholding her War Orphans and Social Security benefits, which he continued to collect. When the psychological examination classified him as a "sadistic, manipulative, compulsive and repetitive child molester," his lawyer offered a plea bargain. He pleaded guilty to second- and third-degree sexual assault, was sentenced to seven to nine years of incarceration at a treatment facility, and walked free after eighteen months.

Grazyna, a thirty-year-old Polish woman working in a restaurant in Yugoslavia in 1991, was promised work in a German restaurant by two of the customers. As the salary was attractive and Grazyna had to support her children and mother back home, she decided to leave for Germany together with the two men she thought to be her new employers. On the way she was raped, robbed of her papers, and brought to a brothel in Amsterdam, where she was kept in virtual slavery. Several attempts to escape were unsuccessful, mainly because Grazyna could not make herself understood, and only led to her being guarded even more strictly. Finally she managed to contact the Foundation against Trafficking in Women. Grazyna decided to press charges against the traffickers, but when she was interrogated by the anti-vice police, she found to her amazement that the police did not believe her. They thought she had made up the charge of trafficking in order to be granted asylum. Meanwhile, the trafficking mafia had already begun to threaten Grazyna's family in Poland. She is now trying to obtain a residence permit in the Netherlands on humanitarian grounds. She is one of the five thousand women estimated to have been trafficked into the Netherlands in recent years.

Nahid Toubia, a medical doctor from the Sudan, is the founder of the Research Action Information Network for Bodily Integrity and has worked for years to get the socially prescribed practice of female circumcision banned for what it is: female genital mutilation. For those who claim that female genital mutilation is only an issue for elite women, she invites all to come and sit with her in the Outpatient Obstetrics and Gynecology Department of Khartoum Hospital, where she is daily confronted with the physical and psychological pain caused by a procedure which millions of girls have to undergo against their will. While there are many forms of sexual oppression, this particular one is based on the manipulation of women's sexuality in order to ensure male domination and exploitation. Together with many other women, Nahid Toubia also calls for a feminist interpretation of religion. After all, neither Islam, Christianity, nor Judaism mention female circumcision in their texts, though followers of all three religions practice it and use religion as a legitimization.

Petrona Sandoval from Nicaragua is one of the approximately two thousand people who have been paralyzed because of being injected with an expired medication. The anesthesia that was used during her cesarean birth in March 1986 was both outdated and inadequately administered, as during the blockade of Nicaragua, clean syringes, sterilization material, and other medical equipment were in scarce supply. For women this meant an increase in the health hazards related to pregnancy and childbirth. Four years later, Petrona ended up in a wheelchair, her back permanently injured, her professional possibilities destroyed, and her family life in jeopardy. She has joined with other women in similar situations and is amazed how many there are and how afraid they are to speak up.

Lesbians are victims of persecution, coercion, and illegal arms. Their personal security is constantly threatened. In some countries such as Brazil, the incidence of violence and murder related to sexual preference is extremely high. *Marty's* case is an example of the impunity granted to aggressors against lesbians. She is from the city of Maceio. In 1983, she was violated with a bottle and killed along with her lover, Rita da Silva. The aggressor was a member of the family, and he remains free. It is only one example of this "social cleansing" that results in the physical extermination of lesbians, homosexuals, prostitutes, and street kids. Despite the changes that have come towards the end of the twentieth century, forced heterosexuality remains the only role for women that is valued by the society.

Consider this testimony shared out of my own experience as well. *Sarika* was a Bosnian refugee woman who was waiting to be granted asylum in Switzerland. During the waiting period it is forbidden to accept employment, a situation which only leads to a black market with extremely low wages. Sarika had found employment as a kitchen helper in a church-related conference center. The work was essential for her, as she was also trying to free herself from her extremely violent husband. Twice she had already sought refuge in a women's shelter, twice she had returned to the husband because of the children. When she demanded divorce, he threatened to kill her, announcing even the day. Sarika went to the police to ask for protection; the police declined as this was considered a private matter. The husband shot and killed her on the day indicated in the presence of her two small children. The conference center where Sarika had worked quickly acted to help in all practical matters, but was also concerned not to make too much public fuss about the case; after all, the center had provided illegal employment! The husband is now expecting trial but may get away with a manslaughter sentence, which will land him in prison for two to four years maximum.[3]

VIOLENCE AGAINST WOMEN'S BODIES: UNDERSTANDING THE PROBLEM

These testimonies, different as they may be, have several features in common: They demonstrate the following: (1) violence against women is often perpetrated by the very persons women trust most: the male members of their family and close friends; (2) it is usually supported by cultural customs, thus making it difficult for the victims to protest against it; (3) it results in a state of physical and psychological subjugation which places the control over the woman's body firmly in the hands of the aggressor; and most importantly, (4) all violence is primarily violence against the body, "an act carried out with the intention, or perceived intention of physically hurting another person,"[4] mostly with the aim to coerce and subdue this person. It is inflicted against the will of the victim.

It is important to remember that relationships of domination and dependence are usually characterized by physical violence. In slave societies, the vulnerability of the body was one of the main distinguishing characteristics between slave and free man. Torture and physical punishments were part of a calculated scheme of terror, intended to brutalize the body and intimidate the soul, until a state of total dependence was created.[5]

Violence against the body was and continues to be the prerogative of the powerful, who define which type of violence is legitimate and who may avail themselves of it. But while physical violence was an attribute of class difference, physical violence against women has an important gender-related dimension. Since patriarchy has constructed woman's body as a sexual body, violence against women's bodies is almost always violence against women's sexuality.

This is recognized by the UN Declaration on Violence Against Women, which defines violence against women's bodies as

> any act of gender based violence that results in or is likely to result in physical, sexual or psychological harm or suffering to women, including threats of such acts, coercion or arbitrary deprivation of liberty, whether occurring in public or private life.[6]

Listing such acts, the declaration states that the definition should be understood to encompass

> violence occurring in the family and in the community, including battering, sexual abuse of female children, dowry related violence, marital rape, female genital mutilation and other traditional practices harmful to women, non-spousal violence, violence related to exploitation, sexual harassment and intimidation at work, in educational institutions and elsewhere, trafficking in women, forced prostitution and violence perpetrated or condoned by the state (such as torture and rape in police custody).[7]

Even a cursory glance at this list reveals that all these forms of violence have something to do with the way society defines the nature and ownership of women's sexuality. If all violence is perpetrated to establish clear power relations, violence against women's bodies has for its aim to ensure male control over women's sexuality. This becomes clear when we analyze the following patterns of violence against women's body and look at the reasons that make women vulnerable.[8]

The social construction of female sexuality and its role in social hierarchy. Because of being female, a woman is subject to female genital mutilation, abortion of female fetuses and female infanticide, food deprivation during childhood, incestuous sexual abuse, and rape and sex-related crimes during much of her adult life. All these aggressions share a long tradition and are well documented in historic and literary writings, even though it was usually not possible to discuss them openly.

Let us take just one example, female infanticide. It was practiced in many societies and under specific conditions, often as a means to keep the ratio of family size and landholdings constant and sustainable. Its practice depended further on prevailing marriage and dowry arrangements and on availability of means of livelihood for women. Infanticide as such was part of patriarchal cultures that granted the father power to decide over the life of his children. In practice, however, a far larger proportion of female children were killed or disposed of in infancy. Roman custom had it that even rich families should educate only one daughter.

As women were usually the ones to execute the decisions of the fathers, we have many literary documents that witness to the suffering of the mothers, and to the miraculous escapes that were made possible again and again by the ingenuity and compassion of midwives.[9] The very fact that these writings could flourish shows how entrenched these customs were in popular cultures.

Today's research demonstrates that in certain countries infanticide is on the increase, often shamelessly so. Indian sex detection clinics recently advertised that it was better to spend $38 now on terminating a female fetus than $3,800 later on her dowry.[10] A Harvard study on the global male-female ratio confirmed that in countries where both sexes receive similar care, the ratio is about 1.05 or 1.06, reflecting women's biological advantage. But in South Asia, West Asia, North Africa, and China, the ratio is typically 0.94 or lower. The study's authors, economist Amarethya Sen and demographer Ansley Coale, estimated that sixty million women are "missing" in this way, all victims of feticide, infanticide, selective malnourishment, lack of investment in women's health and various forms of violence against women's bodies.[11]

The concept of women as the dependents and the property of a male protector. Because of her relationship to a man, a woman is vulnerable to domestic violence,[12] wife battering, dowry murder, sati, and so-called "crimes of honor," which allow a husband/father/brother almost free hand in dealing with a (sexually) misbehaving or aberrant wife, a lesbian daughter, or sister.

The absence, or perceived absence, of a "protector" can also be a reason for aggression. Many women all over the world are afraid of sexual violence and therefore rely on restrictive, isolating tactics (not going out, not going to certain places) most of the time.[13] The specific vulnerability of women considered "weak" or "unprotected" (and that means available for all men) is only now receiving special attention. Disabled women, women in mental-care institutions, women in psychiatric and pastoral counselling situations increasingly speak about the sexual harassment and aggression to which they are subjected.

In the final analysis, the notion that women are "properties" of men can lead to commodifying women for certain purposes. Trafficking in women/enforced prostitution is clearly on the rise, but so is the trafficking of the female body as a sexual body that is shaped, marketed, and sold in ever new versions of pornography.

The idea that woman may be abused as a means of humiliating the community to which she belongs. This idea is closely linked to the notion of woman as property of man, to male control over women's sexuality and over the question of paternity. Rapes, forced pregnancies, and other sexual abuse in times of war (most recently in the countries of former Yugoslavia) and ethnic, caste, and class conflict have traditionally served as a means to attack the very identity of the enemy's male population. They were considered to be so "normal" that they were not even included in the list of war crimes under the Geneva Convention.

After the first reports of mass rapes in the countries of former Yugoslavia reached the press in October 1992, European women's organizations began a campaign to make sure that rape was recognized as a war crime under the Geneva Convention, and that female judges would have a place in the court if a war crimes tribunal should ever be able to work. *The perception that the state itself condones such practices and does not adequately defend and protect women nor punish the aggressors.* Given the fact that the state reflects the social norms and practices which have shaped it, the lack of recognition of gender violence and the special victimization of women is understandable. It is also, however, cold comfort to realize that in the special case of gender violence, the very institutions which are charged to create just conditions for life for all often help to reinforce, legitimate, and legally codify the hierarchical power relations which make possible violence against women's bodies in the first place.

Women themselves have been socialized to accept the cultural norms concerning their own body and sexuality. This has usually made them silent accomplices with male violence. They often accept violence and deprivation as a necessary element of the relationship between the sexes. Silent suffering is the most prevailing female response to male violence. Women often strive to meet the physical, aesthetic, and sexual requirements imposed on them by custom. The beauty industry is a worldwide multibillion-dollar business,[14] complete with its own products, surgical procedures—such as silicon breast implants for cosmetic purposes, vaginal corrections, etc.—and norms. Since thinness has become a cultural and sexual ideal in the West, the incidence of anorexia nervosa and bulimia is estimated at 5 to 6 percent among school and college females.

Women often become staunch defenders of traditional harmful practices. It is well documented that in the case of female genital mutilation, it is often the mothers that insist on the more severe procedure, infibulation, as if the suffering that goes with it would ensure a measure of security for the future of their daughters.

It is particularly those self-inflicted forms of violence which remind us that the old dictum "Women don't have a body, they are body" still holds true. Women are the body that men have defined for them, and that men continue to control. Violence against woman's body must, therefore, be seen as reflecting the existing power relations between men and women, and will only be overcome to the extent that women begin to redefine their body and sexuality on their own terms and take the steps necessary to enshrine these definitions in women's human rights legislation.

WOMEN: BODIES NOT YET BORN

In order to understand more clearly how violence against women's bodies is being constructed as a ritual of male sexual power over women, we have to enter the process of redefinition of women's bodies on women's own terms.

When we do that, we shall soon discover that this is a conflictual process, even within the women's movement, and carries in itself a number of basic epistemological difficulties.

Women's definition of their own bodies is shaped by a tradition of male perceptions of women's bodies and sexuality. These male perceptions were largely fashioned by women's usefulness for men: by their ability to bring forth children, by their ability to work, and by male sexual desire for the body of women. How important it was for men to retain control over the construction of the female body is illustrated by the interesting history of one of the few medieval medical works written for women and ascribed to a woman author. It is *De Mulierum Passionibus* (On the Sufferings/Illnesses of Women) by Trotula de Ruggiero.[15]

Trotula was a woman who probably studied and taught medicine in eleventh-century Salerno. She wrote the book in order to enable women to help themselves in all matters relating to their physical and emotional well-being. In her introduction she mentions that women "have a vulnerable body and are of great modesty, wherefore they often do not dare to see a doctor." Couched in such language is the suggestion that women were probably afraid of being sexually molested by a male doctor. Outward modesty thus acted as a defense mechanism, but it also deprived women of medical help and thus made them prone to many sufferings.

Trotula's book is particularly interesting, as it is a book not only about illness but also about health and beauty. It is the first European primer on gynecology and achieved great fame in the centuries to follow. More than a hundred manuscripts of the medieval text are known and were widely circulated and translated between the twelfth and fifteenth centuries. In the sixteenth century, however, a German scholar, Wolphius, re-edited the manuscript and in the process re-invented Trotula's identity; she became a man. Feminist historians today point out that the "masculinization" of Trotula needs to be seen in the context of changing gender relations in the fifteenth century, which were clearly unfavorable for women, and against the background of increasing male claims to exclusive control over learning and knowledge.

However, the continuing debate among historians about Trotula's identity shows that more is at stake. Trotula, like Hildegard von Bingen (the twelfth-century mystic, theologian, and physician), is one of the few women who enable us to establish a genealogy of women's own perceptions of their bodies. According to Trotula's concept of women's bodies, women's sexuality, much as it contributes to some of their pressing health problems, does not receive primary attention. Greater emphasis is laid on preventive health care and beauty. Two of the three books of *De Mulierum Passionibus* are dedicated to measures to keep the body healthy and beautiful.

In Hildegard von Bingen's *Liber Causae et Curae* (The Book of Causes and Cures of Illnesses), we find phenomenologies of the different body types of women, which are astonishing because of the frankness with which they speak about women's own desires. They certainly do not affirm sexuality as viewed by men as central to women's lives. In describing a specific type of thin women, Hildegard states laconically that "these women are healthier and happier without men, especially as they feel often weakened after intercourse."[16] Could it be that the body knowledge of women had to be silenced (or reclaimed by men) because women may have constructed for themselves a body not suited to the purposes of men?

In this sense, the centrality the feminist debate accords to sexuality may in itself be a reflection of the fact that even reconstruction of women's bodies happens within the symbolic framework, the discourse system, and the language of patriarchy, which in the past two centuries has increasingly sexualized the body of women.

French feminist philosophers have rightly argued that our bodies are social and cultural constructions in which the definitions of what is "nature" and what is "culture" are inextricably mixed. Every single aspect of our biological, sexual, and social being carries with it a universe of meanings and is part of a process that changes in time and space. Even the biological body has changed in the course of history, together with the cultural one. When we look at the history of body aesthetics, we can easily realize that the sexual body has always been a construction. What in the body was considered to be beautiful and sexually attractive has changed over time and proved to be rather culture-bound.

As Mary Daly in her analysis of the Chinese custom of binding women's feet convincingly argues, sexual attraction often had more to do with the power a particular female shape or gesture granted to men than with any intrinsic erotic quality.[17] This is also borne out by the fact that in all patriarchal cultures sadism (physical violence) is practiced as a lust-heightening feature of sexuality. Sexuality as a play of power that asserts dominance (usually of the male partner) is also reflected in the body norms that were considered ideal. Women's small feet came to be seen as highly erotic because they reduced women to a state of helplessness and made them vulnerable to male (sexual) power.

It is interesting to note that the cultural ideal of the small, girl-like female has its origin in nineteenth-century Europe. At a time when the first demands for equality were raised by women, the emerging bourgeoisie created the body image of the delicate girl who needed protection in order to be able to live at all. The corsetted European middle-class women, whose 45-centimeter waistlines naturally made them faint often (and faint deeply enough even to be raped!),[18] coveted the image of the ever young, ever immature woman who needed a man for her provider, protector, and legal representative. In most European legal systems, husbands were the tutors of their wives well into the twentieth century!

The history of the female body is a cultural history of male fantasies about this body, the way it can be used and the way it had to be controlled in the process of deconstructing this "body" and re-constructing it on their own terms. In light of this, women face several difficulties.

They continue to move in the symbol system and language of patriarchy. If they want to describe the "sexual difference," namely, the fact that women are women in a body different from the body of men, they quickly realize that beyond the phenomenological description of the female body, there is no "symbolic representation." Luce Irigaray has attempted a rereading of some basic philosophical concepts through the body of woman and woman's sexuality.[19] She comes to the conclusion that the concepts of time, space, and relationships prevailing in Western thought reflect the self-consciousness of a male body and male sexuality. What does it mean to have an open body whose sexual experience is shaped by providing the limits to the other's expansion, by fluidity, the "mucous" nature of women's bodily discharge, which in itself is no substance but purely enabling quality, always in the state of becoming another, immanent form of transcendence?

It is easy to denounce such concepts as essentialist, as a return to a new biological vision of women's bodies, but the concept of sexual difference does not construct social roles out of body differences. It is a discourse model that tries to think women's "bodies" from within women's bodily experience, and thus to create for women a symbolic universe of their own. It includes the epistemological problem essentialism presents in its process of thinking. In doing this, we gain some important insights for the necessary process of redefining social relations. In this process the "body of women" and the "truth of sexuality" (endlessly discussed by men from Freud to Foucault) must be constructed and codified in a women-centered way.

The other difficulty women face is the conflict of interests among women themselves. A woman's body is also a class and a race body. The ideal of the "delicate woman" was clearly a class ideal. Working-class and peasant women could afford neither delicate frames nor crippled feet. Thinness was and continues to be a value among the "rich," among those who do not have to worry about where to get one square meal a day.

If women submit to body and sexual norms (including the violence that may go with it), it is because they also derive a measure of benefit from doing so: economic security, social status, a clearly defined identity, belonging. German sociologist Christina Thürmer Rohr contends that women become "accomplices" in a status quo which may be unjust, violent, and hurting them because the benefits outweigh the disadvantages.[20] As their solidarity is with the men to whom they "belong," they may even become opponents to the liberation struggles of other women, as they perceive it potentially threatening to their own situation.

In our efforts to reconstruct women's bodies, we therefore have to begin recognizing sexual difference, but also social, cultural, economic differences that have shaped women's bodies. At the same time we must not fall into the trap of constructing a series of seemingly endless differences, each of which is a system of discourse by itself, each competing in a market of meaning with nothing else but its one intrinsic claim that it is "also truth." Indeed, reconstructing woman's body cannot be done only in a perspective of sexual difference. As the aim is a new paradigm of power, we must also introduce the justice dimension of women's human rights, as defined by women themselves.

TOWARDS A NEW PARADIGM OF POWER

Trying to reconstruct woman's body must not let us forget that the vast majority of women in the world suffer social and economic deprivation and various forms of violence because they live as women, in a female body, faced with its biological functions and vulnerable to male aggression. They experience pregnancies, births, and the prolonged periods of child-care shaping their lives and perspectives; they are part of social and cultural traditions that decide on their education, health, and employment opportunities on the basis of their being women.

This reality creates a self-perpetuating consciousness against which the right argument is not enough. A new consciousness therefore has to come together with

strategies to attack the root causes of violence in addition to treating its symptoms. This means challenging the social attitudes and beliefs that undergird men's violence and renegotiating the meaning of gender and sexuality and the balance of power between women and men at all levels of society.[21]

In this process of renegotiation, women have to take the lead themselves.

When I offer a number of criteria for reconstructing woman's body, I think of them as encouragement in a passionate struggle that we as women have to wage ourselves. They draw on Gerda Lerner's concept of "self-authorization": Women must become their own authorities on matters concerning their lives, and grant authority to each other and to their claims.[22]

Women themselves have to think of their body as intrinsically good and beautiful. Women themselves usually do not think of their bodies as good and beautiful [4-15]. The idea that women have to improve, shape, beautify, and purify the body is part of the female socializing process, amply described by authors like Naomi Wolf. Women have internalized the direct or indirect contempt for women's bodies that is part of patriarchal culture. To claim the body as good needs a re-reading of our religious tradition, which has passed on ambiguous messages about the body, particularly about woman's body. There is no doubt that the misogynistic streaks of European culture developed in the matrix of Christianity. The *Malleus Maleficarum,* the theological handbook that appeared in the late fifteenth century and justified four hundred years of witch hunts, drew heavily on some of the patristic interpretations of Genesis 1-3, which had constructed women's bodies as the entry point for the devil. In a re-reading of the creation myths, Old Testament scholar Helen Schungel-Straumann proves that already the inner-biblical exegesis tended to dwell on the Jahwist tradition of the second creation story, with its hierarchical relationship between the sexes. Influenced by certain Hellenistic misogynistic streams, some of the wisdom literature (such as Jesus ben Sirach) and some of the New Testament epistles interpreted Eve's sin as sexual sin and therefore considered woman's submission under the rule of man as chastisement of her unruly body.[23]

The long and complicated debate on God language and images of God usually argued against female images by pointing to the strictly non-sexual nature of God in the Jewish-Christian tradition. However, as it continued to use male images quite unabashedly, it only proved that not "the body," but the sexually identified body of woman was and continues to be the problem.

The scholastic "solution" to affirm woman's being made in in the image of God in her spiritual nature made matters only worse. It left women with bodies that could be considered as mere matter, always in danger of being violated, defiled, destroyed at will. Worse, the destruction of the body was on occasion even perceived as a means of purifying and saving the spiritual substance hidden in such impure vessels. While they seem almost anachronistic, such thoughts do not only continue to have theological influence; they also shape the self-perception many women have with regard to their bodies. In a secularized manner, the "purification of the body" continues in the religiously observed rituals that are designed to make the body more beautiful, more attractive, "good."

The first creation story implies that the intrinsic goodness of all things is derived from the fact that they were created by God. In deeming everything good, God establishes a loving relation between creation and God. Being made in God's image thus also includes the ability to establish loving relations, which enable us to perceive the intrinsic goodness in all created things, in our bodies, and in those of others. In Genesis 1, beauty is understood in relational terms.[24] In love, the other person, indeed creation itself, becomes good and therefore beautiful.

When relations are distorted, the body can be held in contempt and violated in one form or another. Therefore the idea of self-perfection in Christian traditions always centered on the notion of perfecting relationships to God and neighbor. Without this dimension, self-perfection of the body can indeed be a form of self-contempt, in which aesthetics becomes a mere technical problem of how best to achieve an outward norm.

Women must claim their right to bodily integrity (including sexual integrity) and to decisions concerning their bodies. This means that the notion that women's bodies can be owned, used, and abused for whatever purpose must be overcome. This demand is the more difficult to implement, as it is the nature of patriarchy that women depend socially, economically, but also emotionally on the men to whom they belong. The fine line from cultural custom to violence (which is an enforced act, perpetrated against the will of the victim) is not always visible, as violence is also self-inflicted in the name of security, traditional values, even love, and in the face of apparent helplessness.

We, therefore, have to do a critical re-reading of religious texts that explicitly or implicitly condone violence against women's bodies, that define the relationships between men and women as relations of ownership, and that establish a clear hierarchy of power between the sexes. In such arrangements, the care and protection accorded to women were governed by the social, class, and ethnic status of the men to whom they belonged. A slave girl or a concubine was less protected than a free woman and a wife (though it needs to be mentioned that Jewish legal provisions granted a far greater measure of protection to women of lower status than any of the surrounding cultures did).

While hierarchy between the sexes is not seen as the intention of God, it is considered the consequence of the Fall. Though the harsh punishment of Gen. 3:16 was later cushioned by numerous protective measures, the hierarchical nature of men-women relationships cannot be explained away. It still governs the debate of "who owns women's bodies," their sexuality, their right to decide on pregnancies, on the number of children, often on the possibilities of a lifetime.

Women must claim their right to health and well being as defined by women themselves, and their right to special attention on all health hazards that may arise out of their reproductive abilities. Self-evident as this may seem, it is not. Women's health hazards still include lesser care and nourishment in infancy and childhood and health hazards related to early marriage, pregnancy, and childbirth. They also include hazards arising from "fertility control" (including semi-enforced testing of new means of birth control) or the low priority accorded to research on women's diseases. Worldwide domestic violence, wife battering, assault, induced suicide, and similar aggressions are still among the quantitatively most numerous health hazards. In addition to these there are hazards related to the adherence to body norms (eating disorders, surgical procedures intended to make women sexually attractive, etc.).

Women can only claim their right to health to the extent that they define their body and sexual needs apart from their relationship to men. This means that they must create their own body norms and their own aesthetics, which would also include the aging and the disabled body. Rather than focussing on the "moment of perfection" of the ever youthful woman, they can focus on the process of change the body undergoes, and create a process aesthetics of "being alive," being in the state of becoming, fluid, open.

Re-constructing women's bodies must take as a starting point the needs of the most vulnerable women. These needs can be stated in very simple terms: (1) that a girl child has the chance to develop into a mature woman, without being deprived of food and medical care, sexually abused, sold into child marriage or child prostitution, and violated against in any other way, because she is a girl; (2) that a woman must not endure body violence as part of her existence as a woman, especially when she is poor, dependent, and powerless; (3) that a woman must be able to make her own decisions concerning her body and sexuality without fear of being (physically) punished for them.

This means that any effort at reconstructing women's bodies must at the same time be a step towards redefining power relations between men and women. It further means that men must bid farewell to their own body fantasies of potency and violence, endlessly emulated in real and in virtual reality! It means that the family of states and the different religious communities should rethink their ambiguous position on the question of the sanctity of life of all human beings that are born into this world.

As long as violence and killing is condoned as part of conflict solving and wars, as long as violent contempt for the body of the poor and powerless is in order, it will continue to be necessary to train for caring on the one hand and for ruthless brutality on the other [11-8]. Violence against woman's body is often the merging point, the terrain where caring and brutality meet and where men are unable to keep the two messages, the call to care for life and the command to destroy it, apart.

To overcome violence against woman's body, therefore, means for men and women to reinvent their bodies as instruments for mutuality, compassion, and care.

NOTES

[1] Lori Heise with Jaqueline Pitanguy and Adrienne Germain, "Violence against Women: The Hidden Health Burden," World Bank Discussion Paper 255 (Washington, D.C., 1994).

[2] Center for Women's Global Leadership, *Testimonies of the Global Tribunal on Violations of Women's Human Rights at the United Nations World Conference on Human Rights*, Vienna, June 1993 (New York: Center for Women's Global Leadership, July 1994).

[3] Testimony supplied by R. Traitler-Espiritu on the case of Sarika D., killed January 17, 1995, at her home in Hombrechtikon/Zurich.

[4] Margaret Schuler, ed., *Freedom from Violence: Women's Strategies from around the World* (New York: OEF International, 1992), 10.

[5] In the classic studies of slavery in the Caribbean—such as Frantz Fanon's *The Wretched of the Earth* (New York: Grove Press, 1977); or C.S.L. James' *The Black Jacobins* (New York: Vintage Books, 1963)—the connection between physical violence and mental subjugation is well established.

[6] "Violence against Women: The Hidden Health Burden," 3.

[7] Ibid.

[8] The following analysis is indebted to Margaret Schuler, "Violence against Women: An International Perspective," in *Freedom from Violence*, 10.

[9] The medieval novel *Fresne* by Marie de France (ca. 1160) is only one of many that tell the life and adventures of a girl that was saved from infanticide.

[10] "Violence against Women: The Hidden Health Burden," 12.

[11] Ibid.

[12] It must be noted that corporal punishment of a wife was the (legal) prerogative of the husband in many countries of Europe well into the nineteenth and early twentieth century. It still lingers on in the sense that in certain societies it is at least culturally acceptable, if not outrightly condoned.

[13] "Violence against Women: The Hidden Health Burden," 25.

[14] Naomi Wolf, *The Beauty Myth* (London: Chatto and Windus, 1990).

[15] A detailed analysis of the case of Trotula is given by Maria-Milagros Rivera Garretas, *Orte und Worte von Frauen: Eine feministische Spurensuche im europaischen Mittelalter*

(Vienna: Wiener Frauenverlag, 1993) Vol. 23, 112-142. In Spanish: *Textos y Espacios de Mujeres* (Icaria: Barcelona, 1990).

[16] Quoted ibid., 137.

[17] Mary Daly, *Gyn/Okologie: Eine Metaethik des radikalen Feminismus* (Munchen: Frauenoffensive, 1981), 156ff.

[18] Heinrich von Kleist's novella, *The Marquesa of O.* (New York: Unger, 1973). Written in the early nineteenth century, the story is told of an aristocratic woman who finds herself pregnant without being conscious of having had intercourse. It turns out she was raped by her protector while she had fainted.

[19] Luce Irigaray, *Ethik der sexuellen Differenz* (Frankfurt: Suhrkamp, 1991), 11-116. See particularly her re-reading of Plato, Aristotle, Descartes, and Spinoza on the listed pages in the German edition.

[20] Christina Thürmer Rohr, *Vagabundinnen* (Berlin: Orlanda Frauenverlag, 1986).

[21] "Violence against Women: The Hidden Health Burden," ix.

[22] Gerda Lerner, *Die Entstehung des feministischen Bewusstseins von Mittelalter bis zur ersten Frauenbewegung* (Frankfurt: Campus, 1993).

[23] Helen Schungel-Straumann, *Die Frau am Anfang: Eva und die Folgen* (Freiburg im Breisgau: Herder, 1989).

[24] In many cultures (also in ancient Greece), the words for "good" and "beautiful" were interchangeable, thus denoting awareness that ethics and aesthetics belong together.

7

VIOLENCE AND WOMEN'S BODIES IN AFRICAN PERSPECTIVE

Elizabeth Amoah

The Scribes and the Pharisees brought a woman who had been caught in adultery; and making her stand before all of them, they said to him, "Teacher, this woman was caught in the very act of committing adultery. Now in the law Moses commanded us to stone such women" (John 8:3-5a).

In many cultural and religious traditions the woman's body is conceived in such a way that the autonomy of her will and wishes is completely denied. She is seen as an object for unlimited access. It is not uncommon to find that in many cases of rape, the tendency is to blame the woman rather than the man. A particularly fashionable example is the reference to the so-called "provocative dress" of women as if this is a good excuse for violating their persons in cases of rape. Another typical example is what is portrayed in the above quotation. A woman caught in adultery was to be stoned to death as the Mosaic law demanded. The law as stipulated in the book of Leviticus required that both the adulterer and the adulteress should be stoned to death (Lev. 20:10). In the case cited in the passage quoted above, the rule is bent and the woman alone was condemned to be stoned to death. This is a case where rules and regulations are used to control the body of the woman.

In some rural African settings, it used to be the pattern for men to take rather unlimited liberties in touching particular points of women's bodies for amusement and enjoyment without any remorse. This strict control over women's bodies is related to another conception, that the woman's body is essentially and potentially sensual and seductive (Prov. 7:10). This in its extreme form is seen in many restrictions associated with the bodies and persons of women.

In Islamic religious thought, for example, women in this respect are expected to cover as much of their bodies as possible; in some cases, even not excluding the face. In their form of worship Moslem women are expected to be at the back of the congregation,[1] so that as they bend in times of prayer they may not expose their bodies to men. In this way, what to the men seem seductive postures may not tempt men who are with them in the service.[2]

Again, a biblical example in the same vein may be found in Paul's first letter to the Corinthian Church (11:2-5). In the letter, Paul instructed Corinthian women not to expose their hair, which to him was a source of attraction to men. The underlying thought in all these injunctions is that women's bodies are seen as the source of potential seduction and thus they should be strictly controlled.

In many of the African traditional societies, not much concern seems to be expressed about the bodily exposure of females under minority, that is to say, those who are not yet up to the age of marriage. A similar attitude is adopted in relation to certain exposures of parts of women's bodies where these relate to old women, especially those past the age of childbearing. However, in the intervening period, when they are approaching nubility, a great concern and many sanctions are attached to bodily exposures. After nubility rites, women are expected to be extremely cautious about the way they dress and comport themselves. Severe sanctions, both moral and religious, are often associated with deviations from the expected pattern of modesty with regard to dressing and bodily appearances.

In such situations it is considered to be an act of adultery to touch or see specific parts of the woman's body—such as breasts, buttocks, waist-beads, and thighs—or to make any unseemly gestures in relation to actions towards these parts. Sitting on a married woman's bed, talking to her while she is having a bath, or making some jokes about her constitute acts of adultery in many African traditional societies. Such acts, depending on the contexts and situations, have their appropriate sanctions.

The understanding of women's bodies as sensual and seductive seems to be at its peak in the period of nubility. In this nubility period the woman is sexually and socially considered to be mature. The various rites of nubility which abound in Africa testify to this.[3] It is the period within which women are expected to marry and to reproduce. Marriage thus confers on the man exclusive rights over the woman's body and sexuality.[4]

No one from outside the marriage has access to the woman's body. It is this kind of thinking in relation to the exclusive power and rights over the woman's body which often leads to all forms of violence and abuse of women by men. For instance, wife battering and periodic violence, be it physical or psychological, are rampant and often justified in terms of such rights. These acts of violence are accepted as the responsibility and the privilege of men to "discipline their wives" and subdue them to their proper position.

Similarly, the sexual act between spouses is not seen as a mutually participatory act in most cases.[5] More often than not the woman is expected to submit to the act without any complaint and objection. Any attempt by the woman to initiate actions in such matters is traditionally seen as unbecoming and, at worst, something that should be checked.

In this regard some have interpreted female circumcision as one way of limiting, if not eliminating, women's sexuality.[6] Another level of interpretation relates to the idea that women have to bear pain or suffer without complaint. Thus female circumcision and other related rituals associated with bodily mutilation are seen as preparing the woman to be able to absorb painful conditions such as childbirth, an act which is both biologically and symbolically linked with womanhood.

The conceptions which have been outlined above have implications for the consideration of the socioeconomic and political situations of women. This is brought up even more clearly in the context of some of the contemporary issues relating to women. A few examples will be cited below.

Population Issues and Women's Bodies

The recent Cairo Conference on Population and Development highlighted some religious and social conceptions about the bodies of women. One of the central issues at stake was the extent to which the woman has the freedom to make decisions over her body in relation to childbirth.

There was general agreement about the need to control population in the light of the general diminishing of resources. When it came to the discussion on the actual method of the devices for population control, opinions seemed to be sharply divided on the issue of abortion as one such device. Some religious groups, particularly Muslims and Roman Catholics, flatly dismissed abortion as a morally and religiously unacceptable device. On the other hand, some women, especially from the West, took the firm stand that when it came to these issues the woman should have the right over her own body. One sees here a clear challenge to the stereotyped and traditional thinking about woman which denies her autonomy and the right over her body.

Another aspect of the population issue is related to the size of the family, that is, the desirable number of children. Here again religious and cultural beliefs come into prominence as important factors that determine, in one way or the other, attitudes towards women. There are traditions and religious beliefs which have been interpreted literally to mean "be fruitful and multiply" without limit (Gen. 1:28). There are also the traditional beliefs in some societies, especially societies in Africa, that the number of children that couples have is a sign of prosperity and well-being. Having many children also implies that the ancestors are coming back to life.

These beliefs and ideas definitely affect the attitude of people toward family-planning programs.[7] The attitudes range from outright rejection of some of these measures to acceptance. There are many cases where it is also thought that family planning programs are the sole concern of women. Thus the men will not have anything to do with either the use of family-planning devices or any discussion about it. The glaring implication of these attitudes is that in many cases some women go on having children at the expense of their economic survival, health, and life.

Women's Bodies and Prostitution

It is not only in the issue of women's bodies and population that these risks to women are seen. Another area relates to prostitution as a social problem. This is an area where the bodies of women have been abused and violated in various ways. Prostitution has become a very important problem in many developing countries where, because of severe economic deprivations, women have been forced to sell their bodies in order for their families and themselves to survive.

The health hazards and risks involved are extreme, especially the possibility of acquiring the dreadful disease AIDS. In Ghana many AIDS patients are women who have had to migrate to other places for prostitution. There is good reason to believe that this situation is not different in other developing countries. This is a situation where economic factors affect the bodies of women in a very telling way.

Women's Bodies and Drugs

A phenomenon which has clearly emerged in recent times is the use of women's bodies in trafficking hard drugs. There are many instances in which women in developing countries have been arrested and jailed because such drugs as cocaine have been found on their bodies. This has led to very humiliating searches of the bodies of women, especially those travelling from the third world, at immigration points by air, land, and sea.

The popular means for carrying these drugs have included either insertions or swallowing. In both cases serious risks to the lives of the carriers cannot be ruled out. There have actually been cases where women have died in such pursuits. Such cases are a clear indication of the extent to which economic and patriarchal systems can drive women into serious hazards and degrading conditions. It is clear that women's bodies are seriously violated in all such instances even if one may admit that in some cases they themselves get involved in the drug-trafficking business. Surely, the big businessmen behind these deals are taking advantage of the women who are used merely as tools in this risky business.

Women's Bodies and Advertising

In precisely the same way as women are used in drug trafficking, so are they often used in a whole range of advertising. It is not uncommon to see any new product ranging from cars to alcoholic beverages being advertised with models of women. Much pornographic literature and advertising similarly use the bodies or pictures of women as catchy advertisements for their clients. This practice is conducted on a large scale even in multi-national business, especially tourism and the hotel industry. Because of the commercial gains that are involved in these advertisements, women are lured into such business arrangements. Here, too, it is very clear that women's bodies are exploited for economic reasons without any concern for their self-respect and dignity.

Women's Bodies and Alternative Relationships

The stereotyped view is that sexual relations should occur between a man and a woman. This is reinforced both by traditional cultures and also through religious beliefs and norms (Rom. 1:26-27, e.g.). This stereotyped view clearly denies the right of choice by people. Some women have boldly and openly chosen to have other women as partners, thus challenging the traditional stereotyped man-woman relationship. This could be seen as an expression of freedom and the right to decide in matters of relationship with others.

However, this has not gone unchallenged, as seen from the press and other media. Some of those who have made this option have had to face severe odds from opposing segments of the secular and religious society. There have been violent reactions on either side of this issue. These actions and reactions reinforce the dominance of traditions and stereotypes and the extent to which they constitute impediments for new conceptions about the woman's right over her body.

Single Parenthood

Another alternate relationship that has emerged is the issue of single parenthood in the form of the female-headed household. Some women have opted to live outside marriage, have their children, and take responsibility for decisions affecting their own lives and those of their children. This phenomenon is seen not only in the Western world but also in many of the developing countries. What is at issue here is not that they are entirely against marriage, but that they should be allowed to express their own options in relation to matters affecting themselves. The crux of the matter here is the issue of freedom and the right to make independent decisions regarding fundamental issues such as marriage, which affect their lives and identities.

Women's Bodies and Religious and Spiritual Identity

The identities of women are not to be seen as having only biological, physical, and socioeconomic dimensions. The religious and spiritual dimension is also crucial in any discussion on women's body and violence. One significant instance relates to religious and ritual perception of women and biological processes such as menstruation.

In many African traditional religious rituals menstruating women are seen as both polluting and potentially destructive. They are generally excluded from religious rituals, sacred places, and objects.[8] Besides, there are taboos that restrict their movements and social participation during their menstrual cycles. These restrictions on the menstruating woman are also seen in the religious traditions of ancient Israel (Lev. 15, e.g.). However, Jesus, as portrayed by the Gospel writer in Luke, raised questions that challenged this kind of perception by healing the woman with the issue of blood (Luke 8:43-48).[9]

The implication is that these restrictions and perceptions of the menstruating woman are completely out of place and untenable. Modern biological thinking and experience also reinforce this point. The upshot is that women are thus freed from such restrictions, which have no basis yet can completely control their activities and behavior in traditional societies.

Women's Bodies and Witchcraft

Over a long period of time the belief has been held that witchcraft, which is essentially perceived as evil and destructive, is associated with women. Thus forms of inhuman acts of violence are meted out to women who are accused by the system of being witches. Even in most recent times in Ghana, there are some villages described as witchcraft villages, especially in the northern part of Ghana, where any woman accused of witchcraft is sent away and confined. Such women are kept in very small rooms where they are denied some of the basic necessities, including visitors and hygienic conditions. It is not unusual for deaths, or mental and physical disabilities, to occur among such women.

Some women in some of the African-instituted Churches and the charismatic ministries which emphasize deliverance go through similar hardship. Some of these women are accused of having all types of evil spirits and demons. Thus, they are said to be the cause of a whole range of hardships, misfortunes, and sufferings of others. They are made to undergo long hours of exorcism and purification procedures that are, in many instances, violent and humiliating. The central issue here is that as women, they are seen as inherently carriers of witchcraft and demonic spirits. This can be seen as a violation of womanhood. The point being made is that such negative concepts reinforce some of the brutalities which are meted out to women who are characteristically believed to be the source of all problems.

It should be noted that in both traditional African religion and Christianity there are instances of liberating perceptions about women. In traditional African religion, women perform functions of the priesthood, including divination and healing. Similar activities of women can be cited in some of the African-instituted Churches. There are women believed to be endowed with the Holy Spirit and who perform as prophets, healers, councilors, preachers, and so on.

So far, we have attempted an overall survey of some of the ideas about women's bodies and violence in both religious and social contexts. It is clear that there are some long-standing stereotyped conceptions of the body of women which affect their lives. Some of the various ways have been discussed in the light of socioeconomic, political, and religious dimensions. In all these spheres, women are clearly challenging the dominant stereotypes and are breaking new ground in expressing options that emphasize and enhance their dignity, self-respect, and autonomy. One cannot discount, even in the face of all this, the strong counteracting influences and views that still seek to reinforce the status quo. But women have gone a long way towards asserting themselves, and they are supported by some modern developments in education, increased awareness, and unfailing efforts of some outstanding women who act as role models for the further advancement of women. There are such women in the various religious traditions and society in general. Their lives should be the source of encouragement to uplift women from self-pity and absolute conformity against limiting traditional stereotypes, raising them to a position where they can assert themselves in the context of full self-awareness. In this way women will also have the abundant life toward which all humans strive.

NOTES

[1] *The Koran*, 4th. rev. English edition (New York: Penguin Books, 1974), 24:31, 60; 33:59.

[2] Amma Rabiatu, "The Position of Women in Islam: A Case Study of the Position of Muslim Women in Accra," 1981, unpublished paper.

[3] Peter Sarpong, *Girls' Nubility Rites in Ashanti* (Tema, Ghana: Ghana Pub. Corp., 1977).

[4] Elizabeth Amoah, "Femaleness: Akan Concepts and Practices," in *Women, Religion, and Sexuality*, ed. Jeanne Becher (Geneva: WCC, 1990), 129-53.

[5] Ibid.

[6] Scilla McLean, ed., *Female Circumcision, Excision, and Infibulation: The Facts and Proposals for Change*, Report No. 47 (London: Minority Rights Group, 1980), 1-20.

[7] Tom K. Kumekpor, *Rural Women and Attitudes to Family Planning, Contraceptive Practice, and Abortion in Southern Togo* (Legon: University of Ghana, Department of Sociology, 1970).

[8] Cf. Robert Sutherland Rattray, *Religion and Art of the Ashanti* (Oxford: Clarendon Press, 1927).

[9] Elizabeth Amoah, "The Woman Who Decided to Break the Rules" in *New Eyes for Reading: Biblical and Theological Reflections by Women from the Third World*, ed. John S. Pobee and Barbel Van Wartenberg-Potter (Geneva: WCC, 1966), 3-4.

Part Three

ECONOMIC AND MILITARY VIOLENCE

8

ECONOMIC VIOLENCE AGAINST MINORITY WOMEN IN THE USA

Ada María Isasi-Díaz

A few months ago in New York City I was driving with Ivone Gebara through Harlem in an area known as Dominican Heights, since it has the greatest concentration of Dominicans anywhere, including even the Dominican Republic itself. Ivone, who is from São Paulo in Brazil, mentioned the impact of seeing that the same economic oppression the USA has established and maintains in Third World countries is also a reality for racial/ethnic minorities in the USA. Racial/ethnic minority women in the USA do suffer economic violence in a number of ways. They live in situations where their ability to provide for themselves and those for whom they have responsibility is curtailed or hindered. They live in situations where they are abused or coerced by unfair remuneration of their labor, and situations in which, through physical or psychological means or through moral pressure, they are not allowed equal participation in the goods of society, whether those goods are natural or manufactured.

Racial/ethnic minority people in the USA are indeed Third World people living in a First World context. It is obvious to us and to all those who are willing to look at reality through our eyes that most of the strategies of exploitation and domination that the USA uses in Third World countries are first "practiced" on us, the minority groups in the USA.

The term "minority" is used in the USA not to refer to numerical size but as a "status designation," that is, the relative prestige and power of groups in the stratification hierarchy of the social order. The essence of minority group status is "unequal access to the sources of economic and political power in society."[1] In this article I will use "minority" both to refer to the more than sixty million people in the USA who themselves or whose ancestors originated in a common area other than Europe, such as Latin America and the Caribbean, Africa, Asia, and to refer to the indigenous people of the USA. Each of these groups shares important elements of a common culture and participates in activities in which "the common origin and culture are significant ingredients."[2] In the USA a central feature of "minority" groups is distinctive phenotypical characteristics, such as skin color, hair texture, face, and body shape, different from those of the white Europeans who constitute the dominant group. The importance given to race and ethnicity in the USA leads to stratification in terms of access to prestige, wealth, and power, which in turns results in a "structured system of exploitation and social discrimination."[3]

THE DIVERSITY OF MINORITY WOMEN

Following are some demographic and socio-economic characteristics of USA minority women that will begin to make clear what it means to be "minority" women in one of the most powerful and richest nations in the world.

African American women have suffered discrimination and violence, either from their original position as slaves or from the persistent prevalence of racism in this society, having been brought to the USA as chattel slaves. Black women have long suffered from the dual disadvantage of race and gender, especially in the labor force. Initially, they were largely agricultural laborers in the post-slavery period; subsequently, black women worked primarily in domestic service, and more recently, they are concentrated in low-level service and clerical jobs. Many black women are single mothers who earn considerably less than men and experience difficulty in providing for their families.[4]

The three main groups gathered under the term "Latinas" are Mexican Americans, Puerto Ricans, and Cubans. The majority of Mexican Americans were born in the USA, descendants of a population that was indigenous to the southwestern part of this nation before it was taken over from Mexico in 1848. Also considered part of this sub-group are the Mexicans who cross the border searching for jobs. They constitute a large portion of agricultural workers who have only seasonal work and migrate to different areas of the country to harvest different crops. The second most numerous group of Latinas are Puerto Ricans, USA citizens by birth. With few occupational skills, Puerto Rican women work in low-skill manufacturing jobs mainly in the northeastern area of the mainland. The Cubans are mainly an immigrant population who have come to the USA mostly since 1959. Initially Cuban immigrants were "largely professionals and entrepreneurs who fled the communist government in Cuba. They were given special refugee status and provided settlement assistance by the U.S. government, which helped them to do well economically."[5] In the 1980s another wave of Cuban refugees of much lower socio-economic status arrived. Since then, the steady stream of Cubans who have arrived in the USA also belongs to a low socio-economic stratum.

Asian Americans include women from China, Japan, the Philippines, Korea, India, and Vietnam. The Chinese started immigrating to the USA in the 1840s but in 1882 Congress prohibited Chinese immigration and expelled many Chinese. Chinese immigrants have increased again especially since 1965, when national-origin immigration quotas were lifted. Japanese in the USA are mainly second generation, a large number of their parents having suffered the ignominy of internment during World War II out of fear that they would cooperate with Japan against the USA. Filipinos are the most recent Asian immigrants. While initially Filipino immigrants were mostly agricultural workers, recent ones "tend to be professionals, with many among the women being nurses."[6] Koreans and Indians have come mainly since 1960. Both groups are, for the most part, mainly urban, highly educated professionals. Finally there are the Vietnamese, a refugee population that arrived in the USA between 1975 and 1980. Large groups among them, like the Hmong, are mostly rural people with few economic or literacy skills.

Native Americans, indigenous to the USA, have been one of the most oppressed groups. They have been affected by laws unique to them because they are part of separate nations rather than citizens of the United States. In the first half of this century, they lived on reservations and followed fairly traditional lifestyles. Subsequently, they have moved off the reservations in large numbers.[7] Native Americans have low literacy rates and minimal economic skills, traits which result in a pervasive poverty and discrimination against them.

SOME CHARACTERISTICS OF USA MINORITY WOMEN

Examining socio-economic characteristics will give a more concrete picture of the world of African American, Latina, Asian American, and Native American women in the USA. Consider educational attainment. In the last thirty years the percentage of African American, Latina, and Native American women has more than doubled but still remains considerably less than that of women from the dominant group. Interestingly enough, the percent of Asian American women who graduate from high school has always been higher than that of women from the dominant group. But in general, the percentage of minority women graduating from high school is lower than that of women of the dominant group. Besides, one has to take into consideration the fact that in the last thirty years there has been a lowering of academic standards with the result that a high-school diploma nowadays has less than half the socio-economic significance that it had in 1960. A college degree, earned after four years of studies beyond secondary school, now has roughly the socio-economic significance that a high-school diploma had in the 1960s. And though there also have been significant gains in education for minority women, the women of the dominant group are well ahead of minority women, except, again, when it comes to Asian American women.

The following table provides the data for comparison.[8]

Women High-School Graduates 1980		*Women College Graduates 1980*
White/Dominant	68.1%	13.3%
African American	51.5%	8.3%
Latina	42.7%	6.0%
Asian American	71.4%	27.0%
Native American	54.3%	6.4%

When one looks at the role of minority women in the labor force, the first thing that becomes obvious is that gender and race/ethnicity play an important role in the kinds of jobs to which they have access as well as the pay they receive for their labor. The "primary" sector of market labor, consisting of "white-collar salaried or self-employed workers with high status, autonomy and, often, supervisory capacity,"[9] has been monopolized by white males of the dominant group. Jobs in this sector have traditionally yielded family wages that support a wife and children. The "secondary" sector, consisting of "low wages, few or no benefits, little opportunity for advancement, and unstable employment,"[10] is where one finds USA minorities. The jobs in this sector, often part-time or temporary, with the amount of education or experience of the workers not leading to increases in salaries, do not pay family wages. Thus women in the family find it necessary to enter the labor force. A third sector is the "underground" sector. Here is where the most marginalized labor force groups earn their living from illegal or quasi-legal work. This sector contains a great variety of jobs, including drug trafficking, crime, prostitution, work done by undocumented workers, and sweatshop work which violates labor standards such as minimum wages and job safety regulations.[11]

In short, a growing number of minority women are grouped in the jobs that yield less income, have less benefits, and provide less stability. The jobs held by most minority women are in agricultural labor, domestic service, and other kinds of work in the service sector. An increasing number of minority women are single heads of households, totally responsible for their children with no help from the children's fathers and, often, because of distance, little help from the extended family. This fact, combined with extremely minimal job opportunities, results in very perilous situations for minority women in the USA.

An analysis of the economic oppression of minority women has to include a thorough look at the ways in which economic institutions and practices structure the lives of these women, as well as the important role which the economy plays in creating and sustaining racial/ethnic, gender, and class conflicts. Economic status and class are greatly impacted by gender and racist/ethnic exploitation. For example, access to ownership of the means of production and, concomitantly, to wealth greatly depends in the USA on being white and male. In the early history of the USA, white males established their economic dominance, rationalizing their behavior by using racist and sexist ideas prevalent in Europe at the time. Once they had done this, they were able to perpetuate and institutionalize this dominance, first in the emerging capitalist system of the nineteenth century and after that in full-blown market capitalism through the monopolization of managerial and other high-level jobs to which racial/ethnic minorities, particularly women, have little access.[12]

Two of the key ingredients of market capitalism are cheap labor and expansion of markets. The USA at present depends much more on a service economy than on a manufacturing economy, so cheap labor is needed for the service sector, where salaries are significantly lower than for the manufacturing sector. And that is where you will find the majority of the USA Third World people.

It is for this reason that since 1965 the USA has allowed the numbers of immigrants from Latin America, especially Mexico and Central America, to double, and of immigrants from Asia to triple. Women are considered particularly good workers when it comes to service jobs because they are hard workers, attentive to details, subservient, and polite, and their low pay is justified because it does not matter that women be given a "family wage" anyway.

The voracious need for expanding markets drives the USA to create new markets no matter where and no matter at what cost. That is the main reason for the North American Free Trade Agreement with Mexico and Canada (NAFTA). Why is it that instead of expanding the middle class in the USA by making it possible for racial/ethnic minorities to become part of it, the USA prefers to work at expanding middle classes abroad? Does the reason have to do with the racist/ethnic prejudices that continue to reign in the USA? Indeed, it is no wonder that minority women in the USA with their very small buying power are considered surplus people by market capitalism. Only those who consume and those few needed for the advanced jobs of technology are considered important in the USA.

The present anti-immigration sentiment in the USA is linked to this rejection of low consumers. The reason has nothing to do with immigrants costing the federal government because they dip into social welfare programs. Time and again studies have been conducted that indicate that immigrants, even undocumented immigrants, contribute more to the economy of the USA than they drain from it. The sentiment against them is not because they cost the government monies, but rather because they are not consumers.

Capitalist society in its advanced state has no time for non-consumers, no need for them, no use for them. Therefore, society is not willing to invest money, time, or effort in satisfying basic needs for food, health, housing, or education of minority women who consume so very little. The capitalist system views non-consumers as a dangerous sector of society where prostitution, theft, drugs, and AIDS flourish. This leads to being excluded from, separated from, society at large. Indeed, many think that the neglect from society, even neglect from the churches, that racial/ethnic minorities in the USA experience is a strategy of the system to get rid of this surplus people which has no role to play in it.

SNAPSHOTS OF MINORITY WOMEN

A few snapshots of the economic reality of minority women within the USA will help to concretize the economic violence they suffer.

Chinatown in New York City, located on the southern part of the island of Manhattan, is one of the areas with the highest concentration of population in the USA. It is not uncommon for two families to live in the same space. In this situation, one occupies the space while the other one works; when the one in the house goes to work, the second family comes in to sleep and eat. Asian Americans have the highest number of people working per household of all racial and ethnic groups in the USA. In the whole population there is an average of 1.6

workers per household while among Asian Americans the average is 2.23 workers per household. Many Asian Americans work no less than ten hours a day, 6.5 days a week.

African American women have certainly made progress when it comes to participation in the labor force. They now work in almost every job category, but gains are not distributed evenly. "While an increasing share of Black women hold managerial and professional jobs, in 1980, 12 percent were unemployed, 32 percent worked at the bottom of the labor market hierarchy, and almost one-third of all Blacks continued to live in poverty."[13] The progress of African American women is both partial and tenuous: partial, because their employment opportunities are still limited, and tenuous, because a large number of the ones who are managerial and professional women are employed in the public sector, being dependent, therefore, on "the size of the government sector in an era of budget austerity and lessening commitment to affirmative action."[14]

One in four Latino families is poor, and the poverty rate among female-headed families is twice as high: 51.8 percent. Almost one out of every four Latino families is headed and maintained by a single woman. In the USA, 15 percent of white children are poor, while 39.3 percent (or two in five) of Hispanic children are poor and 45.1 percent of Black children are poor. In the first quarter of 1995, the median weekly earning of Latina women was $308, compared to $349 for Latino men, $401 for African American men, and $565 for Euro American men. But to understand that the exploitation of Latinas is not just a matter of sexism, one needs to compare the median weekly salary of Latinas, $308, to that of other women: $343 for African American women, and $416 for Euro American women.[15] This means that for every dollar Euro American men make, Latinas make 54 cents; Latinas make 76 cents for every dollar African American men make, 88 cents for every dollar Latino men make, 74 cents for every dollar Euro American women make, and 89 cents for every dollar African American women make.

Native American women's participation in the labor force rose from 35 percent in 1970 to 48 percent in 1980. But almost two-thirds of Native American women only had "part time jobs—the highest rate for any racial-ethnic group of women except Chicanas (Mexican Americans)—and American Indian women faced the highest unemployment rate (12 percent) of any racial-ethnic group except Puerto Rican women in 1980."[16] Much of the blame for the low occupational status of Native American women is due to "repressive, inaccessible, and inadequate education . . . along with discrimination by employers, and the stagnation of the reservation economy."[17]

"DEVIANT," "OTHER," AND ENTRAPPED BY THE MYTH

The economic violence minority women in the USA experience is part of the imperialism for which this country is so well known. It is important to notice what economic exploitation does to the psyche of people, individually and communally, for imperialism is not only a matter of economics but also about rendering the perspectives of minority women invisible at the same time that they are stereotyped as "other," as "outsider." Imperialism in its concrete form of ethnic and gender-based prejudice against minority women is responsible for making the experiences and culture of non-minority women the norm in the USA. The dominant group of non-minorities, which soon after the turn of the century will be less than half of the population in the USA, "project their own experience as representative of humanity as such,"[18] while construing the experiences of minority women as deviant and inferior.

The culturally dominated undergo a paradoxical oppression, in that they are both marked by stereotypes and at the same time rendered invisible. As remarkable, deviant beings, the culturally imperialized are stamped with an essence. The stereotypes confine them to a nature which is often attached in some way to their bodies, and which thus cannot easily be denied. These stereotypes so permeate the society that they are not noticed as contestable.[19]

The most destructive aspect of imperialism over minority women in the USA, however, is not what it does to minority women but what it makes minority women do to themselves. Little by little they internalize the way the dominant culture sees them, when it sees them, for they are always obliged to act according to the image society has of them. Little by little their own cultures, their self-understandings become as invisible to them as they are to the dominant culture. And that invisibility finds expression in a rejection of their own cultural customs and values, in a rejection of themselves all the more insidious because of how imperceptible it is, even, or perhaps primarily, to their own selves.[20]

The rejection of their own cultural customs and values makes minority women all the more vulnerable to a central and powerful USA myth that says that, because this is the best society in the world, whether one accomplishes what one wants or not depends on the individual. It depends on whether one is ambitious enough, gets a good education (which the myth maintains is available to everyone), and is willing to work hard and sacrifice oneself. This myth is promulgated constantly in the most pervasive way possible. The fact that minority women do not acquire the standards of living that the myth says is open to all those who really want it and work hard to get it often results in a negative self-image for minorities. This negative self-image carries much apathy and fear with it. As an oppressed group within the richest country in the world, minority women view achieving what the myth says is possible as such an immense task that a common response is apathy. Minority women often think of that mythical achievement as being beyond accomplishment; apathy then arises as a protection against frustration. Those with the strength to overcome apathy are then met by fear, the fear of failing, which means one will continue to be considered inferior, but also the fear of being coopted by the status quo, fear of betraying one's own community and culture to "make it" in the USA by living up to the image portrayed in the myth.

THEO-ETHICAL CONSIDERATIONS

Following are a few theo-ethical considerations deriving from the economic violence minority women suffer in the USA. They may also be considered strategies for action, something very appropriate when theology is understood to be a liberative praxis.

First, the suffering of economic violence is inscribed in women's bodies, is experienced through women's bodies. It is the bodies of Latinas, blacks, Asian Americans, that are exploited; it is their bodies that are demanded to produce at such speed that they get sick, are incapacitated for life. Their lives are cut short. Embodiment has to be dealt with seriously in all liberative theological praxis. The dualism that has dominated Christianity has to be denounced; a wholistic view of the person, based on both understandings of creation and redemption, has to be embraced by all liberation theologies and ethics. Corporality has to be looked at in a wholistic way: minority women's bodies are not only a source of joy, a source of creativity. Their bodies are also the vehicle used to impose on them economic control, domination, and exploitation. So embodiment as such (instead of distinct issues such as abortion, homosexuality, extra-marital sexual relations) has to become a central theme in theo-ethical liberative praxis.

Second, we need to recapture the authentic sense of the kin-dom of God,[21] not fully realizable in history but continually unfolding in our midst. What does that kin-dom look like? What are the utopias, the new visions that are to encourage and guide minority women? Here, and set over against the issue of economic violence, one needs to think about something old that is ever new: the common good. For the common good to be good, it has to be common. This means, first of all, that it has to be an order created at the expense of no one. But it is not only that. For it to be common, it has to be created by all. It is not only a matter of an order from which all benefit. It also has to be an order which all participate in creating, an order to which all contribute. The problem with even the best of democracies today is that while they may be representative, they are less and less participatory. So the common good must (1) be at the expense of no one; (2) be a participatory effort to which the greatest possible majority contributes; (3) be good not only for persons but for the whole of creation. For the common good to become a reality, there must be present at all times a preferential option for the marginalized, for the disenfranchised, for the poor, for the oppressed, for the exploited. *If it is not good for the poor and the oppressed, it is not good for anyone.* For the common good to be good, one has to keep in mind that at best such a reality presents to us an eschatological glimpse. This means that by its own intrinsic nature the common good has to be transcended by the truth it seeks to articulate: the kin-dom of God.[22]

Third, justice is a constitutive element of the gospel message, and women's liberation theologies have to help in every possible way to establish justice in society. In the face of the economic violence minority women suffer in the USA, one of the key elements of establishing a just social order has to be reparation and restitution. A deep sense of justice cries for restitution. But, many might argue, could restitution undo the distribution of good that might have been accomplished? If the distribution has been part of a need for restitution, then the common good will have been advanced, but if the distribution has been done at the expense of someone else, then the common good has not been advanced and restitution becomes a key element in reparation.

Fourth, theo-ethical formulations have to keep in mind their consequences. As Native American women ask, what effect will those formulations have to the seventh generation from now? The immediate satisfaction promoted by society today makes it all the more urgent that consequences be kept in mind when one talks about economics. At the same time, possible consequences must not keep one from considering the effectiveness of actions on behalf of justice for women, actions to which all Christians must be committed. Anything we say about violence against women we say while keeping in mind its political effectiveness.

Finally, commitment to struggle against the economic violence minority women suffer demands clarity when it comes to one's preferred future, to the historical project for which Christians need to struggle. Without forgetting that the fullness of the kin-dom of God is not the same as any present historical reality, and without turning theology and ethics into politics, Christians are called to make their options precise enough so people can choose among them.

The economic preferred future of minority women in the USA would, in my opinion, demand the following. First, labor market hierarchies as well as other hierarchical social institutions must be radically changed. This will not happen without the total undoing of patriarchal systems. Second, secondary-sector jobs should be restructured so that they provide dignity and meaning to the workers, pay them more, and provide them with true opportunities to manage and to control their working conditions. Third, worker ownership of enterprises is to be promoted in order for a participatory economy to replace the present hierarchical one.

Democracy in the workplace, though, is not enough. Democracy must be extended to the entire economy through planning mechanisms that give communities the power to determine, for example, what jobs will be located in their midst and what technologies will be adopted. These changes must be accompanied by movements toward democracy in politics, such as greater voter participation, elimination of the power of the corporate media, and public financing of electoral campaigns.[23]

Fourth, there must be a national commitment to full employment together with adequate minimum wages so that those who work can earn a living wage.[24] "Full employment not only strengthens the bargaining power of workers vis-à-vis capital, but the guarantee of a job is a basic human right, which guarantees incorporation into and participation in social life."[25] Fifth, the concentration of wealth in the hands of a few has to be eliminated by taxing wealth and establishing policies that redistribute inheritance. Part of this redistribution of inheritance would pay reparations to the minority groups in the USA whose lands and wealth have been stolen in the course of this country's history. Finally, changes have to take place in the economics of the family and in the relationship between family and work life. This means there is a need for paid parental leaves that can be shared by both parents, widely available sex education, affordable and dependent child care, national health care, and quality education for all.

Somehow minority women in the USA are going to keep their dreams of liberation alive. Somehow they are going to resist being oppressors themselves. Somehow they are not going to seek to belong to institutions that dispense and maintain privileges. That is not easy when one lives "in the belly of the beast." But if oppressed women in Third World countries embrace minority women in the USA as sisters in the struggle, minority USA women will have ever greater reason to find ways to remain faithful to a true vision of the common good, to remain faithful to the kin-dom of God, and to remain faithful to their people.

NOTES

[1] Ronald L. Taylor, "Minority Families in America: An Introduction," in *Minority Families in the United States*, ed. Robert L. Taylor (Englewood Cliffs, NJ: Prentice Hall, 1994), 1.

[2] Ibid., 2.

[3] Ibid., 3.

[4] Vilma Ortiz, "Women of Color: A Demographic Overview," in *Women of Color in U.S. Society*, eds. Maxine Baca Zinn and Bonnie Thornton Dill (Philadelphia: Temple University Press, 1994), 14-15.

[5] Ibid., 17.

[6] Ibid., 19.

[7] Ibid., 20.

[8] Ibid., 26.

[9] Teresa L. Amott and Julie Matthaei, *Race, Gender, and Work* (Boston: South End Press, 1991), 26.

[10] Ibid.

[11] Ibid., 27

[12] Ibid., 22-27

[13] Ibid., 186.

[14] Ibid., 187. *Affirmative action* refers to both initiatives and laws put in place in the 1960s in the USA to insure that racial/ethnic people would be given due consideration in society at large but especially when applying for jobs. Now there is an attempt to do away with such initiatives and laws in the name of "reverse discrimination."

[15] US Department of Labor, Bureau of Labor Statistics, "Employment and Earnings" (Washington, DC, April 1995), 151.

[16] Ibid., 58.

[17] Ibid., 59.

[18] Ibid., 59.

[19] Ibid.

[20] Maria C. Lugones, "On the Logic of Pluralist Feminism," in *Feminist Ethics*, ed. Claudia Card (Lawrence, Kansas: University Press of Kansas, 1991), 35-44; Iris Marion

Young, *Justice and the Politics of Difference* (Princeton, NJ: Princeton University Press, 1990), 60.

[21] Ada María Isasi-Díaz, *En la Lucha—In the Struggle: Elaborating a Mujerista Theology* (Minneapolis: Fortress Press, 1993), 34-45.

[22] I use kin-dom instead of kingdom, for the latter is both a sexist and classist term.

[23] These plans and strategies are taken from Amott and Matthaei, *Race, Gender, and Work,* 345-348.

[24] Ibid., 346.

[25] Ibid.

9

ECONOMIC VIOLENCE
IN LATIN AMERICAN PERSPECTIVE

María Pilar Aquino

In this essay I propose to offer some concerns that were highlighted during our sharing of women's experience of economic violence at the meeting in Costa Rica. I have selected these concerns based on the criteria of relevance and of commonality as they express both geo-political regions: the North and the South. This reflection provides a theological framework that offers a critique of the current neo-liberal capitalist model and advocates a critical formulation of an alternative model of society and of civilization.

My reflection, however, especially seeks to collect some of the major areas of concern and of challenge that were addressed by Third World feminist theologians. Our approach to the reality of economic violence against women is strikingly similar, especially in relation to our critique of the current world market economic model. While this similar critique is clearly found in the reflection of women whose theological discourse is elaborated from the context of the South, it is not so present in the women's theological discourse done from the context of the North. This essay will discuss three major concerns: the violent nature of the current economic system; the frameworks of the free-market economic model; and the sharing of a common theological agenda rooted in justice, integrity, and the well-being of all women.[1]

THE CONTEXT OF ECONOMIC VIOLENCE AGAINST WOMEN

Theological reflection on economic reality must seek out the connection between this reality and religious faith. In the context of Christian faith, the understanding of salvation not only includes the notion of justice and its realization in historical terms; it further accepts that access to salvation is impossible without the actual practice of economic justice, especially for the impoverished and the oppressed. Today, more than ever, the economic system of the current society works against women, their bodies, and their deepest desires for wholeness. If the Christian understanding of salvation is to be operative as "Good News" for women, it demands a transformation of the whole economic system for true justice to be realized. In other words, in the Christian understanding of salvation, all believers must work for the establishment of a just economic system that sustains the well-being of all as an integral dimension of Christian faith.

Our societies continue to be governed by power social relations marked by inequality and conflict, just as they have been in the past. The ruling groups, in both church and society, continue to be composed of a select group of males whose condition may vary in terms of race and social status but who all benefit from the advantaged position they enjoy in patriarchal institutions. The disadvantaged position of women in all areas of church and society is pervasive on a planetary scale, but this is especially true for Third World, impoverished, non-white women who lack fundamental rights. Therefore, our theological task is one of contributing to both the elimination of violence against women and the transformation of present reality.

This task must take into account the polymorphous nature of dominant power. The current social system is characterized by asymmetric social relations in terms of race, gender, social position, sexual orientation, and even religious affiliation. These social relations are established on the grounds that all persons and all nations have chosen freely their own positions in the social ladder according to their own will. In this line of thought, the victims of injustice are in the position of victims because they have chosen to be there. However, as we have pointed out, the production and reproduction of violence against women are possible only by the interaction of multiple social structures that give shape to a social system that is hierarchical as a whole and violent in itself.

The practical and intellectual combination of present neo-liberal capitalism, patriarchal social relations, and neocolonialism has proven to be highly detrimental not only for women but for planetary life as well. A critical approach to the functioning and the outcome of this social system is by far more consistent with true reality when an evaluation is conducted of the effects it has had on the lives of women, of the impoverished and oppressed, and on the earth. The abuse of women around the world takes different forms; it is committed on a daily basis both in public and in private, and this pervasive abuse has not lessened under the recent reconfiguration of the world economic system. Sadly enough, despite the dramatic dimensions of this reality affecting more than one half of the People of God, it does not seem to matter to the ruling groups of most Christian churches.

The economic processes taking place all over the world are placed within the framework of the neo-liberal capitalist model, which is best expressed in the so-called "world market" economy.[2] Because the tendency of this model is to centralize social power, goods, resources, and decisions, it has had a dramatic impact on the lives of the most disadvantaged social groups, especially women, who are the majority of the world's population. Our 1992 Final Statement of the Third General Assembly of the Ecumenical Association of Third World Theologians (EATWOT) states:

> We are under the grip of a market economy that is being directly controlled by the financial institutions of the powerful countries. It is a forgone conclusion that under that kind of economic arrangement the condition of the poor and socially disabled will not become better . . . The disappearance of the Cold War and the break up of the socialist system in Europe have left us in a situation where world politics tends to be under the increasing control of a single power maintained by aggressive militarism targeted primarily at the Third World. In a new military and political configuration, the poor in the Third World are expendable.[3]

In spite of the tendency of the present world economic system to create and exacerbate divisions among people, women have reunited in sisterhood to resist and to oppose its aggressive nature. The same Final Statement of EATWOT observes that women "have also provided a strong critique of the Euro-centered development paradigm, and the untold levels of suffering it causes, particularly to women and children."[4] Although women's participation in action for justice is informed by a diversity of cultural, religious, and theoretical frameworks, the involvement of women against all forms of domination is of major social, political, and theological importance. Since the decade of the seventies, Professor Schüssler Fiorenza has raised concern about the massive reality of violence against women that is committed at a systemic and planetary scale.[5] Nonetheless, even today there still are many nations, cultures, and churches refusing to acknowledge that violence against women is a blatant violation of human rights. In the face of such an overwhelming fact, we call on the theological community to expose the true nature of the present social system for its deceit, dehumanization, and sin.[6]

THE FRAMEWORK OF A FREE-MARKET ECONOMY

The neo-liberal economic model presents itself as the ultimate response to the human search for happiness and humanization. It not only imposes itself as the dominant force of geo-economic, of geo-political, and of geo-cultural reach but also carries a particular conception of civilization, of humanity, and of what social relations should be. In this line of thought, the neo-liberal model contains an anthropological, ethical, and theological framework which is presented as the most valid and reasonable for today's world.

As for the anthropological framework, the neo-liberal model claims that all human beings have the same possibilities and capabilities to obtain a lifestyle similar to the one that nations of European origin have reached in the North. Furthermore, the ruling elites of these nations are presented as the model of human progress, determination, development, and growth. Consequently, the anthropological neo-liberal framework operates with the idea that every person can and should attain perfection only through the appropriation of the social agenda imposed by the elites of northern nations and their allies in the South. Such a social agenda, however, has been and still is overtly colonialistic, patriarchal, homophobic, and highly predatory in nature.

The capitalist neo-liberal conception of humanity understands that the desires, needs, and interests of the power elites are and should be adopted by each individual in society. While feminist theory embraces the principle of the attainment of personal integrity in the well-being of the planetary community as the point of reference for all social constructions, the neo-liberal model supports the principle of unlimited satisfaction of the individual's own desires. To reach a successful satisfaction of all desires, the individual must incorporate into the world market economy through the application of competition, accumulation, and profit. From the standpoint of the dominant culture, this is the most reasonable and most effective course of action for the individual to attain social acknowledgment, honor, and well-being.

The current neo-liberal model maintains that each person has unlimited freedom to obtain what they want, since every human being has the same possibilities and capabilities to do so. The only limitation to both reaching well-being and avoiding exclusion from social life is the individual's will and endurance to compete, to earn, and to accumulate. In this framework, the individual liberty to satisfy one's own desires becomes the governing principle in discerning not only individual choices but the truth of things as well. Each individual conscience establishes the meaning of truth, having as the sole referential point the satisfaction of the individual's own desires. The whole social system offers reward and protection to individuals who more aggressively adopt this idea of unlimited growth. To be sure, they can attain progress and human growth only at the expense of the human deterioration and stagnation of those who cannot compete, accumulate, or negotiate, much less earn. This is the case of the majority of women, and of the world's impoverished. In this light, the anthropological framework of today's economic model shows itself to be detrimental for both women and the planetary community due to its elitist, violent, and antiegalitarian nature. Many women are trying to offer a feminist reconstruction of what it means to be human, using the complexity and richness of women's experience as an interpretive point.[7]

As for the ethical framework, the neo-liberal model comes equipped with its own value system to regulate properly the whole of social living. The fundamental value is the freedom of individuals to choose the path of unlimited access to the goods of the market to satisfy all needs. Only those who have not accepted this fundamental truth suffer today from unemployment and hunger and find themselves in social and psychological chaos. According to neo-liberal ethics, the world market promotes liberty and protects democracy because its doors are open for every person to incorporate without restriction into the life of capitalist economy. Although individual freedom is the foundation of the system, the path conducive to goodness and happiness includes the individual's observance of other values, such as the greatest profit, the accumulation of capital, the perfection of physical appearance, pleasure in possessing, and attachment to public prestige.

For neo-liberal capitalist ethics, the market leads individuals to the source of good if they observe these values. The criterion to establish what is good depends on what makes individuals feel good. In this context, the conception of good bears androcentric terms because it is defined according to the values, needs, and desires of the power elites. Neo-liberal ethics devalues deeply what women understand to be good to overcome our social position of disadvantage and marginalization. Thus, the dominant society interprets every effort to advance an alternative value system as a blind bet for chaos and error. Those who do not observe the value system offered by the world market economy would face exclusion from social living and be refused access to the unlimited happiness that only the market economy can give.

Because neo-liberal ethics understands that social position depends on individual choice, it claims no responsibility with respect to the conditions of survival affecting most of the world's population, much less with respect to the mechanisms that are the root cause of violence against women. While neo-liberal ethics declares the wants of power elites as the main principle of the ethical order, Leonardo Boff offers an alternative ethical principle consistent with ecological views:

The essential principle of an ethics of this kind is the following: That is good which conserves and promotes all creatures, especially living creatures, and among living beings, the weakest; that which is bad is everything that prejudices, debases, and destroys living creatures.[8]

More in accord with our ethical agenda as feminist theologians, E. Schüssler Fiorenza asserts "what is best for oppressed women" as the main principle of a feminist ethics of solidarity.[9]

As for the theological framework, the present model of free market economy understands itself as the sole universal bearer of "good news" for the whole world. Those who believe in its promises of success and well-being have not only overcome the temptation to move into rebellion, which causes confusion and despair; they also enjoy stability and inner peace in the present time. The market offers wealth and salvation to every person who enters the world of competition and unlimited gain through the narrow door of renunciation to emotions akin to compassion for those who are at a disadvantage. A re-wording of the Gospel serves me to express the spirit of the market. Since the days of the European colonialistic expansion up to the present time, the free market has been subjected to violence and the violent are taking it by force (Mt. 11:12). Only those who accept the rules of the patriarchal institutions enjoy honor and receive social acknowledgment. While the Gospel offers as the foundational principle of social life "that they may have life, and have it abundantly (John 10:10)," the world market economy offers the principle of "save yourself those who can and at the cost of whomever." While the Gospel affirms the practice of justice for the poor and oppressed as the ultimate criterion for salvation (Mt. 25:31-46), the neo-liberal model offers salvation now through the unlimited consumption of goods and of planetary resources. If Jesus and his movement understood that the realization of the Reign of God means doing justice for the poor and oppressed, the neo-liberal model understands that the free-market economy has irrupted on a global scale in favor of those who are rich and powerful.

By its own logic of exclusion, today's economic model is the result of and reproduces a dehumanizing civilization. The frameworks on which this model is based operate in concert as mechanisms that distribute unlimited frustration for all social groups forced to survive in a position of social, racial, sexual, cultural, and religious disadvantage. In the end, because of the dramatic impact this model has on the lives of women, we have to assert the impossibility to reconcile it with the Gospel's message of liberation.

A COMMON AGENDA FOR AN ALTERNATIVE EPISTEMOLOGY AND PRACTICE

The present situation of economic violence against women calls attention to the need for theology to stress even more the notion of justice for women as an integral dimension of Christian faith. Moreover, this situation demands that women theologians of the North and of the South not only engage in a rigorous critique of the dominant world market economy but also articulate such a critique with a feminist reconstruction of those anthropological, ethical, and theological expressions that affirm equality and liberation for all the women of the world. In the search for new economic paradigms, our theological discourse must be nourished by and at the service of all oppressed women who, despite being the consumers of patriarchal religion, still experience faith as a powerful source of survival, resistance, and hope. In this sense, our theological work must continue to affirm that every action aimed at the goal to establish justice for all women is a historical expression of Christian salvation.

If economic violence against women takes place in a context of reality that combines multiple power structures, the diverse social practices of women for justice and integrity must be empowered to counter the polymorphic character of patriarchal power. In this line of thought, the contribution of critical feminist theory is fundamental to interpreting the richness of women's experiences, while it helps us to eliminate the intellectual fragmentation among women. The goal of feminist theory and action is the articulation and realization of an alternative society that will eliminate all hierarchies. More than a mere socio-political movement formed by isolated groups of women, the feminist vision seeks to shape a new civilization and a new human community linked by the principles of justice and equal participation for the fulfillment of life. The formulation of such an alternative requires the elaboration of a common identity and common goals that will allow us to define *what* we are opposed to and *against whom* we are allied. Also, the capacity to join efforts and wills lies not so much in defining who we are, or even what we call ourselves, but in the practices the feminist movement initiates considering the complexities of race, culture, class, and religiosity. These practices across differences have the potential to break the traditional patriarchal consensus while allowing for an opening of new spaces that advance the goals of justice for women.

Given the interaction of these coordinates, feminist social practices assume a multiple and heterogeneous character. We must establish the distinct correlation of oppressive forces based on race, class, culture, and religion at a local context, and the possible strategies that will lead to real change. The diverse corporeal configurations and social characteristics of the actors define the contents and the fields of committed action. The available resources also constrain what can be done and which alliances we can establish. Despite the diversity of feminist social practices, a common point of reference remains the theoretical and practical formulation of a social model that represents a repudiation of current hierarchies. No justice for women is possible if we do not establish alliances of values, interests, and common tasks to face the violence of the current patriarchal civilization.

Women must continue the analysis of gender-based cultural constructions and the impact of these on the daily lives of women in the form of economic, social, and sexual inequalities as a central strategy with which to counter effectively polymorphic patriarchal power. However, not every feminist theory offers the analytical tools necessary to criticize rigorously the current patriarchal civilization and its predatory logic. Some feminist theories have not incorporated a critique of neo-liberal capitalism, including its attendant sexual, racial, and social inequalities and the extent of its colonizing global reach. From my perspective as a Latin American woman, the feminist critique of the geo-economic and political hegemony posed by the current neo-liberal model is necessary. The current economic model is deeply embedded and secures its existence through political, technological, financial, military, and intellectual centralization. In addition, the hierarchy of certain religious institutions supports this model by increasing the rigidity of Church institutions and strengthening the symbolic frames that justify patriarchal power.

Any social group or current of thought that opposes this dominant logic is in danger of being co-opted, discredited, or suppressed. This is evident in the increasing control of knowledge and of research. Democratic spaces of inquiry and political activity have been drastically reduced at all levels. In the last ten years, state and ecclesiastical institutions have pressed every alternative social movement to the point of desperation, fragmentation, or collapse. Although this phenomenon affects us directly, both personally and collectively, I often perceive that feminist theory has the tendency to confine itself to matters of argumentation, as if it were a self-subsistent discourse, with no connections whatsoever with geo-economic and geo-political developments. On the contrary, the present situation in society and in religious institutions requires that this connection be made more explicit and that it reach the construction of intellectual apparatuses so that we can more accurately perceive the devastating logic of present civilization and the polymorphic character of its patriarchal power. As feminists, it is ever more necessary for us to expand our ability to create alliances according to common purposes and tasks. Without a transversal common agenda that affirms justice for women on a local, regional, and global scale, we will not have the necessary capacity to generate an alternative epistemology and practice.

In the analytical approach to violence against women, I have noted the importance of developing a feminist reconstruction of the notion of *universality*. Because this reality is universal, the meaning of universality is fundamental in any attempt to establish a common agenda of justice for women. Regardless of our distinct bodily structure and our specific social location, such a reconstruction must embrace the following presuppositions:

1. A *religiously based* universality emphasizes the interconnectedness of all women's bodies as bearers of God's grace, power, and mystery.
2. A *politically chosen* universality has its reference point in a common understanding of an alternative social model that embraces and promotes the fundamental rights of all persons.
3. An *imaginative* universality is a vision of a new civilization that protects integrity, justice, and equality for all.
4. A *critically formulated* universality empowers women's memories and fantasies.
5. An *organically articulated* universality alters the daily life of the majority of the world's population: impoverished and excluded women.
6. A *realistically assumed* universality allows us to perceive the distance and connection between theoretical conceptions and the daily practice of women. This perception nourishes the dialogue between women's experience and the intellectual formulation of that experience.

NOTES

[1] María Pilar Aquino, "Roundtable Discussion: What's in a Name? Exploring the Dimensions of What 'Feminist Studies in Religion Means,' " in *Journal of Feminist Studies in Religion* 11, no. 1 (Spring 1995), 115-119; and "Hearing One Another into Speech: Latin American Women," in *Women and Theology: The Annual Publication of the College Theology Society 1994*, Mary Ann Hinsdale and Phyllis H. Kaminski, eds. (Maryknoll, NY: Orbis Books, 1995), 99-104.

[2] See the following excellent analysis of today's free-market economy: Franz J. Hinkelammert, "Changes in the Relationships between Third World Countries and First World Countries," in *Spirituality of the Third World: Ecumenical Association of Third World Theologians (EATWOT) 1992 Assembly, Nairobi, Kenya*, K.C. Abraham and Bernadette Mbuy-Beya, eds. (Maryknoll, NY: Orbis Books, 1994), 9-19; Pablo Richard, "A Theology of Life: Rebuilding Hope from the Perspective of the South," in *Spirituality of the Third World*, 92-108; Helio Gallardo, "Notes on the World Situation seen from Latin America," *Pasos*, Selected Articles 1994, No. 1/1995, 22-31.

[3] Final Statement, "The Statement of the Assembly: A Cry for Life," in Abraham

and Mbuy-Beya, *Spirituality of the Third World*, 191.

[4] Ibid., 192.

[5] Elisabeth Schüssler Fiorenza, *Discipleship of Equals: A Critical Feminist Ekklesia-logy of Liberation* (New York: Crossroad, 1993), 61, 311.

[6] Maria Pilar Aquino, "Evil and Hope: A Reflection from the Victims, a Response to Jon Sobrino," in *The Catholic Theological Society of America: Proceedings of the Fiftieth Annual Convention,* Paul Crowley, ed., vol. 49 (New York: CTSA, 1995), 85-92.

[7] See the excellent work of Ann O'Hara Graff, ed., *In The Embrace of God: Feminist Approaches to Theological Anthropology* (Maryknoll, NY: Orbis Books, 1995).

[8] Leonardo Boff, *Ecology and Liberation: A New Paradigm* (Maryknoll, NY: Orbis Books, 1995), 30.

[9] Schüssler Fiorenza, *Discipleship of Equals*, 351.

10

MILITARISM: A THRUST TOWARDS GLOBALIZATION

Marlene Perera

"The Croatian army launched a major offensive against rebel Serbs in Croatia," "Tigers blasted two navy boats killing 40 in Sri Lanka," "Fresh fighting has broken out in Rwanda . . ." So scream the headlines. It is said that in Afghanistan an entire generation has been raised amid one of the world's longest and most devastating wars. Do we not live in a savage and brutal world? Is it not war that seems to lead the way in this last century of the second millennium?

Between 1960 and 1988 military expenditure of the poor LDCs (least developed countries) quintupled in real terms; that is twice the rate at which their GDP per head increased. In the decade ending in 1988, the LDCs spent U.S. $439 billion on importing arms, which was more than three-quarters of the world trade in weapons. Between 1984 and 1987, twenty-two countries with a combined population of 1.8 billion spent more on defense than they invested in the education and the health of their people. An estimated 400 million people have been killed in more than 125 wars in the Third World since 1945.[1]

Grim figures indeed! And if this trend continues, we can be almost certain that it will be nothing but war, LIC (low-intensity conflict), MIC (middle-intensity conflict), and HIC (high-intensity conflict), that will herald the dawn of the third millennium. Certainly, the future looks bleak, with massive military buildup and industrial complexes. Yet, are we not taking things too much for granted? And do we not treat these realities as isolated events, refusing to see the web into which they are woven, and thus shut our eyes to the evidence of our own continuing violence? I wish to probe some of the aspects of this savagery. At the same time, I maintain that this essay is not exhaustive and there is scope for further development.

THE SRI LANKAN EXPERIENCE

We in Sri Lanka have been caught in the throes of continuing violence and immense human suffering these past two decades, living through two youth uprisings. Since 1983, the country has been trapped in the struggle of the Tamil youth in the North and the East due to the aggravation of their social and economic situation and certain discriminations suffered at the hands of the majority Sinhala state. This has now developed into civil war, with the North being virtually cut off from the rest of the country. As a consequence, the small ceremonial Sri Lankan army has now become a mighty army over a hundred thousand strong. The process of recruiting goes on endlessly and new recruits are easily gained due to the poverty and unemployment prevalent in our villages. "The military expenditure has risen from 2.9 percent of the total expenditure in 1982 to 20 percent in 1992 and when compared to expenditure on health and education, the emerging picture is very disturbing."[2] The buildup of the National Security ideology and the state with the "Prevention of Terrorism" Act and other repressive legislation has made dissent almost impossible throughout the island. Hence it was possible for the state to redirect our economies so as to be sucked into the global capitalist system with no hindrance whatsoever. Though at times they give the image of coming to the peace table, peace seems to be elusive, without even a glimmer of an end to the protracted war.

The other insurrection was the second irruption of southern Sinhala youth between 1988 and 1989 that had been building up due to poverty, unemployment, and popular grievances, but was precipitated, through the advent of the Indian Peace Keeping Force, (IPKF), on the issue of the northern war. This was crushed within a few months, mercilessly massacring nearly sixty thousand boys and girls, taking thousands as detainees, and subjecting them to inhuman torture, sometimes involving innocent citizens. It was a time when numerous *pajeros* roamed the land by night, hounding their prey; numerous paramilitary groups of various hues and stripes mushroomed overnight. It was then that we saw the youth of the land burning on tire pyres by the highways and byways, and the mutilated bodies that kept on floating on our rivers, reddening their waters with blood! All this manifested the determination of the former regime to suppress any form of dissent or self-assertion. Yet, no one would lift a finger or raise a voice. Fear psychosis gripped the nation. Yes, Mother Lanka continues to weep for her youth, Tamil and Sinhala and Muslim, too, whose lives have become so cheap.

We need to question why one conflict was quelled with such ferocity and the other allowed to drag on for years and years with no political will to arrive at a solution. There may be many reasons for this. But isn't it evident that a revolt by the majority, a real threat to the system, had to be nipped in the bud, even by resorting to inhuman atrocious genocide? Yet the struggle of the minority, on the other hand, is being maintained at a manageable low-intensity level, as it inevitably helps to stabilize the status quo under emergency rule and repressive laws. Does this not help to boost and fatten power-hungry, corrupt politicians and their cronies through arms deals? Does it also not help these politicians to grab for themselves the maximum of security? Yet, what about the people? The ordinary citizen in a country where the voice of the gun is decisive?

WOMEN TRAPPED IN SITUATIONS OF WAR

Conflicts may irrupt within countries through the resurgence of nationalism and minorities for self-determination. At best it seems the nation-state is in crisis. Conflicts also may arise between countries for border disputes. On the one side, armed struggle in the so-called Third World countries could be due to religious, ethnic, racial, or tribal differences. On the other side, they could be caused by ideological differences due to increasing discrepancies in the socio-economic system. Very often these conflicts have a tendency to spread with the intervention by neighboring states and by super- or regional powers. They are also fuelled by sales of arms and military equipment to both combatants and regimes by not only superpowers but also by other Third World countries. They often involve cross-border affiliations and networks among militant groups. At times, even chemical weapons may be used, with neighboring states providing shelter, arms, and training to militants. Whatever form they may take, these conflicts cause unimaginable havoc and bring untold misery to a large portion of humanity, among whom women and children are the worst affected. The mass displacement of people within the country itself brings a situation where, paradoxically, one becomes a refugee in one's own country, housed like cattle in temples and kovils and makeshift shelters and forced to exist on the bare minimum. Conditions in refugee camps make women vulnerable to inhuman and outrageous situations, physical discomfort, and psychological tensions; they are forced to bear the burden of protecting and fending for themselves and their children, whose education is disrupted.

The mass exodus of people from conflict areas to foreign countries is today a very complex phenomena. Forced to flee their countries at short notice, women flood the labor markets of foreign countries with hardly any skills or knowledge of the language and conditions in those countries. Since they have no bargaining power, they are highly exploited in factories and homes and are forced to work in unhealthy conditions with low pay. Their plight of being refugees and illegal workers renders them voiceless and helpless even in the face of sexual abuse and cruel manipulation by unscrupulous elements in society.

Those women caught up in war situations become easy prey to rape, sexual slavery, torture, genocide, and other forms of gender-specific violence. The much publicized case of comfort women, including Koreans and Filipinos, during World War II speaks volumes on the atrocities committed against women in wartime. It is said that civilian casualties have far exceeded those of the military in the last fifty years. Surely women and children form a big percentage of this, notwithstanding psychological traumas due to terrorizing tactics used by both guerilla groups and state apparatus. Children as young as ten or twelve are forcefully conscripted by militants and are hardened for war by passing through blood-chilling training programs. Thus drawn into the conflict as combatants, they are often used by guerilla groups as frontline cannon fodder and ultimately become fierce fighters. The hatred thus inculcated into them makes one anguish about their future.

There is no doubt whatsoever that these conflicts not only destabilize the countries concerned but also disrupt their economic and developmental thrust. Ecological disaster that is the outcome of modern armory and chemical weapons is a serious blow to poorer countries whose economy is dependent on agriculture. The health hazards incurred by the population due to pollution are enormous.

WAR, PART OF THE GLOBAL SPIDER'S WEB

During the past fifty years or so, war has shifted stage from developed countries to the developing countries. There is today a staggering increase in the scale and frequency of armed conflicts in our part of the world, where state militarization becomes a desperate response to the violent expressions of the increasing societal contradictions of class, religious ethnicity, caste, tribe, and clan that have increased during colonial times and been aggravated since independence. Violence today is an endemic phenomenon in our countries, tearing apart the delicate fabric of our cultures and civilizations as militarization takes hold of us by leaps and bounds, with powerful tendencies at work to accentuate differences. Hence, as fears of superpower conflagration recede, the specter of nuclear and conventional arms proliferation in Asia and the Middle East is growing. Most countries in Asia and the Middle East are seeking to acquire long-range ballistic missiles and combat aircraft which have a greater strike capability than ballistic missiles. Disarming and de-escalating the arms race in Europe has meant that some of these arms are being sold cheaply to Third World governments.[3] When we probe critically into this reality, we realize that economic power and militarism go hand in hand.

ECONOMIC POWER AND MILITARISM

In the 1960s and 1970s most Asian and other Third World countries, following the non-aligned principle and with the desire to protect themselves from international exploitation, followed a more or less closed socialist economy.

The last decade saw a reversal of these policies with the coming into power of rightist blocks who now attempt to re-direct our countries according to the dictates of the World Bank (WB) and the International Monetary Fund (IMF). Their Structural Adjustment package includes an open economy, no control on imports, tourism, privatization leading even to the alienation of our lands to foreign multinationals, and initiating new cash crops and small industries by setting up numerous FTZs (Foreign Trade Zones) in a situation of low wages and unhealthy working conditions. All this is done in the name of development and the search for foreign exchange. On the other hand, these countries are discouraged from producing their food requirements: rice, onions, chilies etc.— which can be grown very well there. Is this a strategy to make smaller nations a mere cog in the big wheel of the international economic machine, making them dependent on and subservient to the big powers even for their sustenance, and, in addition, disregarding their own historical process, cultural aspirations, and humanity? Could this be development or an effective way of maintaining control and getting others to serve one's own hidden agenda?

The flooding of our markets with glittering foreign goods and the accompanying advertising create superficial needs in a population that has become poorer in the process. In this context the minority rich become richer and even the middle class becomes poor as the disparities continue to widen. To allow for the thriving of foreign industries, there is strong repression, and laws have been enacted prohibiting the organization of workers. National Security in this context has become the idol and ideology, and the presence of illegal and underground armed death squads and the rigid anti-people practices make dissent impossible. Thus the atmosphere is conducive for corruption among politicians who are easily allowed to go uncensored. Random use of force by the powers that be and the violence of militant groups together lead to the brutalization of culture. The frustration among the masses thus gathers up until at some point it explodes. Hence it is vital to grasp the connection between National Security ideology and the world militaristic ideology and the economy.

THE VULNERABILITY OF THIRD WORLD COUNTRIES

After centuries of colonialism there is an anguished search in our countries for a lost heritage and identity in reaffirming national cultures and languages. The globalization of capitalist ethics and the influx of the global consumer culture has a drastic impact on our societies, and there is strong resistance from certain sectors to this process. Yet, our countries regrettably remain vulnerable to this influence for many reasons. Some of them are (1) the increasing contradictions in our societies; (2) the heterogenous nature of our societies; and (3) colonialism and its legacy.

There is no doubt whatsoever that it is mainly through colonialism that Western powers were able to amass wealth, power, and control over other nations. Colonial rulers' methods of dividing arbitrarily even continents among themselves are at the root of many problems and especially that of alienation in Africa. Their policy of divide and rule led to the benefitting of minorities over against the majority. The promotion of Western culture to the detriment of our own cultures and religions has had serious effects on our societies. Our subsistence economy was turned into a cash economy, bringing us into the world market and making us dependent. Colonialism produced a Western-oriented elite who continue to be hand in glove with the former powers, striving to serve the vested interests of both parties. The importation of foreign labor and the open-door policy of the colonizers have changed the population patterns and made our societies more heterogenous. Adverse trade arrangements on the international sphere have brought about an increase in the external debt which is strangling us. Hence, it could be said that colonialism has made us subservient for many years to come.

In "Rwandan Tragedy Not Just Due to Tribal Enmity," Michel Chossudovsky posits that under the free market system imposed through Structural Adjustment programs in Rwanda involving macroeconomic reforms recommended by the Bretton Woods Institutions, neither cash crops nor food crops were economically viable. He continues:

> No sensitivity or concern was expressed as to the likely political and social repercussions of economic shock therapy applied to a country on the brink of civil war. The W. B. Team consciously excluded the non-economic variables from their simulations. While international donor communities cannot be held directly responsible for the tragic outcome of the Rwandan civil war, the austerity measures combined with the impact of the IMF sponsored devaluations contributed to impoverishing Rwandan people at a time of acute political and social crisis. The deliberate manipulation of market forces destroyed economic activity and people's livelihood, fuelled unemployment, and created a situation of generalized famine and social despair. To lay the blame solely on deep-seated tribal hatred not only exonerates the great powers and the donors, it also distorts an exceedingly complex process of economic, social, and political disintegration affecting an entire nation of more than seven million people . . . Rwanda, however, is but one among many countries in Sub-Saharan Africa which are facing a similar predicament.[4]

The further globalization, with world trade organizations (WTOs) having a big impact on trade, investment, and production, would inevitably lead to a type of domination hitherto unknown, leaving no space for small nations to decide on their own development and way of life. The whole process would depend largely on imposed adjustments to assure debt payment, making nations and peoples objects of macroeconomic policy and slaves of a sovereign market. The attempt seems to be to build a uniform world on a unique economic system reducing humans to mere commodities. But the very fragmentation that is taking place today all over the world belies this endeavor and demonstrates the hypocrisy and unsuitability of the development model imposed on us. This is part of the crisis of modernization. Doesn't this conspiracy lead to the liquidation of peoples, nations, and states? In this so-called "New World Order," UN-related institutions become more and more ineffective as the grand trio of WB, IMF, and WTOs begins to act together to maintain this death-dealing order.

DOCTRINE AND STRATEGY OF LOW-INTENSITY CONFLICT

The response to the resistance mounted against the globalization of Western capitalist ethics seems to be the ideology and strategy of low-intensity conflict. In this type of conflict even human rights and humanitarian and economic aid could easily serve as useful weapons. LIC and MIC are devastating processes, no doubt aiming to thwart any attempt not to fall in line, and youth, militant groups, and even religions are co-opted through disinformation, covert action, psychological warfare, etc. The Third World is thus kept under the thumb of world powers in establishing U.S. hegemony over the entire world. Crying "Peace and human rights" from the rooftops, their thrust is rearmament and the building of huge military-industrial complexes.

Dr. Meera Nanda, an Indian journalist specializing in science and technological issues, in "U.S. Revises Weapons Systems for Future Wars in Third World," maintains that the U.S. is redesigning its Star Wars program to make it more suitable for middle intensity wars in Third World countries such as the Persian Gulf Conflict.[5] James Petras, Professor of Sociology at the State University of New York, Binghamton, in "Gulf War Reveals Nature of New U.S. Foreign Policy," says the "U.S. is relying more on military and ideological forces to expand its global influences." Simultaneously, the U.S. projects itself as the policeman of the world while promoting international armed violence in the name of "democracy," involving thereby a fusion of eco-political and military intelligence. Do the peoples of the world accept this U.S. projection of being chosen by God to keep order in the world? But really it is disorder and chaos that are being realized. How does one justify America's self-proclaimed right to control the production of arms by countries of the world? For whose benefit is this being done? And who is to control and supervise the production of arms by the U.S. and her political allies? What is the role of the UN in all this? How far has it become the pawn in manipulations by the mighty? The events in the Gulf War have led to the loss of UN credibility in most parts of the world. The reactions to the Gulf War show that not negotiations but firepower and force are going to be paramount in international affairs. Former U.S. Attorney General Ramsay Clark in his letter to the Secretary General of the UN pointed out that the assault on Iraq was uncivilized, brutal, and racist.

ACTION TOWARDS PEACE

It is an urgent and impelling task to mobilize world opinion towards a lasting and constructive peace all over the world. However, we must address the root causes of military violence by constructive action on three essential fronts: economic, military, and ideological. The high-handed manner in which the Western powers interpret and act contrary to principles that maintain equality of sovereign states in international relationships and unilaterally impose sanctions, using the big stick on those who do not toe the line, has to be confronted. Though the five major nuclear powers continue to retain nuclear weapons, the Nuclear Non-Proliferation Treaty they have signed makes it obligatory that they, too, work towards complete nuclear disarmament, and we should bring pressure worldwide that this is achieved sooner rather than later. The ludicrous attitude that might is right must be wiped from the face of this earth as we agitate unceasingly that the creative genius of humans be directed towards the building of a stable, global future for all of humanity.

"I refuse to be an accomplice." With these words the Belgian Pierre Geland has come out from the working committee of the non-governmental organization of the World Bank. He reproached the World Bank:

It has become more arrogant. After being in dialogue with the World Bank as a member of the working committee for three and a half years, I announce my quitting. It has become very clear to me that there is no way to humanize the World Bank. Africa dies and the World Bank enriches itself. Asia and East Europe see how their wealth is plundered and the WB protects the interests of the IMF and GATT, which dictate the plundering of their material and intellectual wealth. Latin America looks with horror at how their children are used as a work-force; still worse, as forced organ donors of a blooming transplanting market in the United States.[6]

Geland refuses to be an accomplice of this merciless fatalism that the World Bank preaches. He thinks that the fifty years of existence of the World Bank is enough and calls the WB the main enemy of the poor. He suggests creating another institution in place of the WB that promotes the worthiness of peoples and guarantees development in partnership. Refusal to be an accomplice is a constructive action that would touch the deadened conscience of the world and shake these inhuman structures and ideologies from their very foundations. As women, we need to build solidarity for justice and peace by refusing to become accomplices by our passivity and exposing and protesting against the hypocrisy that operates relentlessly to rob the Third World through diverse ways, including the trafficking of arms to fill the coffers of unscrupulous arms dealers, thereby dealing death to so many millions.

We need to raise our voices loud and clear, demanding that money spent on military hardware be diverted to meet the urgent needs of poverty and disease so as to preserve life. Concrete action for justice is a must if we are to eradicate poverty and also preserve the ecological balance. We need to agitate for a just code of conduct for multinational and other international organizations operating in the Third World. We need to direct our efforts towards a comprehensive planning of the use of resources to serve humanity, not leaving it to the vagaries of the market, and promote equity in the distribution of wealth and greater participation of peoples in building a New Humane World Order on the principle of unity in diversity. In this New World that we dream of, all humans and human societies would have access to all necessary resources and tools and have the possibility and also support to work out their own destiny in freedom, engaging together in meaningful interaction to build a more dignified human life in harmonious local and international communities respecting difference. For this, we must make use of everything available, information, media, etc., to disseminate correct information and promote new values of justice, reconciliation, truth, understanding, appreciation, interconnectedness, partnership, and opting for the good and the beautiful.

It is clear from recent history that violence does not pay, and hence there is a great need to rethink the situation of so-called liberation movements themselves. Though the situation seems hopeless, we need to keep the flame of hope burning brightly against all odds in our search for new alternatives—alternative lifestyles, institutions, structures, models of relationships, especially international—while acting on the local manifestations of this global disorder, noting the failure of its present economic and political structures and development models to provide basic improvement in sustainable livelihood.

It is an hour of crisis but also of creativity. People yearn for a positive and more humane vision and thrust of society. We need to use our powers of imagination to the maximum in developing and expanding such a vision. Let us come together as concerned women and men, sharing leadership and taking the initiative to be in tune with the fundamental and deep human and religious spirit in creating alternative images of power, order, and leadership and move away from hierarchical, patriarchal, and bureaucratic structures. Let us strive to network and establish a supportive and fostering climate for innovative ventures for revisioning and rebuilding society and World Order.

Our quest to build authentic community and communication across existing barriers should be a persistent effort to fight against the commodification and the liquidation of peoples and nations as well as the liquidation of humanist values as we struggle to maintain an enabling environment. Former U.S. Defense Secretary Robert McNamara admits in his memoirs that the U.S. was wrong in its military thrust in Vietnam. Well, it should not stop there. We women need to press that these big powers learn from their great historical mistakes that have brought about untold human suffering, not only to review honestly and critically the ongoing military thrust and ideology they have at present vis-à-vis the entire global community but also to make concrete reparation for the great devastation they have caused and continue to cause.

In the modern world there is hardly any regard for morals or ethics in guiding human behavior in economic and political life. Deep spiritual insights and religious contributions are cast aside in this modern rat race for money, power, and prestige. One would not even hesitate to manipulate these insights and contributions to suit this modern craze. William C. Chittick, in his address to the Conference on Islamic Civilization and Culture held in Teheran, says, "Scientific rationality allows for no moral distinction whatsoever. Post modern observers of this situation, however, do not conclude that anything is wrong. On the contrary, they have simply concluded that there is no such thing as right and wrong." He continues:

The fundamental characteristic of modern scientific knowledge is to be empty of unifying principles . . . There is no unity in modern thought because unity is strictly a divine quality and without the knowledge of God it is impossible to understand the nature of unity, much less establish it . . . In their concern for establishing God's incomparability, rational theologians abstract God out of the cosmos . . . The good and the beautiful cannot be perceived without a myth and mythical thinking is beyond the range of reason. People cannot live without myths because myths provide concrete ways of understanding the meaning of life. Reason can never supply meaning from within itself. Rational structures with their enormous accumulation of power produce no mythology. The traditional function of myth and imaginal thinking was to allow unity to be seen permeating all levels of the Universe, society and the human. God was never absent and through his presence God was constantly concerned for the welfare of his servants.[7]

Accordingly, is it not evident that the thrust of the modern world to advance purely on rational knowledge, which is never neutral, has brought about this chaos? We women, who are so close to life and nature, have the potential within us to unleash this holistic understanding that comes from within and bring a true wisdom to a world that is groping in the dark. Our theology must be uniquely directed to the search and the manifestation of wisdom and bring back God into the very core and mainstream of life, bringing vital meaning to life, affirming the cosmic interconnectedness. It behooves us then to go into our cultural roots and value systems rooted in a philosophy that stresses the need to strike a balance between material and spiritual development and the elimination of unbridled selfishness in creating a dynamic culture of justice, peace, and prosperity for all, which enables people to be attentive to their own space and time, to their own history, culture, and local situation in defining the forms of their social life, grasping what it means to be truly human and to build a way of life that also is in harmony with the Cosmos.

NOTES

[1] Ariya Abeysinghe, *"Military Expenditure in LDC's: A Case Study of Sri Lanka,"* *People's Bank Economic Review* (January 1992), 33-47.

[2] Ibid.

[3] Kumar Rupasinghe, *Lanka Guardian,* vol. 13 (March 15, 1991), 22.

[4] Published in *The Island* (March 24, 1995), 17.

[5] *Lanka Guardian,* vol.13 (April 1, 1991), 23.

[6] Ibid.

[7] Published in *The Island* (March 28, 1995), 23.

11

MILITARISM IN NORTH AMERICAN PERSPECTIVE

Susan Brooks Thistlethwaite

In its first three centuries, Christianity was both anti-militarist and pacifist. One of the key theological issues in sustaining this anti-militarist and pacifist stance was the doctrine of the human being that developed out of the first century. The human being was deemed capable of divinity. The incarnation of God into a human body and Jesus' insistence that the Kingdom of God is "in our midst" vested the human person and human society with tremendous value.

That human beings could become divine can be seen biblically in Jesus' admonition to be perfect even as God is perfect (Matthew 5:48), or in the Christian resistance to the divinity of the emperor. The centrality of the Kingdom *(basileia)* to Jesus' preaching and teaching supports the notion that this world has value and we are not to value only the world to come.

Christians were to understand themselves as created in the image of God and falling "upward" toward salvation (Irenaeus). The equality in image of divinity of all humanity replaced the image of the emperor as image of divine power. This was rightly held by the Romans to be subversive, and the deification of an uneducated Jewish carpenter executed by Romans for treason against the state unleashed the whole power of Rome against Christians for three centuries of persecution.[1]

In the first three centuries Christians were regarded as able to choose the good and not cooperate with the demonic military power of Rome. Therefore, their theological anthropology produced a practice of political and military resistance against the empire.

When Christianity became the official religion of the empire, however, then it was the Pax Romana that became the model of human society, and "order" becomes the definition of the good. Human beings, according to St. Augustine, far from being understood as images of the divine, are fallen and have lost all capacity for free will. They are, then, in divine providence, to be ruled. This theology dovetails nicely with obedience to a Christian-sanctioned totalitarianism, the Holy Roman Empire. Participation in the military, then, is not only permitted but the duty of Christians to the empire, now dubbed "holy."

The so-called "left wing" of the Reformation reinstates the emphasis of the first three centuries on the freedom of the Christian and the non-cooperation with militarism. The attitude of a Luther or Calvin, however, represents the dominant Protestant position, which is to continue the notion of the hierarchical order of society, as the remedy for the hopelessly depraved human condition, and the participation of Christians in the military.

Vitor Westhelle, a Brazilian theologian, faced not with Pax Romana but its more modern version in Pax Americana, has protested that

in Latin America . . . "order" is not a positive concept. "Order"' is most often an ideological disguise for domination, repression, and persecution. Order becomes the moral parameter to speak about God's will in the midst of the cosmos, justifying the organization of the state. Where order is granted by the head of the state, where order is the result of the "invisible hand"' of capitalism, where order is the patriarchal hierarchy, the stability and control of the whole society is guaranteed.[2]

Militarism is the way in which the hierarchical ordering of political, social, economic, familial, bodily, and even biological life is constructed and sustained. It both constructs and sustains certain understandings of who the human being is theologically.

In the method of liberation theology, it is necessary to expose these constructions through ideology critique and then to reconstruct alternative doctrines of the human being. In this reflection paper I will consider four such constructions: 1) the construction of body and sexuality; 2) the construction of economics; 3) the construction of race/ethnicity; and 4) the construction of culture.

MILITARISM AND THE CONSTRUCTION OF BODY AND SEXUALITY

In our research for our book on prostitution, Rita Nakashima Brock and I have been repeatedly struck by the significant role that militarism plays in creating the conditions for the sex industry and not only, as is often thought, in creating the market for sex work.

One of the primary ways that militarism constructs the conditions that create the sex industry is in the forced separation of the sexes in military life. Men in the military are taken out of the intimate familial patterns of human relationship and no longer are governed by civilian community norms for sexual and moral conduct. They are placed in contexts that mimic the ascetic; physical symbols of individual identity, such as clothing and hair, are removed, and sleep deprivation and intense physical demands teach a denial of the body and its needs. A soldier in uniform is to be a "lean, mean fighting machine" and not a limited, embodied human being.

The military ideology of the body says that the body is to be suppressed and controlled. Contempt for embodied human life is the necessary splitting of consciousness required to kill another human being. The power and dominance of military ideology becomes identical with masculinity and posed in direct opposition to femininity, portrayed as weakness or softness. Sex then becomes a vehicle for overtly denying embodiment by asserting dominance over it, and the need of the lonely, stressed, and vulnerable recruit for relationship remains unacknowledged. The need itself, however, does not go away but gets reconfigured as power and dominance through the use of force. Sexuality and relationship then get constructed as violence, as the chant taught at many U.S. boot camps attests:

This is my weapon, this is my gun,
One is for shooting, the other's for fun.

Militarism is both a support for and a product of the gnosticizing tendency in Christianity to denigrate the body and sexuality and to exclude them from the realm of the spirit. Rape or forced sexuality in war underlines the separation between power and embodiment and relegates the body to that which must be controlled. Military life itself is an alienated existence and further reinforces the denial of relationality that purchased sex illustrates. Militarism helps to support theologies that rigidly separate body from spirit and atomize human beings one from another.

This separation of the spirit and the body must be reconstructed in Christianity toward an integration of sensuality and spirituality. This is what is meant by the womanist and feminist re-definition of the erotic as sensuous spirituality.[3] Relationality must be re-claimed as well, as constitutive of the human being, for, as Beverly Harrison writes, "we have the power through acts of love or lovelessness literally to create one another."[4]

MILITARISM AND THE CONSTRUCTION OF ECONOMIC RELATIONS

Militarism also helps to create the population for prostitution in that warmaking disrupts local economies and produces refugee populations or prisoners of war who can be made into brothel prostitutes or the euphemistically termed "camp follower" or "comfort women," as the Korean, Philippine, Chinese, and Japanese women forced into prostitution by the Japanese army in the first half of this century were called.[5] The story of these women is powerfully presented in Chung Hyun Kyung's chapter in this book.

The disruption of local economies and the production of dislocated populations also contribute to the general reduction of human beings to commodities in a world where the market is the defining metaphor. It is easier for multinational organizations to exploit indigenous workers where the community norms have been disrupted by militarism and the increased poverty makes any job welcome.[6] Prostitution is on a continuum with other forms of the commodification of human beings.

Marilyn Waring, member of the New Zealand Parliament from 1975 to 1984 and member and, finally, chair of the Public Expenditure (Public Accounts and Budget) Select Committee, was stunned to find that what she valued about her country, the clear air, safe drinking water, the parks, the beaches, lakes, and forests *all counted for nothing* when she was called upon to tally up her country's gross domestic capital. These figures, under a system called the System of National Accounts, are used to inform entities such as the World Bank, the International Monetary Fund, or the United Nations agencies of the need for aid. In short, she could not borrow to protect her country's environment; she could only borrow to clean it up if it were polluted. She could not borrow to maintain her country's status as a nuclear-free zone; she could borrow to make weapons. Waring writes,

The current state of the world is the result of a system that attributes little or no 'value' to peace. It pays no heed to the preservation of natural resources or to the labor of the majority of its inhabitants or to the unpaid work of the reproduction of human life itself not to mention its maintenance and care. *The system cannot respond to values it refuses to recognize.*[7]

An otherworldly Christianity that does not recognize the "*basileia* in our midst" works well with a capitalism that sees the world as having no value in itself as the creation, but only as a material commodity for exploitation. Militarism facilitates such a devaluation of the world, since its reason for existence is destruction, not construction.

To resist such theology of world devaluation, we must assert the world as God's creation. We can then offer an economics of "household," a world where the chief economic problem is not the managing of scarcity, but the creation of abundance.[8]

MILITARISM AND THE CONSTRUCTION OF RACE/ETHNICITY

Militarism has a profound investment in attempting to construct racial and ethnic identities. Certainly race has always functioned, in both ancient and modern war, to construct the identity of the enemy as other, as not fully human, and therefore to remove any moral impediment to his or her extermination. The enemy is a Gook, a Nip, or, in the Gulf War, a camel jockey or sand nigger. It may have taken the Western powers longer to "stop Hitler" precisely because Hitler's explicit use of racial supremacist solidarity against the Jews played to Euro-Atlantic constructions of race dominance and anti-Semitism. Racism against Asians fueled the Japanese internment camps; anti-

Arab racism was marshalled to get support for the Gulf War.

In the complicated construction of race in the United States, the military has functioned to define racial otherness and, as in the case of gender, also to provide the education, status, and rhetoric of racial betterment. This can appear to be a contradiction, but it is not. Racial/ethnic minorities are defined as the surplus people of a society and therefore a ready supply of impoverished people who need a chance at economic improvement. As the U.S. military increasingly becomes the only employer hiring in minority communities, the logic of the military construction of race becomes more visible.

Militarism uses racism to form rigid boundaries between the self and the other. Indeed, racial otherness is one of the major supports for the "hardened self," in Catherine Keller's useful phrase, a self that cannot let the other in for fear of losing identity. Theologically, this means that "the separative ego expels the world from himself, projecting the sphere of immanence onto the fleshly woman below him, [and] he simultaneously projects his transcendence onto an otherworldly spirit above him."[9]

The ability to be permeable to other people is the foundation of community and what we could mean theologically were we really to allow ourselves to hear the radical embodiment of ecclesiological constructions such as "body of Christ."

MILITARISM AND THE CONSTRUCTION OF CULTURE: MAKING THE WORLD SAFE FOR HYPOCRISY

To know and not to know, to be conscious of complete truthfulness while telling carefully constructed lies, to hold simultaneously two opinions which are canceled out, knowing them to be contradictory and believing in both of them, to use logic against logic, to repudiate morality while laying claim to it, to believe that democracy was impossible and that the Party was the guardian of democracy, to forget whatever it was necessary to forget, then to draw it back into memory again at the moment when it was needed, and then promptly to forget it again, and, above all, to apply the same process to the process itself— that was the ultimate subtlety: consciously to induce unconsciousness, and then, once again, to become unconscious of the act of hypnosis you had just performed.[10]

Gustavo Gutiérrez has called the United States a "liar society." One of the most important constructions of militarism is a culture of double-speak, where war is named peace and what passes for peace is really war, where totalitarianism masquerades as democracy and democracy is in reality oppression, where economic practice creates poverty and is presented as the cure for poverty, where violence in the home is called family values, and family values are the barest kind of contempt for children, women, and the elderly, and the supreme doublespeak and doublethink—death is more productive than life, and the living death of most of the people of the world is life.

These reversals take tremendous effort both to establish and to maintain because the experiential base of life finally cannot be denied: when people starve, they know it is not abundance: when they are abused, they know it is not love, when they are shot, they know it is not peace; and when death is all around, they know it is not life. But for those whose access to the experience of what their culture is actually up to is only secondhand, through the news media, these reversals can more easily be made.

Language and images are the key ways in which the culture of militarism is achieved. Language is extremely important, as the terminology "New World Order" attests. The New World Order is the Pax Americana with only one superpower, a world in which U.S. power will not be checked militarily. It employs a code word for peace, but does not dare use the term "peace" itself. Those responsible for the development of these terms have learned their lesson; when they named the Cruise Missile the "Peacekeeper," they provided fuel for peace activists to ridicule the military for years. And so they have learned to siphon even more meaning off the top of terms so that all that remains is the hypnotic effect.

Without the New World Order imperative, military power around the world was in imminent danger of being curtailed. The so-called "peace dividend" had a brief life where even politicians speculated on what domestic agendas could now be achieved with the former Pentagon budget. The situation was dire.

It was necessary not only to claim a higher purpose for continued military expansion but to denigrate the possibility of social justice where more money was to be spent on social programs. As one of the most acute critics of these tactics, Marian Wright Edelman of the Children's Defense Fund (no stranger to strategic language herself!), put it:

> One of the most corrosive lies we face is the pervasive argument that "nothing works," the War on Poverty failed, social programs don't succeed. It is as though our entire nation had been put in one of those spirit-squelching, hope-destroying schools in which we bury so many students . . . These teachings inspired a "can't do" spirit.[11]

The Children's Defense Fund has estimated that it would have cost $26 billion to bail children and families out of poverty in 1988, and to eliminate all poverty would have cost just under $54 billion. This is just about half the current estimates of the cost of bailing out the savings-and-loan industry.

Militarism demands that we tear the spirit from the body. The body can be held in contempt as the cause of corruption of the will. But it is truly not all bodies that are so held in contempt, but the bodies of the vulnerable, those who do not have power or access to power in our societies: women, children, the elderly, the minority races, the poor, the non-heterosexual, the surplus other. We must expose these body-denying theologies for what they are: the rejection of the gift of the creation and the barest kind of contempt for the creator. Instead, we must re-construct Christian theology, drawing on the "hidden histories," the many places in our Christian history where a theological construction of the human person has been as one who is body and soul together, a creature destined for community with God and with one another. We must re-construct with intent, we must delegitimize militarism and its constructions before the separation of the body and the spirit is complete in a world-destroying spasm of violence and greed. And I suggest that we hurry.

NOTES

[1] Elaine Pagels, *Adam, Eve, and the Serpent* (New York: Random House, 1988), 39.

[2] Vitor Westhelle, "Creation Motifs in the Search for a Vital Space: A Latin American Perspective," in *Lift Every Voice: Constructing Christian Theologies from the Underside*, ed. Susan Thistlethwaite and Mary Potter Engel (San Francisco: Harper & Row, 1990), 131.

[3] Rita Nakashima Brock, *Journeys by Heart: A Christology of Erotic Power* (New York: Crossroad, 1988).

[4] Beverly Wildung Harrison, *Making the Connections: Essays in Feminist Social Ethics* (Boston: Beacon, 1985).

[5] This case has received press recently because a Japanese historian found documentation which proved that the Japanese government had authorized the use of women for sex with soldiers as a policy. The prime minister of Japan has apologized to Korea, but the Japanese government has refused any form of redress or reparation. Cf. "Sexual Slavery by Japan's Imperial Army," in *Against Prostitution and Sexual Exploitation Activities in Japan* (Tokyo: Japan Anti-Prostitution Association, c/o JWCTU, 2-23-25 Hyakumin-cho, Shinjuku-ku, Tokyo 169, JAPAN), 20-39.

[6] Cf. *Chicago Tribune* series on Asia and the plight of workers (Nov. 7, 8, 1994).

[7] Marilyn Waring, *If Women Counted: A New Feminist Economics* (San Francisco: Harper and Row, 1988), 3-4.

[8] Douglas Meeks, *God the Economist* (Minneapolis, MN: Fortress, 1989).

[9] Catherine Keller, *From a Broken Web: Sexism, Separation, and the Self* (Boston: Beacon, 1986), 44.

[10] Cf. George Orwell, *1984* (New York: New American Library, 1977).

[11] Children's Defense Fund, *S.O.S. America! A Children's Defense Budget* (Washington, D.C.: 1990), 11.

Part Four

WOMEN'S STRUGGLE FOR LIFE

12

YOUR COMFORT VS. MY DEATH

Chung Hyun Kyung

Her name is *Noh Soo-Bock*. She was born in a small southern village, Ahn Shim, in Korea in 1921. She was the first daughter of a poor farmer's family. Her father's name was Noh Back-Bong. She cannot remember her mother's name because people never called her mother by her own name.

It was during the time of the Japanese colonial occupation in Korea. Because of severe taxation by the colonial government, Soo-Bock's father, a poor landless farmer, could not feed his family even with his back-breaking work. Soo-Bock's memory of her childhood, therefore, was filled with hunger. She spent many hours a day gathering leaves, wild vegetables, and plant roots in the fields and mountains. It was a difficult time to grow up as a girl-child. She could not even imagine herself attending elementary school. She never learned how to read or write the Korean language. Instead, from her grandfather she learned a few Chinese letters and the Confucian way of womanhood, especially the importance of chastity. In spite of all the hardships of her childhood, however, she still remembers vividly the magnificent colors of spring flowers in the mountains behind her shabby house and the beauty of the calm lake in her village.

When Soo-Bock became fourteen years old, her parents married her off to a family in the next village. Her parents' poverty forced her into this early marriage. One more mouth in the family meant one more bowl of rice which they could not afford. Following the custom of her time, she obeyed her parents and married a man she had never met. Without knowing him, she slept with him in deep darkness on her wedding night, as all Korean women did in her time. The next day she got up and saw her husband's face for the first time. He was a leper, and she fainted.

It was torture to sleep with her leper husband. Fear and disgust filled her life. Ignoring Soo-Bock's pain, her mother-in-law made her work all the time, but she did not give Soo-Bock enough food to eat. Fear and hunger overwhelmed her, and she decided to run away. As if she were possessed by a ghost, she ran and ran through the mountains and streams and finally arrived at her father's house, the home where she had grown up with her brothers and sister. Her father was so angry with her shaming the family's reputation by running away from her marriage that he chased her away, saying, "If you want to die, go and die in your husband's house. You are not one of our family any longer. You belong to your husband's family."

Weeping, Soo-Bock walked and walked to the nearby big city, Tae-ku, without having any plan or knowing anybody. She became a maid. With the hope that her family might accept her if she had money, she saved all her meager earnings and one year later visited her family again. Her father still did not allow her even to enter the house. Her mother pleaded with him to allow Soo-Bock to stay just one night with her brothers and sister. Her father's response was the same, "Go die in your husband's house," and he chased her away again. Her mother followed her to the edge of the village, weeping and beating her breast in sadness and helplessness.

In despair Soo-Bock went back to the big city and became a maid once more. She moved from house to house and ended in Pu-San, the second largest city in Korea. There she met her second husband. She was now seventeen years old. She visited her family again with her new husband, expecting that her father would accept her now that she had a new husband. But her father was the same. He kept telling her, "What shame you brought upon our family!" She was chased away again. This was the last time she ever saw her home.

It was autumn 1942. Soo-Bock went to the well to wash her clothes. It was dusk. When she tried to draw water from the well, four Japanese policemen appeared. First, they asked her for water, then one policeman tried to grab her. When she escaped his advance, other police joined him and tied her with rope, yelling and threatening to kill her. She resisted them with all her power, but they pulled her by a rope and put her in their vehicle.

Finally she ended up in a police station. There were already five or six young Korean women there. The Japanese policemen said to them that they were chosen to be sent abroad as representatives of the Japanese Emperor. Then they gave military uniforms to these women. The Korean women pleaded with them to get a message to their families before leaving Korea, but their requests were denied. If the Korean women talked about or did something which the Japanese policemen or soldiers did not like, the women were beaten severely.

Soo-Bock and the other Korean women were forced to travel in the bottom level of a Japanese military ship and they sailed for forty days. Then they arrived on a shore with many palm trees. It was Singapore. Upon their arrival they were transported to a military base. The next morning, when they awoke, they found many Japanese soldiers trying to look into their tent. Seeing the women getting up, the soldiers began to shout and tried to get into their tent. The Korean women held one another tightly and trembled with fear. Then a soldier came in and told them to prepare for the song party.

When evening came, thousands of soldiers filled the military field while Soo-Bock and the other Korean women were forced to go on stage and sing for them. The Japanese soldiers became so excited they began to shout and sing and dance. As soon as the women returned to their tent, a Japanese lieutenant came in to Soo-Bock's room and tried to rape her. When she begged him not to, he hit her with his fist and kicked her in the stomach until she fainted. When she regained consciousness, she knew what she had become: she had become a so-called "comfort woman" for the Japanese soldiers. Soo-Bock saw the other Korean women, to whom the same thing had happened. They burst into tears. They wailed together. Then the soldiers came in and hit them as if the Korean women were their punching bag; they went out, locking the door from the outside.

This was the beginning of her life as a "comfort woman." Korean women had to clean the military bases, wash the soldiers' clothing, and carry their bullet boxes in the morning. Starting in the afternoon and through the night they had to receive Japanese soldiers. Sometimes they received more than sixty soldiers a day. If they resisted, they were stripped and whipped in front of Japanese soldiers in the military field. Japanese soldiers also called them "cho-sen-pee," a derogatory term for Korean women (which literally means "Korean pussy"). Many of the women started to die of starvation, exhaustion, and venereal diseases, and from their wounds from being battered by the Japanese soldiers.

After many days of despair and crying, Soo-Bock determined that she would survive. She could not die like a dog in this strange land. She started to eat as much as she could, and she also became very obedient. She did everything the soldiers asked her to do. She knew they were ready to kill anybody. Some of them even struck their sword on the "tatami" (Japanese floor) when they raped Korean women. It was better not to provoke them. Soo-Bock was transported from one base to another. On one base in Thailand she saw other Korean women, but they were not allowed to be together. Japanese soldiers were afraid that if Korean women got together, they might make plans to run away.

Early in 1945 Soo-Bock began to hear rumors of Japan's imminent fall. With that rumor more Korean women were gathered from other bases and brought to Soo-Bock's base in order to "comfort" Japanese soldiers. The more they heard about the impending fall of Japan, the more they were raped by nervous soldiers. In June of 1945, Japan surrendered at Singapore, and English soldiers came onto the base. The Korean women were transported to refugee camps. There were many other women from Thailand and Burma. More than two hundred of them lived together, and there they heard the story of Japan's defeat on August 15. They shouted, "Long live Korea!"; they jumped for joy, embraced one another, and wept together.

Finally the day came, the day of returning home. When Soo-Bock heard of the plan of return, she became very anxious. "How can I go back home and meet my family with this dirty body?" she asked. She became very depressed. Her father's strict face appeared in her dreams again and again. After many days of agony she decided not to go home, and she ran away from the refugee camp.

She ran through the jungle and became a beggar in a land where she knew no one and could not speak the language. A man called Mohammed, a devout Muslim, rescued her and she became a maid in his family. After working in his house in Malaysia and receiving his family's encouragement to work for her own independence, she left for Thailand, landing in Hot Chai, where a new mining business was flourishing. She found a job in a Chinese restaurant there and also met the husband she was to keep for life, a poor old Chinese bachelor, Mr. Chen. He could not marry because he was so poor. It was the first time in her life that Soo-Bock had felt that strange feeling called "love." In the autumn of 1947, she married him in a lotus flower Buddhist temple. For Soo-Bock it was a moment of rebirth. She was determined to bring her own beautiful lotus flower of life to bloom out of her muddy past.

Their restaurant business flourished, but Soo-Bock could not become pregnant because of the many rapes she had endured. She persuaded her husband to take a young second wife to give them children. Although he refused her offer in the beginning, he later gave in. They took a young Chinese woman, who gave birth to three children. The two women, their three children, and the one husband lived together happily, helping and appreciating one another. Soo-Bock often said, "Korean, Japanese, Chinese, Thai—we are all friends."

Soo-Bock is now seventy-four years old. She misses Korea, but is still afraid to go back. She wants to come home at least once before she dies. She asked herself, "Is it really all right to visit home now?" For many days she could not answer that question. Then suddenly peace came into her heart. "Why not? It is my home. What happened to my life was not my fault. Now I am not afraid of anything. I will go home."[1]

THE "COMFORT WOMEN" SYSTEM

This is the story of a Korean woman. It is the kind of story which is both ancient and contemporary for any Korean woman. We all know this story, a story both strange and familiar. It haunts each of us every time we hear it just because we are Korean women. We are still deep in the story even today [13-2].

Any group of women must have their "root story" of what it means to be women in their own specific history and land. African-American women remember stories of slavery, brutal kidnappings, rape, forced breeding and labor, and intentional destruction of their family and dignity. Jewish women remember the story of the Holocaust, Nazism, Hitler, German nationalism, Auschwitz, stripping, the gas chambers, and medical experiments with their bodies. European women remember the story of witch-hunting. In the name of holiness they were captured, tried, tortured, drowned, burned alive. Women from Asia, Africa, Latin America, the Pacific, and former European colonies remember what it means to be "other," "primitive," and "savage" in their own land, slowly losing their language, culture, and memories.

As a Korean feminist liberation theologian who refuses any kind of colonial domination in my life, I have to remember and re-tell Soo-Bock's story, the

Korean women's root story, again and again so that we can exorcise this haunting ghost of debilitating rage, fear, and helplessness to bring our full womanhood to bloom like a lotus flower of wisdom from the mud of suffering.

Soo-Bock's story, the story of the comfort women, had been erased from both Korean and Japanese history for the last fifty years until a group of persistent Korean feminists looked for survivors all over Asia and gathered evidence [11-5].[2] Neither the Korean nor the Japanese government wanted to talk about what happened to Korean women during World War II. For Korean men it was too shameful for their ego to accept what happened to Korean women, and there were more important things they needed to talk about in relation to Japan. And for Japanese men it was too guilt-provoking to confront what really happened. They preferred to deny the whole thing because they did not want uncomfortable guilty feelings nor did they want to give material reparation. Not surprisingly, Korean churches also kept silence about these women's lives.

According to research by a Korean feminist group, the number of so-called "comfort women" from Korea was more than 200,000. The exact number is not available because the Japanese government still refuses to release their military documents. The "comfort women" system was created by the Japanese military in 1932 and maintained until August 1945, when Japan gave in unconditionally to the united army of the West.[3]

Research indicates that comfort women's bases were located in China, Hong Kong, Indochina, the Philippines, Malaysia, Singapore, Borneo, the East Indies, Burma, Thailand, Papua New Guinea, Saipan, Guam, the Coral Sea Islands Territory, and Japan.[4] Those who served as comfort women came from Japan, Korea, Taiwan, China, the Philippines, Indonesia, Vietnam, and the Netherlands.[5] These women mainly acted as sexual slaves for the Japanese military. They also worked as cleaning and laundry women, manual laborers and cooks. The number of soldiers they received a day ranged from one to ninety. "Comfort" bases were established in military tents, small houses near a base, in the mountains, in small ditches, in halls, etc. One out of three women are thought to have died during their slavery, and there are no records for the women who survived. Only a few women have surfaced as witnesses in several of the involved countries. Most of their recruitment was done by force or deception (a good-paying job, enough food, clothing, education, etc.).

The reasons why the Japanese military needed "comfort women" were as follows:[6]

1. During the Japan-China War many Japanese soldiers engaged in killing, stealing, burning, and raping. As a result, many Chinese who were victims of these crimes became intensely hostile to the Japanese. Rape especially was most disturbing to them. The Japanese military leaders needed a system of sexual release for their soldiers if they were not to rape women in the occupied land.

2. The Japanese war was a causeless war from the beginning, and there was not much possibility of winning. Many soldiers became restless, and they did not receive the vacations promised them. Therefore, military leaders tried to give them some "comfort" and recreation.

3. Sexual disease was their big concern. Most of the Japanese prostitutes they hired were experienced professionals with a high possibility of having venereal diseases. The military needed "clean women" who had not been exposed to sexual activity. Therefore they chose "chosun" women (the name of Korea at that time) who were raised in a Confucian ideology of strict chastity. Korean women constituted 90 percent of the entire force of comfort women.

4. In order to preserve military security, authorities needed comfort women based in the military. Otherwise soldiers would visit local brothels and spread military secrets by accident to local people. They needed tight control.

When we critically analyze "military sexual slavery by Japan,"[7] there are four important factors which made this cruel system possible: state, nation, class, and gender. Without looking at the dynamics of these four factors, it is impossible to name the evil of military sexual slavery by Japan clearly.

1. The Emperor State had been the backbone of this sexual slavery since 1889. Japan established a state where the emperor had absolute power over all people, including the military. What the state required from the people was absolute obedience. This state stabilized a pyramid-shaped, hierarchical society where discrimination among people of different status was emphasized.

In the process of militarization this state began to have the character of fascism. Therefore, young soldiers felt tremendous repression in being only a "yes" man, and they vented their frustration on women with the most raw and cruel forms of violence. For example, kamikaze pilots forced Korean comfort women to commit suicide one day before the pilots themselves had to go to bomb the united army.[8] Korean women were also forced to say, "Japanese and Korean are one people under the emperor's lordship," before they were raped by Japanese soldiers.[9] Therefore, if kamikaze was a holy, patriotic sacrifice for the emperor's altar, the rape of Korean women by Japanese soldiers was considered holy, patriotic sex at the emperor's temple, which was the military base.

2. Colonialism, which promoted Japanese supremacy, was also the backbone of the sexual slavery of Korean women. Japan's ambition for expansion was based on its early adaptation of capitalism and its political agenda to assuage the restlessness of the Samurai by attempting domination over other nations.[10] Since Japanese capitalism was not as well developed as that of Western colonial countries, Japan's colonial policy was most exploitative and violent to accumulate the most capital from the colonies.[11] Japan controlled Korea and Taiwan and tried to destroy peoples' national identities by changing their names, language, religion, and culture into the Japanese style.[12] Using hundred of thousands of young Korean women, who would become the future mothers of the Korean nation, as sex slaves and making them barren was one of the most effective ways of humiliating, confusing, and finally destroying the Korean people.

3. The development of capitalism in Japan was state-controlled. The expansion of capitalism means the invasion of more colonies for capital accumulation and the rise of many poor people (a proletariat class) in Japan and its many colonies. The development of capitalism was accompanied by the development of public prostitution. In this system, many poor Japanese women were forced

into prostitution, and many young women in the colonies were forced into sexual slavery.

4. The patriarchal Emperor State was like a big "family" state where the emperor became a national father of all the people. According to their law, a wife was the property of her husband. Because of her gender, she was not allowed any economic activity or ability to make legal decisions. Also she could not act on her own without her husband's permission.[13] The Emperor State legalized public prostitution, which flourished with the rise of capitalism. It thought the establishment of public prostitution was helpful for two reasons. One was the release of sexual desire, especially for the Samurai caste, because of their own anxiety and psychological instability, which was explosive because of the continued situation of war. A second reason was to protect the maintenance of a strict family system.[14] It was presumed that if men could have access to many sexual adventures in public, they would not leave their wives.

In this process they used three different gender ideologies for three different classes of women. For upper- or middle-class women who were educated, they used "the ideology of motherhood." Their motto of female education was the combination of state, family, and motherhood. They trained women to be the mothers of Japan, the mothers of militarization, the mothers of warriors, the mothers of a healthy nation, the mothers of the Japanization of Asia, etc. There were many lectures and books published in praise of motherhood.[15]

For unmarried middle-class or lower-class women, the ideology they imposed was "the ideology of the productive worker." With all kinds of special decrees they recruited young unmarried women as workers.[16] For lower-class women who were excluded from the above two ideologies, "the ideology of comfort" was given. They were necessary members of the Emperor Nation, giving comfort, peace, and stability to the big, abusive, dysfunctional, repressive emperor's family.

A "ROOT STORY" FOR KOREAN WOMEN

Why, then, is Soo-Bock's story, which happened fifty years ago, still a "root story" for Korean women? Because it is happening here right now in the everyday lives of Korean women and many other Asian sisters. We still have poor fathers who want to get rid of their daughters. We still have fathers, brothers, and comrades who honor our chastity more than our life itself. We still have our leper husband who thinks his maleness can cover any flaws in his life. Even though prostitution is illegal in Korea and many other Asian countries, we still have a state which sells our women's bodies shamelessly, this time in the name of national progress.[17] We still have colonialists who come to our land and destroy poor women's lives in the name of development, the Uruguay Round, GATT, WTO, MTV, CNN, the peace-keeping army, and tourism. We still have capitalists who commodify everything under the sun: our women, our children, our brides, our workers, our earth. And we still have soldiers who call us "a little brown fucking machine fueled by rice."[18]

After the series of wars in Asia, World War II, the Korean War and Vietnam, Asia became the brothel of the world. Indeed, *Bananas, Beaches, and Bases* went together hand-in-hand.[19] Where the militaristic state, colonialism, the patriarchal family, and capitalism thrive, modern-day comfort women and sexual slavery flourish.

Why are we little? Because in five hundred years of colonialism we have become little physically and psychologically. Five hundred years of malnutrition, oppression, and repression can make anybody little. The most difficult disease we have in our psyche is five-hundred-year-old internalized colonialism. Come to Korea and see that all the models for the best clothing companies are white Western women and men. Come to Asia. Most of us communicate with one another in English, a colonizer's language. With the CNNization of the world and all the rhetoric of internationalization and globalization the world became one humongous market. Our young people do not grow up with Tagore, Gandhi, Lao Tzu, or Chang Zu. They grow up with Madonna, Michael Jackson, and Hollywood movies of sex and violence.

Why are we brown? We became a brownized people by the symbolic representation of a graded color system in this racist world. We became brown people who are closer to earth, nature, primitiveness, wildness, and chaos. We are the ultimate oriental mystics, exotic natives, and the "other" by the orientalist formation of world civilization. Orientalism is a form of cultural imperialism, manufactured inside the mind of Westerners.[20] One of the main reasons Western men come to Asia for prostitution or why they buy mail-order brides from Asia is: they want "a real woman," a real feminine woman. They blame the feminist movement in the West. They say there are no more woman-like women in the West because of the feminist movement. Women have become man-like, no more softness, no more vulnerability, no more obedience! So they come to Asia to find small, brown (more natural), soft, vulnerable, obedient, real women. A San Francisco dating service listed its hottest item as young professional Asian women. Professional white men usually seek Asian women. Asian women also prefer professional white men to upgrade their social status. White men seek psychological and personal happiness by hooking up with Asian women in spite of the downgrading of their social status. They say they are willing to *sacrifice* a little bit of status because they feel happier (feel more like a normal man) being with Asian women because of their femininity, a trait which white women do not have any longer.

Why are we a fucking machine? We became a fucking machine because we never have been a subject for the soldiers, capitalists, and colonialists. We have been a machine for them. When Western men made the whole earth into a battlefield and became brutally violent warriors as hunters of the world, they began to mechanize the whole world, including us. And people who lose subjectivity (the right to act as subjects) become mechanized. "Discover, conquer, dominate, exploit, and manipulate!" Fucking has never been sex. It is not making love. It is violence.

SPIRITUALITY FOR LIFE

Then where was our subjectivity? Where were our power to resist and our legacy of victory? Are we only the passive victims of complex systems of oppression? Where were Korean men and women when Soo-Bock and her friends were dying in the battlefield? What could the Korean church and Korean Christians have done for so many Soo-Bocks in Korean history?

When Soo-Bock ran away from her leper husband; when she determined not to die and began to eat as much as she could and became extremely obedient to violent soldiers, when she ran away again from the refugee camp in Malaysia and never went home, when she found her work and love in a foreign land, she became an agent, *a subject for her own life.* Her mere survival from sexual slavery to the Japanese military is itself a legacy of victory in the history of Korean women. Like her wish on her wedding day at the lotus flower Buddhist temple, she brought her own lotus flower to bloom out of her suffering.

In her old age she told us, "Korean, Japanese, Chinese, Thai are not different. We are all friends!" Where did she find this *power of forgiveness?* Why did she choose to forgive the Japanese? Was it her Buddhism with its wisdom, compassion, and loving kindness? Or was it her experience of being loved by Malaysian, Chinese, and Thai in her new homeland? I do not know. What I know is she cut the vicious cycle of violence and revenge with her power, which I cannot easily name.

Then she came home in her heart, the home which starved, deceived, and rejected her. She decided to come home to Korea, saying, "*It is my home.* What happened to my life was not my fault. Now I am not afraid of anything. I will go home." Finally, after fifty years of exile, she knew she had the power to go home, that place of poverty and abandonment. She claimed that place as her home. She accepted her life as it was, seeing that what happened to her life was not her fault. Suddenly she was not afraid of anything, and she came home.

From Soo-Bock we learn her legacy of survival, forgiveness, and acceptance. Her survival was her liberation. Her forgiveness was her best revenge, and her acceptance was her best resistance.

There are many other Korean women who followed the legacy of Soo-Bock, choosing life in their own predicament. Lee Ock-Soon is one of them. Lee Ock-Soon is an ex-prostitute. Now she is an adviser for Magdalena House, a resting place for prostitutes founded by the Maryknoll Sisters. What Magdalena House does for prostitutes is give them a safe place to rest, talk, share, and just be. It is a ministry of presence. Sisters or volunteers in the house do not teach the Bible or impose worship. They actively *are* with anybody who comes to see them.

Lee Ock-Soon's life as a prostitute began with rape, too. After retiring from prostitution, she became a big sister to other prostitutes. She counsels young prostitutes. If any man treats a prostitute violently or does not pay the fee, she organizes other prostitutes to hit him back, to stop him from abusing women, or to make sure he pays her fee. Therefore, it is clear in her circle of prostitutes that men can buy sexual service, but no violence against women is allowed. She also organized an English class for prostitutes so that they will not be cheated by foreigners, who are their major customers.

While Ock-Soon was doing this kind of "sisterhood work," one man, a taxi driver, joined her group. He helps her by providing the speed and mobility to get her work done. After some years of working together, he confessed his love to her, and she to him. One spring day they were married in the Catholic cathedral in Seoul. Ock-Soon wore a white wedding dress, which is the dream dress for most prostitutes. Prostitutes have an intense longing to marry the one they love while wearing a white wedding dress, the symbol of chastity and purity. Even though they sell their sexual service, they believe they are always keeping their purity and chastity of heart for someone they love.

When Ock-Soon got married, all of us got together and we read a poem on Mary Magdalene at her wedding. Everybody cried. For the first time I thought it was good for some theologians in church history to have taught us that Mary Magdalene was a prostitute. That teaching may be wrong, but how wonderful to have that teaching for Korean prostitutes who identify themselves with Mary Magdalene, the beloved disciple of the good news of Nazareth, Jesus.

Many of the prostitutes at Magdalena House became Catholic, inspired by the "presence" they received from the Maryknoll Sisters there. However, they are not the obedient, ordinary Roman Catholic Christian. They have their own hermeneutics of suspicion coming from their experience. According to their joke, among their customers the clergy and scholar-professor types are the most stingy and demanding customers, for whom prostitutes do not have much respect. They select what they want to hear from the pastors' sermons, remembering what happened in their workplaces.

I wanted to ask Ock-Soon the same question I put to Soo-Bock: Where did your power of survival, wisdom, and courage come from? What is it in your presence which heals and empowers other prostitutes so much? What is the name or the nature of that power? For these are the questions at the root of spirituality for life.

Rita Nakashima Brock has helped us with these questions in her discussion of the importance of innocence and the power of willful nurturing for the empowerment of women.[21] According to Brock, Western Christianity's emphasis on innocent victim and oppositional relationship between good and evil is not helpful to solve the complex problems in women's lives. Rather, it is more empowering to women to lose their childlike innocence and transform it into the willful nurturing of motherhood that embraces the complexity of both good and evil. Brock drops some hints towards new directions for feminist power for problem solving. She observes that the Asian way of problem solving has *esthetic direction* rather than *ethical direction*. By esthetic direction she means the longing for harmony and balance. In ethical direction, what is good or evil and what is right or wrong are the main concern. But in esthetic direction, what restores balance and harmony is the most important concern.

When I look at the present situation of worldwide violence against women, I feel deep despair. Then I become impatient. After all these years of the feminist movement, of women's studies, and feminist theology, is women's situation, especially violence against women, getting any better? Does my work make any difference in women's lives? With all these questions I am searching for that healing power, that life-sustaining, liberating, transforming power which my foremother and sister, Soo-Bock and Ock-Soon, lived out.

What is that power then? More and more I am inclined to Rita's hint of *the power which restores balance and harmony.* Yes, we need feminist social, cultural, political, and economic analysis to name the evil and to see the alternatives. Yes, we need an organized mass movement of women to change laws and customs and to stop the injustice which destroys women's lives. However, we need still more. That "more" might be the energy of raw life: Ki, Chi, Shakti, prana, *ruah,* the Tao, mysterious female, the spirit of the valley which never dries up.[22] How do I really know that power? I am still searching, but I feel something is growing in my womb.

NOTES

[1] Story comes from Kim Moon-Sook, *Mal Sal Doen Myo Bee-Yeo Cha Chung Shin Dae* (Destroyed Tombstone: Comfort Women) (Seoul: K.W.S.J., 1990), 91-122.

[2] A group of Korean feminists formed The Korean Council for the Women Drafted for Sexual Slavery by Japan (K.W.S.J.). They are the main women responsible for elevating the "comfort women" issue to a national and international level. For more information, contact them at: Room 802, Christian Building 136-46 Yunchi-dong, Chongro-Ku, Seoul, 110-701, Korea. Tel. 822-763-9633. Fax 822-763-9634.

[3] *Chong Kun We An Bu Moon Che Eui Yeok Sa Hak Chuck Kyu Myung* (A Historical Research on the Comfort Women Problem) (Seoul: K.W.S.J., 1990), 1.

[4] Ibid.

[5] In addition, there was a witness that some Australian nurses were forced by the Japanese military to be comfort women.

[6] Jin Sung Chung, *Ill Bon Kuk We An Bu Jung Chack Eui Hyung Sung Kwa Byunwha* (The Formation and Change of Comfort Women Policy in Japanese History) (Seoul: K.W.S.J., 1990), 1-2.

[7] This term was developed by K.W.S.J. because they perceived that what happened to Korean women under Japanese militarism was not just being "comfort women" to them. It was systematized, intentional slavery. Therefore, they named it "military sexual slavery by Japan." Young feminists insist on using this term, but old comfort women themselves refuse to use the term "sexual slavery." They prefer the term "comfort women."

[8] "A Historical Research on the Comfort Women Problem," chap. 5, 11.

[9] Witness by a comfort woman; her name cannot be traced.

[10] Masako Fukae, "System of Buying Prostitutes and Emperor System," in *Woman, Emperor System, War,* ed. Yuko Suzuki and Kazuko Hen Kondo (Tokyo: Origin Publishing Center, 1989), 202-205.

[11] Chung, "Formation and Change," 4.

[12] See the witnesses in K.W.S.J., *Witnesses of the Victims of Military Sexual Slavery by Japan* (Seoul: K.W.S.J., 1992).

[13] Yukiko Tunoda, "Sexual Violence and Emperor System," in Suzuki and Kondo, *Woman, Emperor System, War,* 197.

[14] Chung, "Formation and Change," 4.

[15] Yuko Suzuki, "Mr. Horoshito, 'Showa, and Women' " in Suzuki and Kondo, *Women, Emperor System, War,* 23-25.

[16] Soon-Choo Yeo, *Ill Che Malki Cho Sun In Yeo Cha Keun Ro Chung Shin Dae Ae Kwan Han Yeonku* (The Study on Korean Women Workers in the Late Stage of Japanese Colonialism), MA thesis, EWHA Women's Univ. (Seoul, 1993).

[17] Korean Minister of Culture Min Kwan Shik once congratulated Korean prostitutes for bringing foreign currency to the Korean economy. He called them "patriots" who work hard for Korea's economic progress. Similar comments were made by politicians in the Philippines and Thailand.

[18] This was a name for Filipino prostitutes used among U.S. soldiers based there.

[19] Cf. the excellent research on multinational corporations, tourism, and militarism, Cynthia Enloe, *Bananas, Beaches, and the Bases* (London: Pandora, 1989).

[20] See Edward W. Said, *Orientalism* (New York: Pantheon Books, 1978).

[21] Rita Nakashima Brock, "Loss of Innocence and Willful Nurturance," a keynote speech given to the Violence against Women Conference organized by the Center for the Prevention of Domestic Violence (Chicago, 1993), unpublished. Cf. Brock, *Journeys by Heart: A Christology of Erotic Power* (New York: Crossroad, 1988).

[22] Lao-Tzu, *Tao Te Ching,* trans. Gia-fu Feng and Jane English (New York: Knopf, 1972), chap. 6.

13

THE ALCHEMY OF RISK, STRUGGLE, AND HOPE

Denise M. Ackermann

I remember the evening in San Juan, Costa Rica, vividly. It was cool after the rain. We had returned from a picnic on a hillside above a beautiful valley of coffee plantations. We gathered, women from many parts of the world, at our conference center with the quaint address "300 meters from the cemetery." Chung Hyun Kyung introduced her presentation by showing slides of paintings by a Japanese artist on the theme of the exploitation of women. Stark images conjured up acts of brutality and terror. It was hard to watch. Then, dressed in a striking grey robe, she read her paper. First came the riveting and tragic story of Soo-Bock, followed by incisive and comprehensive analysis. Well reasoned and beautifully presented, it was an excellent example of how we women do theology in our own distinctive ways.

For two reasons the memory of that evening will stay with me: first, the merit of the analytic content of the paper and, second, the pain I experienced. On previous days we had had several immersion experiences. I had visited a state agency engaged in working for the alleviation of violence against women. We had all heard two Costa Rican women share their stories of resistance and triumph over great suffering and violence in their lives. As Soo-Bock's and later Ock-Soon's stories unfolded, there was a searing rage in my gut and a series of vivid images flashed through my mind: women in brothels in Thailand, the Bosnian women, the Sudanese women and children in camps in northern Kenya, women and children in Rwanda, women battered in their homes, women working as domestics abused by their white "masters" in my own country. Unremitting and interminable, the obscenity and brutality of violence suffered by women are named, only to occur, again and again and again. Will it never end? The pain permeates the being of all women when we confront the unrelenting evil done to women in war and in times of so-called peace.

On reflection, the cause for my pain was also personal in a very profound sense. Hisako Kinukawa, a Japanese feminist theologian, shared a room with me for this historic EATWOT meeting. As Hyun Kyung began to show the slides, Hisako dropped her head into her hands and wept. Two days previously she had presented a brief paper on the comfort women as a case study on violence against women in the Japanese context. At the end of Hyun Kyung's presentation, Hisako, in a pain-wracked voice, acknowledged Hyun Kyung's work. Two women from very different contexts: the one speaking for the oppressed and violated, the other wrestling with belonging to the oppressors; one speaking, the other listening and then responding in vulnerability. It was impossible not to be moved. I felt deeply for Hisako, not only because I like and respect her, but because her place is familiar to me. I, too, belong to a group of people who have achieved world notoriety for the exploitation of others. I know her pain.

In grappling with the questions raised in Hyun Kyung's paper, "Your Comfort vs. My Death," and the hideous contexts out of which they arise, two reactions are common. The first concludes that silence is the only authentic response to such suffering and that discourse, even theological discourse, is at best impossible and at worse obscene. The second views every attempt at interpretation as a type of optimism which, in the face of the enormity of suffering, appears a mockery. How dare theologians interpret what is so unspeakable? The only conclusion can be that there is no God. "Atheism arises out of human suffering," says Dorothee Soelle.[1] Together with Hyun Kyung (and Hisako) and many other colleagues, I believe that despair or fear must not prevent women theologians from speaking out, from naming the terrors, and asking the questions, even if we know that such questions have no ready answers.

Fuelled by moral outrage, we begin by telling the stories of women's suffering, followed by committed and constructive analysis. Then the taxing and sensitive question remains: What in fact constitutes "a spirituality for life"? Or more aptly, what constitutes "spiritualities for life," as there are clearly many different such spiritualities determined by diverse experiences and contexts? What is that "energy of raw life," that something "more" that Hyun Kyung is still searching for and that she feels growing in her womb [12:20]? What enabled Soo-Bock to decide to eat so that she could survive? What provided strength to countless women in my country as they experienced forced removals, imprisonment, and even torture? What in fact enables certain people to choose life rather than death?

When we dare to probe what enables and sustains survival, we may at no time imply that those who did not survive were less courageous or less worthy. Survivors of the concentration camps have testified that "the best did not survive." In our speaking out, women theologians honor the memories of the countless women, known and unknown, who have died from the multifarious forms of violence perpetrated on them *simply because they were women*. We honor those who have survived, known and unknown. Together we tell the tales of terror in memory of those who have died and use our anger to sustain action to end this terrorism even as we analyze the causes of it.

Frankly, I do not know what enabled Soo-Bock and countless other women to survive the tragic litanies that dog women's lives. I am awed by their courage and their will to live. However, as I grapple with my lack of understanding, certain themes surface in my consciousness. Doubtless they are dictated by my own experience in the South African context. As a contribution to this conversation on spiritualities which enable women not only to survive but to embrace life, I would like to explore these themes. I shall do so in dialogue with Soo-Bock's story, quite simply as I read and understand it. I suspect that we women whose privileges enable us to pursue such reflections do so from a deep existential awareness of our own frailty and vulnerability, as well as from a desire to connect to our own power to overcome. In our hearts we all ask, "Could I endure such suffering? If I had to, what would fortify and sustain me?"

The themes which emerge for me as I contemplate the bare details of Soo-Bock's life are *risk, hope,* and *struggle.* The more I reflect on these three concepts, the greater the difficulty I have in separating them. They are intertwined in a relationship of tense synergy. Risk and hope are inseparable because to hope is to risk, and both demand a commitment to struggle to sustain them.

RISK

Life itself is a risk. However, for those who live in circumstances of severe oppression and exploitation without freedom or material means, risk is not a matter of choice. Here the key issue is survival. Clearly, we are all perennially and involuntarily at risk, for instance, from polluted air, from motor vehicle accidents, from disease, and from the consequences of corrupt political practices. The poor, however, are always at greater risk than those who enjoy privilege, as they lack the means to acquire the necessary buffers against the risks which face all of humanity.

Voluntary risk, unlike the "life risks" described above, involves choice and is actively embarked on. It is the opposite of fatalism, the resigned acceptance that events will take their course. It is risking for the sake of justice as an act of calculated resistance. The decision to risk is made in the face of conspicuous structural evil with the knowledge that change is not imminent and that the struggle will be long and hard. Thus risk concerns future happenings as they are related to present practices.[2]

On a certain day Soo-Bock, who appeared to have no choices in regard to her existence of misery and violation, chose to begin eating. As I read her story, this moment appears crucial in her determination to survive. What led to her making this choice, I do not know. When I hear stories of women and men who have survived torture and imprisonment in my own country, I am struck by how often the determination to survive is coupled to daring to hope. It is risking to believe that there may be a future. Somewhere in the deepest recesses of the human spirit there lurks the gift, the power, of hope in the face of the most wretched circumstances.

HOPE

What does it mean to hope? The capacity to hope appears to be part of the very fibre of our humanness, present from the beginning of life and continuing to influence our development throughout our lives.[3] It is hope which sustains life even when our trust and confidence are assailed. South African philosopher Johan Degenaar, an Afrikaner and radical critic of apartheid, speaks of hope as "creative expectation." "Hope," he writes, "is that attitude which enables us not to become encapsulated within a particular state of affairs which, by claiming finality over our lives, condemns us to inaction. Hope encounters this enslavement by nature of its being a creative expectation of a future in which justice prevails and which, precisely through the disposition of hope, one commits oneself to bringing about."[4]

Dare one speak of hope when sheer survival is the issue? I cannot begin to understand what hope meant for Soo-Bock or for the black rural woman in Natal sleeping in the bushes with her children to avoid the carnage around her, bereft of her meager possessions, fearful, hungry, and shocked as the gunfire and burnings continue. Can one speak of hope when survival is the priority? Yet, survival implies hope. Hope is our human response to evil, adversity, and destruction, and it claims accountability from the One who holds out promises of justice, peace, and wholeness. It is our refusal to accept defeat.

Hope is to be lived. While acknowledging the realism of violence, brokenness, of anger and despair, to hope means to engage hour by hour with life in such a way that one's deeds express that which one hopes for. To hope for justice and peace means to work to eliminate injustice and to be a peace-maker. Our actions again reinforce our ability to hope. Hope without action in the belief that all will probably turn out well is the best possible formula for ensuring that the worst will happen. We have to make our hopes happen.

Hope is risky. The logical conclusion of total hopelessness is suicide. To choose life is to choose to risk. As disappointment follows disappointment, we risk losing our vision. We are tempted to despair. The challenge is to dare to hope and, in this daring, to wrestle with all that seeks to deprive us of hope and thus disempower us. Wrestling is risky. Our strength may fail us, or we may emerge with further wounds and scars. Hope is not mere optimism, which sees the future through rose-colored spectacles, negating the harshness of the present reality. This toying with illusions diminishes our humanity "for we are indulging in a flight from reality."[5]

Hope is nurtured in community. When tempted to despair, when God appears silent, we need to be reminded that to lose hope is to lose life. Hope is also learning to wait. This requires patience and endurance, which are the opposite of resignation. Expectant waiting, unlike waiting for Godot, is nurtured in community, and from it a spirituality of life can emerge.

So I wonder . . . Did Soo-Bock have a friend with whom she could share her dream of something other than the unspeakable misery of her circumstances? Did she risk holding on fiercely to a vision of justice, daring to hope that one day her torture would end? Did Soo-Bock one day reach deep inside herself and find the power to name her desire to survive? Was she sustained by images, dreams, or visions of what she hoped for? I do not know. But one day she chose to eat in order to survive.

STRUGGLE

As hope is resistance, the struggle begins when the void of hopelessness is actively resisted. The title of our dialogue in Costa Rica included the idea of struggle. In the South African context the word "struggle" has a particular political connotation. For many years "the struggle" signified the battle for liberation from political oppression and disenfranchisement and from economic exploitation. When the Federation of South African Women gathered at the Union Buildings in 1956 to protest the pass laws, they understood the nature of struggle and resistance. Proclaiming, "You have tampered with the women, you have struck a rock," they not only defied the powers ranged against them; they dared to hope for a time when all people in South Africa would be accorded their rights and dignity. When the women of the Black Sash continued for forty years to struggle for their vision of a just society, they had no guarantees about the eventual outcome. What sustained them was their involvement in the active praxis of their hope for human rights for all South Africans.

In the search for justice and peace, the struggle is first against apathy. *Apatheia* in Greek literally means non-suffering. The ultimate crisis of human existence is reaching the point of simply not caring any more. Michael Parenti calls apathy "an unconscious adjustment to powerlessness."[6] Herein lies its danger. The state of apathy is embraced unconsciously. All potential for hope vanishes. Second, the struggle is against despair. Despair is ceasing to believe that that which we would hope for can or will ever come about. It is a state of hopelessness into which we spiral ever deeper as conditions of violation and tyranny continue unabated. Last, the struggle is against shame. Shame is not the same as guilt. Shame is directly involved with our sense of self, with feelings of inadequacy or humiliation. Shame relates to the innermost integrity of the self, while guilt derives from feelings of wrongdoing.[7]

We women know that the self is embodied. Our bodies are not simply entities. Our bodies are ourselves and control of our bodies in everyday situations is crucial to protecting and sustaining our sense of our selves. When women's bodies are violated, the struggle is against succumbing to self-destructive shame.

"How can I go back home and meet my family with this dirty body?" asks Soo-Bock when faced with returning home. She runs away, becomes a beggar in a strange land. Then finally she discovers affirmation and loving companionship with Mr. Sen. Many years later she finds the power to act on her hope, which branches and blossoms anew when she sets aside shame: "What happened to my life was not my fault . . . I will go home," she says.

AN ALCHEMY

From our diverse experiences, women continue to ask questions that are the threads which can help us unravel and reweave the tapestries that are our spiritualities for life. We know that our efforts are tenuous, incomplete, and revealing of the one who does the probing. We acknowledge our accountability to those who have gone before us and to those who are brave enough to tell their stories. We know that we cannot ignore the legacies of the past. We insist on restitution, knowing that for some of us this means admitting our complicity in structures of oppression. We hold to the redeeming quality of hope and devote ourselves, with passion for the possible, to a future in which justice will flourish. The more often women's stories of suffering are told in the ever-growing outer circles of discourse and the more women struggle to find meaning in these tales of terror, the greater is the potential for healing for those who are scarred, beaten, and abused.

Soo-Bock's "spirituality for life" in the face of overwhelming odds flowers again at the age of seventy-four. Was the foundation for this spirituality laid long ago when she risked running away from her leprous husband, when she decided to eat in order to survive, and when she married despite her past experiences? I do not know. Could it be that the mysterious alchemy of risk, hope, and struggle was at work in this woman's life? And the question remains: What is the source of this mysterious alchemy? In reflecting on Hyun Kyung's list of divine powers, such as Ki, Chi, Shakti, prana, *ruah*, and so on, I am thrown back on my faith concepts. I have a hunch, and more than a hunch, that God is the breath inside the breath, the source of all that is life-giving.

NOTES

[1] Dorothee Soelle, *Suffering,* tr. E.R. Kalin (Philadelphia: Fortress Press, 1975), 143.

[2] Anthony Giddens, *Modernity and Self-Identity: Self and Society in the Late Modern Age* (Stanford, CA: Stanford University Press, 1991), 117.

[3] Erik H. Erikson, "Human Strength and the Cycle of Generations," in *Insight and Responsibility* (New York: W.W. Norton, 1964), 118; quoted from Donald Capps, *Agents of Hope: A Pastoral Psychology* (Minneapolis: Fortress Press, 1995), 30, who describes hope as "the enduring belief in the attainability of fervent wishes, in spite of the dark urges and rages which mark the beginning of existence."

[4] Johan Degenaar, "Creative Expectation," in *Book of Hope* (Cape Town: David Philip, 1991), 4.

[5] Degenaar, "Creative Expectation," 6.

[6] Michael Parenti, *Power and the Powerless* (New York: St. Martin's Press, 1978), 99.

[7] Giddens, *Modernity,* 65.

14

SPIRITUALITY FOR LIFE

Ursula King

It was an experience of deep joy and great significance for me to be part of the EATWOT women's process of dialogue as we wrestled with the theme of "Women Struggling to Resist Violence." I was thrilled when I received the invitation to speak on "Spirituality for Life" not only because of the historical importance of this meeting but also because I had been in personal contact with several of the participants, through either corresponding or speaking to them about women doing theology around the world.

From the *mujerista* theologians I learned the expression "spirituality as a *struggle* for life," an expression which appeals greatly to me because it proclaims so strongly the power of transformation which spirituality can and must be within the context of *all* of human life: a force for survival and a power for change. Among Asian women theologians I found frequent reflections on "the newly emerging spirituality" within the multiple contexts of religious and cultural pluralism, a theme which resonates with me because of my years of study in India and my ongoing attraction to the rich religious worlds of different faith communities, especially those of Hindus and Buddhists.

Within my own European context, the European Society of Women in Theological Research chose the theme "One Household of Life" for its 1995 conference, a theme which acknowledges and explores the interdependence of all life forms and human communities. We reflected there on the place of spirituality in the multi-cultural and multi-religious household of one earth community. We were seeking a new awareness which can strengthen our resistance against all forms of exploitation and exclusion, all manner of oppression and dehumanizing violence.

We hear so many different voices on the destructive powers of violence. What can we do to overcome them, to transform them? How can we draw on powers for help, for healing powers for the good? Several women theologians have critiqued central elements in the Christian theological tradition which have contributed to legitimizing violence among individuals and communities. This is not a theme I shall further pursue here. Instead, I want to explore positive resources and possibilities for change which will enable us to move from too narrow a focus on victimization and violence to a vision of strength and empowerment; an appreciation and celebration of life which can assist us in our struggle to overcome violence.

EUROPEAN CONTEXT AND PERSONAL GROUNDING OF MY REFLECTIONS

Before I explore some of the spiritual resources and strategies which may help us in transforming women's lives, I would like to say something about the European context and the personal grounding of my voice in experiences of violence and pain. Europe is, at least nominally, still 68 percent Christian, but it is also marked by profound cultural, political, religious, and economic differences and by deep scars of historical and contemporary forms of violence. Women's experience in largely urban, emancipated, secularized Europe is no doubt very different from the experience of many women in other parts of the globe. Yet European women have their own sources of pain, their stories of being maimed and marginalized, of experiencing personal and structural violence, injustices, suffering, different forms of exploitation, and oppression.

Women's experience of violence and oppression can be documented by many examples. Such oppression does not only take physical, material, and economic forms; it is often structural and situational, related to language, concepts, aspirations, and choices. For Christian women there is also the oppression experienced in the church, in theological education and, at the deepest level, through the image and concept of God itself, transmitted by traditional theology and Christian preaching. Women doing theology within a European context must take up these challenges. European Christian women, as women elsewhere, ask with urgency today how to articulate a theology and spirituality which speaks to women's concrete life situations, a theology and spirituality which can be a true "bread of life" feeding us the seeds of liberation and transformation. How do we women experience God's face and saving grace in our lives? Where do we encounter divine presence and its empowering spirit in our lives?

Before I go any further, I would like to share briefly with you something of my own situation. I cannot speak for all women in Europe, nor all women in Germany, where I was born and grew up, nor for the women in England, where I now live. I can only tell you my own story as I now understand and can describe it. This access to the power of words—concepts, ideas, images with which we can unlock the meaning of our own experiences and make sense of them— seems to me absolutely essential in what we are trying to do. It relates to the power of mind, spirit, and imagination, all of which are connected to the power of healing and hope.

I was born a year before the Second World War began. During that war, I experienced as a small child the intensive civilian bombing and utter conflagration of the city of Cologne. We were evacuated, lost all our belongings, and later all means of income and livelihood when my father died as a result of a bombing. We had, so to speak, lost our "existence," as my mother used to say over many years. She had to bring up two small children on her own in a situation of poverty and great loneliness, struggling hard to give us an education. I remember my childhood as a happy time in rural surroundings, with a sense of space and freedom. If you had asked me some time ago whether I had experienced personal or domestic violence, I would definitely have said no.

But reflecting now on the intricate web of violence and deprivation, I can see that there is much I can recognize in my own experience which relates to structural and systemic violence, as well as physical violence. The experience of poverty, of a subsistence level of existence in post-war Germany, of material and cultural deprivation, growing up in what were slum conditions, the experience of being an evacuee, and later an immigrant in a different country with a different language. The experience of living in a one-parent family, the experience of death and bereavement, the loss of my father, the physical punishment meted out by my mother, but deepest of all the scars of war and bombing, the military violence which gave me nightmares throughout all the years of my youth.

Comparatively speaking, my experience of all these was limited and remained contained, and it was eventually redeemed and transformed by other experiences. I often think, however, of the experience of war and bombing, of violence and violation, writ large a million times around the world in the minds of the children of Africa, South America, India, Pakistan, the Middle East, Ireland, Bosnia, and all the numerous places of fighting and war, wherever they are. I know that the dreams of so many thousands of children have been singed by the fires of destruction, by hatred and violence which have maimed their imagination and hope for life. It is perhaps more difficult to survive struggling with such memories than to be dead. The violence which women experience is often linked to such violence, which affects children so debilitatingly and painfully.

At one level, our post-war situation in Germany was a hopeless one which could have destroyed our moral resistance and fibre. Yet we lived out of a hope which sustained us, out of a strength not our own, nourished by the resources of our Catholic faith. It is such spiritual resources of the Christian and any other faith which can help us to live and make sense of life and its struggles.

Let me say something about this experience of faith, faith not without doubt and also mixed with pain, especially today when I experience more and more the narrowness with which basic Christian beliefs are often preached and practiced. Like many other women, I was brought up in the Roman Catholic Church, of which I am still a practicing member. It is a church which I love and which has given me a great deal. I feel a part of its world-wide web of members and admire its rich historical and cultural diversity. As a child I grew up in a narrow Catholic village milieu in Germany where I took the Christian faith on trust, without doubt or questioning. That came much later when, through studying and travelling, I realized how different the Catholic Church is in each European country, and how much it varies in different cultures around the world. Even though our life in post-war Germany was a daily struggle and the quest for education was linked to many a sacrifice, I was fortunate in being able to follow my desire to study theology and philosophy, first in Germany, then in France, and later in India and England.

Yet the path to becoming a trained theologian was arduous, often linked to the experience of being a minority among an always exclusive majority of men. How well do I remember being refused admission to study in a German theology college run by Dominicans because I was a woman. How clear was the message when on arrival in London, after I had graduated in theology at the *Institut Catholique* in Paris, I was told by a male theologian, an eminent Jesuit whom I consulted about job opportunities, "I am afraid there is no place for you in England." I feel one truly needs to be blessed with a strong faith and a determination not to be overcome by adversity in order to survive such negative experiences without scars and resentment.

My personal biography is one thing; the scale of non-recognition, refusal, and hurt suffered by all women within the church as a whole and society at large is quite another. My identity as a Christian woman has been shaped by the Christian community, by the church. Now, however, it has also been called into question, shaken up, and reaffirmed in a challenging way by the new consciousness of women. This consciousness is marked by the power of pain, the pain of being misunderstood, marginalized, vilified, and made invisible in a church whose faith and teaching are deeply committed to the mystery of love at the heart of creation.

Today Christian women around the globe are breaking through centuries of imposed barriers of silence by speaking in their own voice and by rediscovering the rich heritage of their Christian foremothers without whose presence and participation the church would not have become what it is. Today Christian women around the globe are doing theology in a new way, and our meeting is a living proof of this.

The dynamic reinterpretation of Christian faith and practice rooted in the experiences of women is a sign of life, a sign of hope and prophetic vision for the church, a sign of the presence of the Spirit among us, a sign of resurrection and new life. Any faith full of fire, any faith worth having, must have the creativity and dynamic, the powerful hope and zest, to respond to and make sense of the exigencies and struggles intrinsic to the mysterious pattern which is human life. The creative, transformative potential of faith to shape and transform human life at all levels, personal and communal: that is what Christian feminists are giving witness to today. It is this potential of faith which I consider to be an empowering and transforming *spirituality for life*. Let us explore together what such spirituality is and is not, especially in the context of reflecting on how to resist and overcome violence.

REFLECTING ON VIOLENCE AND SPIRITUALITY

Violence maims and dehumanizes us. Much of life is deeply wounded, weak, precariously violable, and in need of support and healing. How can such healing be done? How can wholeness and health of mind, body, and spirit, of the whole woman, be found?

To live in harmony we have to maintain a precarious balance of the dynamically interrelated natural, social, personal, and interpersonal dimensions of our life, of all life on our planet. This balance, though, is often injuriously and violently ruptured through violent human acts and unjust systems of personal and social relations. Systemic social, personal, and interpersonal violence affects women, men, and children, the animals, and natural world. The marginal and oppressed position of women in society, in the churches, in theology, means that women suffer intensely as victims of violence. Most obviously this happens at the physical and mental level, but the splinters of violence penetrate into the moral and spiritual levels of our being and poison our thinking.

I want to underline the presence of *ambivalence*—the ambiguity of all our experiences and actions, as well as of the interpretations we assign to them. What is the nature of our accounts on violence? How far are we objectifying other people's experiences rather than our own? How far are we violating further their pain and shame? Is our criticism negative only, or does it lead to positive, transformative action and help to change given situations? How far is our very discourse about violence and resistance truly empowering to those we wish to help? Or is it not more often a debilitating discourse?

We have discussed many different forms of violence, but let us not forget the existence of mental and spiritual violence as well as the fact that physical violence can harm and destroy not only the body but also the human spirit. Whilst we are in the process of critiquing all forms of violence, we also must become aware of the violence of much of our own discourse, and that includes even such words as "struggle" and "resistance." The word "struggle" in particular is linked to military language. Because of this, I prefer other words, such as "transformative action," "change," "strength," and "courage," to build up and nourish the power of the good, that which is truly virtuous in the sense of inherent power and strength. We have to struggle and resist violence, but that alone is not enough, for it will only confirm our victim and at best our survivor status. We need more to transform ourselves and our world; we need to recognize, foster, and gather empowering resources of strength for new cultural creation and transformation. That is why we *need new forms of spirituality: a spirituality for life* which helps and sustains us in choosing life, to affirm, increase, and trust life, and to recognize the energy and power of God's Spirit in all the movements of life.

WHAT SPIRITUALITY IS AND IS NOT

For many people spirituality is a soft word, something idealistic and dreamy, even sugary, like the icing on a cake, or it is understood merely as something inward, personal, private, or escapist, but this is not its right meaning. We must not consider spirituality as something abstract, divorced from life, as a far-flung saintly ideal for the devout and few; on the contrary, it is something very concrete, strong, physical and material, embodied, something we can really *touch* and *be in touch with*. Wherever spirituality is spoken of, we have to ask ourselves: What kind of spirituality is meant? In what context is it sought?

There are different kinds of spirituality, good and bad ones. Much of traditional religious spirituality, Christian and otherwise, has a great deal to answer for in diminishing women and legitimizing the exploitative use of power and violence, of pain and suffering. But there exists also a strong tradition in spiritual teaching about the necessity for a *discernment of spirits:* what is good and what is bad, what is a debilitating, distorting spirituality, and what is a strengthening, nourishing one which can bring about growth, lead us to the fullness of life, and endow us with the strength of wisdom.

The widespread contemporary interest in spirituality is linked to the emphasis placed on the human subject, on the discovery of the self, and a more differentiated understanding of human psychology. Many religions do not possess a precise word corresponding to the term "spirituality," whose roots are found in the Christian tradition, where it has a long history in theology and religious practice. Today, though, the notion of spirituality is applied *across* different religious traditions; it is used inside and outside particular religions as well as in an interfaith and secular context. Thus spirituality has become some kind of universal code word to indicate the human search for direction and meaning, especially at times of crisis, widespread uprootedness, and confusion. In contemporary society, spirituality is being rediscovered as a lost or at least hidden dimension in a largely materialistic world. This process is facilitated and heightened by the exploration of numerous traditional writings on spirituality which are being made widely available across the different religious traditions.

Spirituality is deeply grounded in human experience, but it is also linked to the belief that there is a greater, fuller reality which surrounds, beckons, and calls us. Spirituality can thus be understood as a calling as well as a process and a goal. Christians speak of the call to holiness and perfection implicit in the gospel, which says, "You must be perfect as your (Parent) in heaven is perfect" (Mt. 5:48). From the beginning of Christianity the search for spiritual perfection, of life lived in the spirit of God, has led to new forms of life, to asceticism, monasticism, and mysticism. Countless Christian writers, from the desert fathers and mothers to medieval and modern saints and mystics, have written about their spiritual quests and struggles, left instructions and teachings, and provided us with models of Christian discipleship and holiness. Thus spirituality can also be described as "the theory and practice of the Christian life," although spiritual writers, theologians, and scholars have taken markedly different positions over the centuries on what this theory and practice consists in.

Many people around the world are asking today *what kind of spirituality* we must develop in order to bring about the profound personal and social transformations our world so desperately needs. Many are the voices that speak out on spirituality, however differently understood. Spirituality is a topic as much addressed by new religious movements as it is by the ecological, the peace, and the women's movement; it is raised by those interested in psychotherapy and the transformation of consciousness, and by those working for the renewal of Christianity or in interfaith dialogue. Yet contemporary understandings of spirituality can sometimes appear as too nostalgic and imitative of the past without being sufficiently linked to contemporary society. Much contemporary interest in spirituality, especially in traditional religious circles, is too individualistic and static, too much focused on revival rather than creativity and renewal, too much concerned with the individual self and personal inwardness than the transformation of both the inner and the outer world.

Evelyn Underhill, the well-known British writer on spirituality (one could describe her as a true "mistress of the spiritual life") has written on the "great spiritual truths for everyday life."[1] She does not reflect on spirituality in relation to violence, but she emphasizes that spirituality is at the heart of all real religion and therefore of vital concern to all ordinary women and men. It is this emphasis on spirituality within the ordinariness of life, within the struggles of life, which allows us to connect it to all experiences, including violent ones, which can be powerfully redeemed, transformed, and healed.

Another writer, the French Jesuit paleontologist and mystic Pierre Teilhard de Chardin (1881-1955), also reflected much on the power of spirituality in transforming all life. He regards spirituality as our deepest energy resource for shaping the world and ourselves, and he speaks very movingly about its life-transforming power in animating and transforming all our activities and passivities.[2] He used to say, "Trust life," the forward-moving, dynamic growth of life and its vivifying force, the divine energy at the heart of creation. Thus God is active in all of life, and for Teilhard the great Christian feast of Easter was a celebration of the feast of the Risen Life, a day on which he wished to die and did die.[3]

Spirituality has been defined in a very general and open-ended way as an exploration into what is involved in becoming fully human. Since this search for full humanity is one of the main goals of the women's movement, spirituality appropriately figures as a strong personal and political process of transformation among contemporary feminists. Spirituality has also been more specifically described as "an attempt to grow in sensitivity, to self, to others, to non-human creation and to God who is within and beyond this totality."[4] This is quite a helpful definition (although some will no doubt want to mention the Goddess here), because it emphasizes the understanding of spirituality as an integral, holistic, and dynamic force in human life, for both individuals and communities.

I want to explore a few metaphors which indicate the power of transformation inherent in spirituality for giving women strength. Spirituality has to do with centering, building up, connecting, weaving threads, all activities much stressed in developing the agency of women and their self-determination, which must also include their religious and spiritual self-determination.

As an interpretative, existential tool, spirituality is the attitude and interpretation we adopt towards our experiences to give them meaning, to make sense of them. This can be done by drawing on the resources of a religious faith, on a program for action relating to justice and peace, on an ideal of being fully human, on a relationship of love and forgiveness. We have to discover the ever transcendent and yet so near horizon which surrounds us, envelops and cradles us. In this sense *spirituality as the struggle for life* is quite literally the immense effort, labor, and pain to produce and bring life into this world, as women always do, but also to attend to all its details of growth, to nurture it with love and care, and struggle to make it grow into a fuller, more abundant life. Spirituality is also the struggle to live and survive against all odds, to make ends meet, to produce the food needed for so many mouths, to calm down fights and quarrels. Furthermore, it is more than merely struggling to survive; it is also the tremendous effort to live a fuller, more abundant, richer, and more meaningful human life. Understood in this sense, spirituality is the *breath* and *blessing of life;* it is *the very bread of life.*

Many women's stories, songs, and voices have expressed this powerful characteristic of spirituality. I can think of many similes to describe its nature. Spirituality is like a fine *silken thread* which women can spin with great strength. It can be *a key* with which to open the obstacles of doors and windows obstructing women's path, which must be opened to give us access to a new and different world. Spirituality is like a *diamond,* hard, indestructible, and full of strength, with which women can cut through the confusing mass of their distractions and confusions and test the strength and integrity of their relationships. More than anything else, though, spirituality can be likened to a *leaven* which makes our life, with its sufferings, violence, and pain, rise anew and transforms it. We must understand this alchemy of transformation as a process which can give us strength and sustenance as well as a new freedom and identity.

Spirituality thus understood and lived is neither a patriarchal nor a kyriarchal patrimony handed down to us in the form of traditional, well-known sets of religious beliefs and practices which must be defended like a closely guarded fortress. No, women's spirituality is an ongoing process; it is like a continuous journey and quest, an adventure and experiment to make and find new patterns of meaning. As women from all over the world, we are so much involved with the preparation of food. We possess and exchange many different recipes for cooking, but we also continuously create new ones to be added to the old. I like the idea of stirring, mixing, and kneading the dough of our daily life experiences into food that is truly nourishing and strengthening, food that is truly spiritual in the sense of putting us in touch with, and being the sustenance of, the whole world and each other.

WOMEN ENCIRCLING THE GLOBE—A SPIRITUALITY FOR LIFE

Women around the globe are seeking full humanity. We are thirsting for the fullness of life, a life worth nurturing, sustaining, and strengthening at a historical moment when so much of our life seems so fragile and threatened. We women are in search of strategies, or rather, to get away from the military language, in search of processes and resources for spiritual empowerment and strength to shore up life and bring it into fuller flowering. Our new consciousness and vision make us dare to dream and act together to affirm ourselves, to affirm the powers of life and of our ecological interdependence.

There is much strength and tenacity in women, in our self-determination and action, which also encompasses spiritual agency and self-determination. Women's strength is not that of unbending steel, but of elasticity and adaptation which can relate to others and work together with them. "The future is female," as a British television documentary on current research into gender differences regarding innate language and relational capabilities declared. It is this positive image of women's strength, of women as actors rather than victims, which I want to stress. If we dwell too much on the idea of resisting, we follow a reactive trend of thought and action. To resist means to strive against, to oppose, to refuse, to comply with, to keep off, to prevent, be unaffected or uninjured by. Such courses of action must be taken at times, but they are not enough by themselves.

A spirituality for life means more. To enter the struggling process of the flow of life requires above all strength, the active strength of being involved, engaged, committed to as well as affected by, the active strength of taking initiative, making life-directing and life-enhancing choices. We need women strong of body, mind, will, memory, and judgment, women who possess endurance, patience, and measure, but above all the strength of courage, women who are determined, persistent, energetic, women who can strengthen each other and encourage the world to seek equality, justice, harmony, and a desperately needed peace.

Violence is not an abstract academic subject which we can dispassionately analyze and examine. No, it is part of the horrible underside of the struggle of life as daily breathed, lived, and experienced around the world in its thousand-fold diminishments and violations. We must recognize the lineaments of violence, wherever they are found. We must diagnose the symptoms and causes of violence so that we can find a cure for them and make the struggle for life one of growth and positive enhancement rather than one of mere resistance. To achieve this requires social and political as well as spiritual transformation. In her essay, Rosemary Ruether speaks of the need to move from violence to biophilic friendship, the need to bring about a *metanoia* for creating a new global community, but this can only be done if new forms of an integral and holistic spirituality centered on the fullness of life undergird all our thoughts and action [30].

We women from around the globe have tremendous resources for this. As a European woman I cannot speak for Asian, African, Latin American, North American, or other women around the globe, but I would like to mention some of the powerful glimpses I catch from these visions which are so inspiring and strengthening.

I am attracted by the dignity, strength, and affirmations of life found among so many African women and their traditional heritage of bonding and community-building, the rich and diverse resources of tradition, history, and culture of their great continent. Among the Latin American women I admire their struggle for justice and peace, their immense courage in fighting poverty, militarism, and all forms of colonial exploitation, their efforts in feeding, sustaining, and strengthening their communities. This is true of many Asian women, too. They preserve a deeply rooted reverence for life which is so much a part of the integral horizon of their multiple spiritual traditions. It is the extraordinary strength and richness of the Asian spiritual heritage and its potential for inner and outer transformation in the context of global encounter and dialogue which seem to me particularly precious, for more than anything else these spiritual traditions so much stress the oneness of our world and of all of life.

North American women, too, are rediscovering the rich diversity of their cultural traditions with an integral, nourishing vision of the wholeness of life. They can also draw on the abundant historical resources of women's recent past, where women worked for the fullness of life by struggling for the abolitionist cause and for their own emancipation and liberation.

We also have the witness of the women's voices at the 1893 Chicago World's Parliament of Religions, the first global encounter of members of different faiths, where women spoke out about freedom and against the injustices and violence of their own time. They spoke about women's great spiritual task for shaping a more human future for the whole world and pleaded vigorously for women's full participation in the life of the Christian churches.[5] That was a hundred years ago, and yet we do not seem to have come very far since then. These voices can be a strengthening inspiration for us today, and they also link up with some of the historical heritage we women in Europe can draw upon and cherish.

For contemporary European women, it is historically most inspiring that women organized themselves so early into a women's peace movement through the founding of the Women's Peace League in 1854. Particularly vigorous were the peace initiatives of the Austrian Bertha von Suttner, who created a stir with her influential book *Down with Arms,* published in 1889. Between 1899 and 1914, she relentlessly travelled, lectured, and wrote on behalf of peace. She pleaded to establish an international arbitration court to settle disputes between states, to end the armament industry and all militarization, and to influence those in power through an inter-parliamentary conference, a peace summit. She was actively campaigning at a time when women neither had the vote nor were allowed to form a political party or take part in political meetings. Her efforts led eventually, shortly after her death, to a meeting of over two thousand women in The Hague in 1915, in the middle of the First World War. This was the first ever collective peace initiative, out of which evolved the Women's International League for Peace and Freedom.[6]

Women recognized early that wars are first born in the minds of men and that women pay the main cost of the annihilating violence of war. Women rejected the concept of the enemy as the demonic other; they mounted a highly organized and articulate campaign of "War against War" during World War I, in which they pleaded for the end of the arms industry, the need for demilitarization, the dissemination of the peace movement, the growth of international links, and a new consciousness, a profound psychological transformation whereby the will to kill is transformed into a will to change the world. But women knew then, as they know now, that such a new social order cannot be developed until women have an equal part in government and foreign relations, and a real political effort is made to settle disputes without recourse to war.

We have, alas, not come very far, although the peace movement among women has grown stronger since then. Yet how many more powerful and violent war machines have we seen since then, exponentially enlarged through the development of nuclear weapons. All the different forms of violence are interstructured and held together by the violence of military power, as is underlined in other contributions to this volume. Environmentally speaking, the greatest violence occurs through the rapacious exploitation of our natural resources, caused by the greed of the capitalist consumer economy, whose evil face we meet in the global militarist industries so closely linked to the violence of war. The destruction and annihilation wrought by wars scar the face of our globe and wound the lives of its peoples. Daily we watch the immensely diminishing and dehumanizing suffering of people not only affected but annihilated and destroyed by wars, whether in Europe, Africa, Asia, or Latin America. When will this madness ever end? Do we as a species take a particular delight in destroying ourselves and all the fruits of our labors, when for women these fruits include especially our children?

As women we have to ask ourselves how we can create a more harmonious and wholesome environment at all levels of our experience. What can we do to teach and learn to practice peace among ourselves and within our global environment? Some years ago the women's peace movement at Greenham Common in Newbury, England, in its courageous stand against nuclear missiles, caught the imagination of the world. It was a powerful, prophetic movement which brought the political and spiritual close together [178]. This is starkly expressed in some of the stories and poetry which came out of that movement. As Viv Wynant says in her *Memo for Peace,*

> we rattle and keen
> cry out one voice
> for peace.[7]

From my perspective, peace is the greatest issue of our time. We need the active promotion of a peace culture, of peace-building and revolutionary cultural transformation, not only to resist but to overcome the continued reproduction of militarism and warfare, of patriarchal institutions and the cultures of violence they foster. For that to happen, we need a major transformation in gender relationships so that we can live more justly, more humanly, more fully with each other. Women researchers have undertaken pioneering work in peace studies involving redefinitions of power and security and the very notion of peace itself as a process linked to action, and peace-building as a pioneering adventure. Creating cultures that promote peaceableness implies a spiritual option to enhance and foster life.

One of the most inspiring efforts in this direction comes from Elise Boulding's writings and her workshops on "Imagining the Future." Participants are asked to step thirty years into the future in order to imagine a world without weapons, a non-hierarchical world based on local group decision-making, a world in which everybody belongs and people care for each other and celebrate together in community. This is not some kind of utopian vision, but the experience of such dreaming is meant to empower participants to work for the future so envisioned now.[8]

We women from around the globe can inspire and empower each other to work for peace and create new local and global conditions which promote greater peaceableness. This is part of the ongoing process of education and learning. Such learning also implies the fostering of greater sensitivity and awareness, which can energize us to knead through, make rise, and transform our daily strugggles of life and bread.

Spirituality, rightly understood and practiced, is a force for survival and transformation. It can give us an empowering vision of strength and courage which makes sense of all the struggles of our lives and nourishes us to make life grow to greater fullness and wholeness. The roots of such dynamic, energizing spirituality lie in faith, for us in our Christian faith, which affirms the mystery of life in its story of death and resurrection, so closely associated with the presence of women. The Christian tradition, together with other patriarchal religious traditions, has an ambiguous double heritage of both dehumanizing and empowering women. But we need to build on the positive elements, the horizons of hope, and on our great spiritual heritage of countless "women of spirit" to develop strength and vigor for weaving strong strands in the joint patterns of our lives.

I feel grateful for all help and encouragement that has already been developed. A great step forward, though far from enough, is the World Council of Churches' Ecumenical Decade of Churches in Solidarity with Women (1988-98).[9] The solidarity of women and the search for new forms of spirituality that are free from gender hierarchies and strengthened by the newly emerging bonds are also created through interfaith encounter. This makes me plead for the promotion of another Decade of Religions in Solidarity with Women.

A friend of mine and I tried to launch this idea at the 1993 Parliament of the World's Religions, the centennial celebrating the Chicago Parliament a hundred years earlier. We collected well over four hundred signatures, including some from the major religious figures and male speakers. The effort was supported by about a dozen women from different faith communities, but we were not influential enough to get our proposal into the plenary of religious leaders. They were too preoccupied with discussing the *Declaration toward a Global Ethic*, drafted by Hans Küng.[10] This is an important declaration with a strong commitment to a culture of non-violence and respect for life. It speaks of solidarity, a just economic order, a culture of tolerance, a life of truthfulness, and an explicit commitment to a culture of equal rights and partnership between men and women. This is helpful and encouraging but it is not enough.

Elsewhere, Küng has forcefully expressed the view that there can be no human life together without a world ethic for the nations, and that there can be no peace among nations without peace among the religions, fostered by dialogue among religions.[11] These noble principles for overcoming the violence of war have been pronounced without any attention to gender differences, nor do they make clear that dialogue always happens between individual people and members of communities, not between religions as such.

Women are very active in interfaith dialogue at the grassroots level, but they are singularly absent among religious leaders who, moreover, often deny or diminish the full humanity of women. If we really want to work realistically for peace and for the creation of a more humane, more just, new social order, it is imperative that women are affirmed, empowered, and made more visible in all the religions on our planet. It is for this reason that we need a Decade of Religions in Solidarity with Women so that women around the globe may work together for peace and collaborate in developing a transformative, realistic, and concrete spirituality that puts us in touch with each other and with the roots of all life. Such a spirituality is what the world needs, and such a spirituality can help us to change radically the overall context and conditions of our personal, social, and political lives.

We women cannot annihilate violence, but we must seek to diminish it. We cannot condone it, but we must try to transform it by nurturing stronger women and men, more egalitarian relationships, and more participatory structures and communities. Women are developing a new spiritual vision; they also possess many spiritual resources within themselves and within their traditions of faith.

The women's movement has been described as a spiritual movement of great prophetic power. Women's voices express the deep human longing for, and the possibility of, a new spirit on earth. Now that we have the technological facilities to transmit any word, sound, and image almost instantly around the globe, have we the determination and will to be closely in touch, to be in communion with each other, so that we link our minds and hearts and work together to create a new world?

We women across the world have to reach out to join our hands from East to West and South to North to encircle the globe and create a web of co-operation and love. We women need and seek a spirituality which is in touch with the realities of our lives, with the realities of our world; we want a spirituality which is nourishing and strengthening, not debilitating. Such transformative strength will empower us not only to resist violence, but to overcome it!

NOTES

[1] Evelyn Underhill, *The Spiritual Life: Great Truths for Everyday Life* (Oxford: Oneworld, 1993).

[2] Cf. P. Teilhard de Chardin's spiritual classic *Le Milieu Divin* (New York: Harper and Row, 1960). For Teilhard's understanding of spirituality, cf. Ursula King, *The Spirit of One Earth: Reflections on Teilhard de Chardin and Global Spirituality* (New York: Seabury Press, repr. 1994). Cf. also my illustrated biography of Teilhard de Chardin, *Spirit of Fire: The Life and Vision of Teilhard de Chardin* (Maryknoll, NY: Orbis Books, 1996).

[3] This trusting in life is more fully discussed in Thomas M. King, *Teilhard de Chardin* (Wilmington, DE: M. Glazier, 1988).

[4] This definition is taken from the Working Party Report on "Spirituality" by the Scottish Churches Council (Dunblane: Scottish Churches House, 1977), 3.

[5] Ursula King, "Rediscovering Women's Voices at the World's Parliament of Religions," in *A Museum of Faiths: Histories and Legacies of the 1893 World's Parliament of Religions*, Eric J. Ziolkowski, ed. (Atlanta, GA : Scholars Press, 1993), 325-53.

[6] Gisela Brinker-Gabler, ed., *Kampferin für den Frieden: Bertha von Suttner*, (Frankfurt am Main: Fischer Taschenbuch, 1982). For a rich documentation of European women's work against war and for peace, see Gisela Brinker-Gabler, ed., *Frauen gegen den Krieg* (Frankfurt am Main: Fischer Taschenbuch, 1980).

[7] Quoted from Alice Cook and Gwyn Kirk, eds, *Greenham Women Everywhere: Dreams, Ideas, and Actions from the Women's Peace Movement* (London: Pluto Press, 1983), 78-79.

[8] Cf. Elise Boulding, "Women's Experiential Approaches to Peace Studies," in *The Knowledge Explosion: Generations of Feminist Scholarship*, Cheris Kramarae and Dale Spender, eds. (New York: Teachers College Press, 1992), 54-63; also "The Concept of Peace Culture," in *Peace and Conflict Issues after the Cold War* (Paris: Unesco, 1992), 107-33.

[9] Mercy Amba Oduyoye, *Who Will Roll the Stone Away?* (Geneva: World Council of Churches, 1990).

[10] Hans Küng and Karl-Josef Kuschel, eds., *A Global Ethic: The Declaration of the Parliament of the World's Religions*, (London: SCM Press, 1993).

[11] Hans Küng, *Global Responsibility: In Search of a New World Ethic* (New York: Crossroad Publishing, 1991).

15

SPIRITUALITY OF RESISTANCE AND RECONSTRUCTION

Mercy Amba Oduyoye

Between 1967 and 1974 an intensive involvement in ecumenical youth work brought me face to face with an African reality that shocked and irritated me. *Youth Without Work* and *Flight from the Farm* were two cartoon booklets that I produced because I needed to get young people talking about their lives. Only later I realized that I, too, had needed to give a visible expression to my own frustrations with regard to the so-called "school drop-outs" and the unemployment of young people produced by the structures of education that we operate in Africa. I am no artist, but the need to externalize the experience could not be met with words. Too many had been spoken already. I was already spending hours upon hours talking with young people, so I co-opted an artist who was also as concerned as I was to communicate that much-talked-about phenomenon in some medium other than writing. We got our two books written and accompanied them with a poster which was meant to be the first episode of a cartoon serial with the title "The Struggle for Survival." With this last instrument I joined the unemployed, out-of-school, disadvantaged young people, victims of an economic disaster, to say "no" to despondency and devastation and dehumanization.

"Life is war," and not to fight it is to succumb to defeat and death. Survival was the prerequisite to staying human. Survival, the young people knew, was not only a matter of food, water, and shelter, but it helps to have them. Survival is not only the absence of life-threatening diseases and the insecurity of war, but it helps to be rid of these. Surviving is not living fully, but one needs to survive in order to be fully human to face the challenge of living as God intended for us to do. It is from the perspective of the refusal of young people to stay on the margins of power that I view African women's lives. Life, living, becoming fully human is a challenge. Doing so in a hostile world has been the lot of Africans for generations. Placed on a continent whose rivers refuse to be tamed, whose deserts creep in on one, and whose forests are awesome to behold and frightening to traverse, a people has evolved who respect the nature around them and who seek to live in harmony with their surroundings.

If the hostility had been restricted to the ecological challenge, Africans, like all other peoples on the surface of the earth, would have creatively responded to the divine admonition in Genesis: "Take care of the rest of nature, and the rest of nature will take care of you." The fact is that we live another story. History has made Africa the continent from which all is taken and nothing is put back. In Africa we live in a hostile world of meager returns for enormous input; a world of giving good in return for receiving evil; a world that debases one's very humanity by the invention of race and racism; a world that places the onus of human survival on women but slights them, and exploits the weak to enrich the strong; a world that seems to know nothing of what it means to share community with God, the Beginner. This hostile world produces communities that do violence to the humanity of women, the very people expected to care for community and its cohesion. In Africa, one of the most persistent challenges to women is how not to allow violence to poison their thinking and their doing.

The young people of Africa responded to the challenge of living in a hostile world by creating cartoons expressing their anger and their hopes. This generated a spirituality of resistance that enabled them to hold on to their humanity. This was a spirituality of resistance born out of a refusal to be marginalized and discarded. Bernadette Mbuy-Beya, writing on charismatic and feminist trends in Zaire, cites instances of women whose resistance to the crisis of survival in Africa led them to create spiritual homes where the power of Jesus and the Gospel could be experienced in a more vivid and dynamic way than the official Church provides. The charismatic movement and the rise of African Instituted Churches are the most organized forms of spirituality for the resistance of anonymity and the sense of having been abandoned by God. Bernadette defines spirituality as "what permits us to make sense of life."[1] My thesis is that in the struggle to build and maintain a life-giving and life-enhancing community, *African women live by a spirituality of resistance which enables them to transform death into life and to open the way to the reconstruction of a compassionate world.* African women live by a resurrection motif or, rather, by the assertion of the Akan spiritual fountain of "Nyame nnwu na mawu" (Should God die I would die). With this affirmation African women confront, survive, and overcome violence.

From the above description of the violence experienced by Africa, some Africans would say that isolating violence against women is like complaining that one had stepped on hot embers when one's house is on fire. True, in Africa we have on our hands violence that brutalizes the humanity of all who are African, but experience of liberation struggles indicates that we cannot have the whole free if the parts are still in shackles. We also know that whatever the situation, socio-cultural norms demand of women submissive and subordinate behavior that exposes them to violence and predisposes them to accept the violence done to them. It is this violence against women that generates a spiritual-ity of resistance to dehumanization. Women's spirituality is developed in the larger framework of violence in Africa and violence against Africa. The Afri-can scene calls for a total reconstruction. The marginalization of women's pain is part of the patriarchal construct of reality which African women need to resist even more vigorously. While doing this, we keep in mind always the Hausa proverb "The silk cotton tree in the middle of the compound, on the day it is cut down, the people in the house grieve, outsiders rejoice."[2] Patriarchy is the silk cotton tree and the majority of women are outside the compound.

The violence that Africa suffers because of racism and exploitation that are built into her relation with the Euro-American world moves African women to cultivate and to feed on a spirituality of resistance that avoids the smooth talk which hides the violence among women. In any global dialogue of justice-lov-ing women the violence arising out of class, education, and race cannot be over-looked. African women draw empowerment from a spirituality that urges them to think through what it means to be partners with women struggling for a world free from violence and for human communities that honor humanity and the environment that sustains us. They draw on a liberation analysis that unveils a wide range of violent situations not the least being that against nature, them-selves, and children and, in some communities, that done specifically against the girl-child.

WHAT IS SPIRITUALITY?

How do women survive all this to challenge the hostile world, to break the culture of violence, and to build up life-enhancing communities? What consti-tutes a spirituality of resistance and reconstruction? Indeed, what is spirituality? At the EATWOT meeting in Costa Rica, one woman concluded:

Spirituality is a holistic and continuous process of becoming. It enables me to look at others with mutual respect. Spirituality is always coupled with justice. The more I grow spiritually, the more I am concerned with justice and taking action for justice. My spirituality sustains and empowers me to relate in a hostile and patriarchal Church and society.[3]

Her group emphasized that women's spirituality must be holistic and cosmic and must embrace our own being. "Spirituality is both passionate and compas-sionate" has become an adage of the Women's Commission of EATWOT since their Oaxtepec meeting.[4] What indications do we get from this use of the word and how it functions in African women's worldview?

For me spirituality has become a notorious will-o'-the-wisp that I need many handles to hold down in order to attempt its description. One of the handles I have found useful is that it is a theological concept, more accurately a trinitarian one. It is God moving in and through us to accomplish a mission of peace with justice which will result in a beautiful world, a new creation, no longer hostile.

From the irritation at the wasting of young peoples' lives, I have come to understand spirituality as "externalizing" the anger and the hurt so that one might look them in the face, say "NO" to them, and thereby be filled with power to struggle for transformation. It is what enables one to break the silence that makes continued dehumanization possible. Spirituality has nothing to do with the perpetration or the acceptance of death and evil.

There are many words in English that do not translate into Fanti, the language I speak and in which I pray. So high and low I have searched in the language of African religion (traditional) and worldview to find an appropriate expression for spirituality. What I have come up with is that the names and attributes of God are what sustains life in Africa. The evidence that religion propels people's particular attitudes and actions is overwhelming. Professor Paris, a Christian ethicist, writes, "The 'spirituality' of a people refers to the animating and integrative power that constitutes the principal frame of meaning for individual and collective experiences."[5] Both Professor Paris (an African-American) and Archbishop Milingo (a Zambian) recognize the pivotal role that the African religio-culture plays in the shaping of this spirituality. The emphasis on the survival of the people, the need to maintain unity in diversity, the primal need for a cohesive community, and the practice of hospitality and integrity are but a few of the marks of African spirituality.

In Professor Ursula King's essay on "Spirituality for Life," she describes the contemporary references to spirituality as pointing to "some kind of universal code word to indicate the human search for direction and meaning, especially at times of crisis, widespread uprootedness, and confusion" [152]. "By what authority do you do these things?" Jesus was once asked. In this hostile world we have become conscious that some people cope better than others. "Better" here means they are able to transform and reshape adversity into advantage, using it as an anchor to secure their humanity or even as a launching pad for the journey towards full humanity. "Better" because, as King says, "there are different kinds of spirituality, good and bad ones," and we have to discern the spirits [152]. Spirituality of resistance is not one of acquiescence; a spirituality of empowerment is not one that disempowers self and others. A spirituality that negates humanity's call to be the image of God cannot derive from God, and has to be resisted. Indeed, for me, it does not deserve the label that it bears.

In Africa, spirituality was never lost, so we do not need to organize a search for it. I see the current vogue as resulting from a realization that we need to clarify the sources of our actions and attitudes. For the traditional African the world is spiritual and human existence is part of it. King reminds us that in European cultural history, a form of spirituality derived from Christianity has been at work "diminishing women and legitimizing the exploitative use of power and violence, of pain and suffering" [152]. Such, too, is the African traditional spirituality that explained all with the disharmony created by non-conformity with tradition, a spirituality that resists change and subordinates our present to our past. This King would describe as "debilitating, distorting spirituality" [152]. It exists also in Christianity, giving the African Christian woman a double dose of an energy-sapping consciousness. Nevertheless, in Christianity as in African religion, spirituality can and is understood as what propels us to resist death and to foster and create life.

With King, I would agree that today spirituality is being used as an "interpretative, existential tool." In this context, spirituality, she says, "is the attitude and interpretation we adopt towards our experiences to give them meaning, to make sense of them" [154]. She speaks like an African woman when she describes spirituality as

quite literally the immense effort, labor and pain to produce and bring life into this world, as women always do, but also to attend to all its details of growth, to nurture it with love and care, and struggle to make it grow into fuller, more abundant life [154].

Yet it is this very spirituality that can be employed for the disempowerment of women, as shown in the examples of marriage and child-bearing. For African women this "breath and blessing" of life, this "very bread of life," is also the shackles they wear as they try to walk away from debilitating traditions. A spirituality of resistance and reconstruction not only removes the shackles they wear as ornaments but enables them to reject being treated as ornaments and to refuse further shackling. A life-enhancing spirituality is that which frees us for mobility. To some it gives wings. It puts roller skates on the shoes of others, and for some, moving and changing space and pace are slow. The freedom to change towards living fully impels, inspires, and beckons them to life-giving creativity. It clothes and encompasses them with power to promote life, and cradles them in the divine love that gives them confidence to carry on in the company of the God of life and, thereby, to part company with living as if they were dead.

I think it is possible for an African woman to work with King's statement that "spirituality, rightly understood and practiced, is a force for survival and transformation" [158]. Africa's triple heritage is a complicated scenario for transformation. But one could if one dared to use Jeremiah's imagery of pulling down and building up (Jer. 1:10). Like apartheid, much of Africa's needs demand the dismantling of current constructs (including the global economic ones) to make way for reconstruction, a creative approach to transforming Africa from a hostile space into a nurturing womb and cradle provided by God. Nothing short of resurrection spirituality can cope with the demands of Africa. Meanwhile the daily experience is one of resisting death.

African women know that to resist death one must be ready to risk death, and so the Esther types take their lives into their hands as they declare, "If I perish, let me perish, I am going to see the King" (Esther 4:16). Such is the stance of one impelled by a spirituality for life, one who seeks the transformation of relationships. But, meanwhile, the spirituality of resistance directs our response to this hostile world. We need to observe that not all resistance is active and frontal. Africa has its share of the Vashti types who simply refuse to comply with the dictates of those who would dehumanize them (Esther 1:9-21).

They face the cross in the hope that the humanity of women will rise from the silence and peace of the graveyard. Both these queens and many African queens and spiritual leaders of the colonial era demonstrated various types of this spirit of resistance to dehumanization.[6] Many more types of the spirituality that urges resistance will be found among contemporary African women.[7]

The spirituality of resistance is demonstrated by Chung Hyun Kyung's article, which bears the uncompromising title "Your Comfort vs. My Death" [129]. It dramatizes women's reality wherever a socialization against "shame" makes women accept and perpetuate injustice against themselves, as a way to life. True spirituality anchored in the God of Life is that which moves one to generate a spirituality of resistance and reconstruction. It is in this respect that a tension develops in the lives of African women, when giving life and nurturing it mean dying to one's self. In fact, on the non-metaphorical level it is a taboo in Akan culture to die giving birth, so an internal critique of the culture by women begins to give birth to a spirituality of resistance for the sake of life. There are women taking the risk to live in the eschaton, and the consequences of that stance are not mean. Professor Dolphyne narrates the traumatic experiences of a Kenyan woman whose mother had refused to have her "circumcised":

When asked if she would have her daughter circumcised, she said she was not sure. Her better judgement told her she should not. But, when she remembered what she had gone through . . . she sometimes wondered whether it would be wise and fair for her to put her daughter through the same misery.[8]

Her parents had taken a step which another woman, a Nigerian, states clearly she was not ready to take. Her parents complied and so does she. As long as her community remains unsympathetic to changing the custom, the most she would do is to seek the services of improved technology. To live today as if God's reign is fully manifested demands absolute confidence in the God of life. It is the commitment to this ultimate goal that sustains one in the penultimate task of disclosing, challenging, and questioning tradition and its provisions.

RESOURCES FOR RESISTING

One needs a spirit of truth to resist. It is not easy to tell the truth about a culture one is brought up to love and respect, nor is it easy to do so with a culture you have been taught to despise as primitive and inferior [17]. Truth telling about African women and especially about cultural violence is costly. From the "insider" it is often misunderstood by other "insiders" as disloyalty if it is negative. Critique by the "outsider" smacks of ethnocentrism and imperialism. On the other hand, there are often some misgivings on the part of both insiders and outsiders when one presents empowering aspects from traditional culture. It is not easy for us to accept that we did not invent these problems and that others before us produced a spirituality to nourish their lives when faced with the agents of death. We find empowering myths in African tradition as we find in biblical prophetic texts. Given the complexity of the scenario, one does well to place more worth on internal critical discourses. What women do in Africa is a critique of our own culture so that we may identify and utilize the values and voices that empower us and give us a sense of dignity and worth. This way, a life-giving hermeneutic is derived from the mixed bag of our culture. From the same bag, we can find resources against the demonization and scapegoating of women. There are myths and stories and sayings in this bag that are liberating for women, or may be re-read from a liberative perspective. Resistance to sickness, disease, and natural disasters is found in women's prayers, sacrifices, and rituals that strengthen them and move them to pick up their lives. There is no time or space for despair.

When invading, peoples with strange religions struck the Akan at their original home. It is the legends of women leaders of migration that have come down to us. When white people from over the seas made uncouth demands that insulted the ancestors and spirit of the Asante nation, it was women who urged and led rebellion against the ungrateful strangers. Of African women's resistance to death and disgrace, from the resources of their religion, history, and culture, not half has been told, and they are there to be selected for our empowerment. To date, however, resistance has taken the form of law reforms and a lot has been achieved in terms of legislation. The question is, are these provisions justifiable, and can they be adequately monitored?

African culture demands community compliance if change is to be effected. The UN Decade for Women empowered African women to seek direct involvement in legislations that affect them and to work for the enactment of new ones to remove traditional religio-cultural disabilities. National Councils for Women's Development were created by many African governments. In Ghana, the Ghanaian members of the International Federation of Women Lawyers were instrumental for new legislations and legal provisions on inheritance of property, legitimacy of children, the definition of who is a wife, and in the abolition of widowhood rites. The challenge that remains here, as in the much publicized sexual mutilation issue, is a spirituality powerful enough to resist the tradition of the people and the religio-culture that informs it. These are theological issues, but the advocates of equality rarely consider the religious dimensions of the struggles for women's rights. We are faced with the task of pulling up the traditional religious construct for a critical review, with a view to rebuilding an empowering one. From within the culture there are resources for transforming it. The oversize sense of worth given women for being nurturers can be exposed. The Hausa have a proverb that many African women need to hear. It goes like this: "They pat the cow before they milk her." So beware of adulation. For Christian women it is the theology of the cross that they have to suspect. A spirituality of the cross without resurrection is promoted among women. But we know that projecting the cross is not true to its Christian origins unless it means a commitment to an Easter of new and life-bearing beginnings, an Easter of dignity and strength, an affirmation of life, and a heritage of bonding and community. Pastoral counselling for marriage which is unashamedly patriarchal is often anchored on a theology of cross and suffering, making it risky to resist aspects of traditional marriage that support the same ideology.

When one is cutting at the roots of a people's culture, the question always is, with what do you replace it? The vision of mutual respect, of loving and bonding in marriage, and of lifelong companionship in a world that begins to know more and more leisure is simply greeted with benign dismissal, because it is far from the African reality, in which there is no leisure to worry about. Christian women have made Bible study and prayer their source of strength. They compose and sing songs from their Christian faith. They expect God to enter into our human experience, to know how it feels in order to make the appropriate response. Prayer becomes a real "telling it to God" and usually begins with the "strong names of God, some of which come from the Traditional Religion." Women know that daily living depends on God, and so one cantor expresses herself as follows:

Jesus, when we touch anything it breaks.
When we pull it snaps
You who still the sea, control the elements,
Aid our efforts, direct our ways.[9]

From the African Instituted Churches, where many African women have found a spiritual home, many songs expressing confidence in Jesus in spite of all the harsh realities may be heard. Here the power of Jesus is the real and only "superpower." They weave songs from traditional idioms and proverbs to express their faith. In the midst of poverty women will sing lustily:

The spoon of my house is not on vacation.
There is still fish in the market.
To the woman who sells Eko' I owe no debt.
The goodness' of Christ to me are many.
I will praise and thank Jesus.

They will sing and dance with Rev. Acquaah's harvest hymn, "Amason hom mbra (Come from All the Nations)."

Hen anum nkofuw	Weeds will not grow in our mouth
Hen atam nkusum	Our clothes will not turn to rags
Ma daa yaaka de	So we can always say
Onso Nyame ye.	It is not too much for God to do.

When all is truly bleak, they will call upon the God, who heard Jonah from the belly of the whale. The God who hears prayers from the deep is the African

Christian woman's God. And when all is well again, women bring every success before the whole community to celebrate in song:

Come join me to lift up my sorrow,
God has done a lot for me.
My legs dance, my heart should rejoice
My mouth should sing the glory of God.

This is the spirituality of traditional Christian faith that encourages and inspires us to expect life from death and should enable African women to seek a transformation of the ambiguities of our triple heritage. The task is that of distilling the empowering aspects to serve as a resource for reconstruction. Total discontinuity is an illusion, though there is an ambiguity in the exercise of continuity. Having had one's heritage violated by Euro-imperialism, one feels like a traitor when one questions one's own traditional culture and lifestyle. The strength for discerning can only come out of a search for justice that is motivated by a sense that one is within the design of the God of compassion, who moves us to have a passion for truth and to live by justice.

RECONSTRUCTING COMMUNITY

It is not enough to survive violence by coping devices or by resistance. There is need to take the initiative to transform the relationship that breeds violence. Reconstructing African communities on liberative and empowering lines demands that we approach life in a holistic manner. There are no issues that are exclusively women's issues, and there should not be any areas of life that demand that men alone meet to resolve the present or to map out the future. Reconstruction demands a community of women and men making a concerted effort towards building up an empowering society that upholds and promotes the full humanity of every individual. Reconstruction will call for a healing process, for the hurts of the people are many, and the powers that operate in their lives are sick with the negative use of power and the fear of empowerment.

In seeking reconstruction, I am conscious that the "we African women" language does not hold. The cleavage that has been observed between women of the South and those of the North is a real one, and I wish to say this applies in all communities and all nations. We do not agree on what constitutes women's issues and especially on the method of seeking reconstruction. Above all it is very exasperating to have impatient liberators on one's back. Professor King states in her paper:

I am attracted by the dignity, strength, and affirmations of life found among so many African women and their traditional heritage of bonding and community-building, the rich and diverse resources of tradition, history, and culture of their great continent [156].

At different levels, African women are learning together about their religio-cultural context and are seeking to discover how to make it empowering for women. The solidarity we seek from the global sisterhood is that we get our rightful space to say our own word. It is no small task to undertake a critical examination of the religio-culture, especially if one hopes to move from knowing to living as one empowered to participate in reconstruction. Seeking to function in this way is like the biblical image of disarming the strongman who is guarding the gates to his stronghold.

Professor King reminds us that in seeking and talking about our new vision for human interaction, we should avoid the militaristic violent language of what we wish to leave behind. She suggests we talk about a spirituality that feeds acts of transformation. She suggests that we put our emphasis on praying, studying, and working for justice. On a theoretical level I am in entire agreement with her; only we should not forget that often the language of struggle and resistance is the only language that penetrates the barricades of the powers of domination. I agree entirely that we should do "No More" violence, and that we should say to all, "No More" violence. This is the stance of many African women for whom every confrontation is violence. And yet, when occasion demands, African women resort to traditional "shaming" devices to say "ENOUGH." In other words, we can affirm that it is possible to attain a violent-free world by an "alternative discourse," one that anchors on renewing the face of the earth and promotes walking together as women and men towards the community envisioned by life and justice-loving women. Such a transformative project calls for working with men, a moot point in the women's discourse. But surely we cannot say that there are no men who seek life and justice for all.

In the search for liberating hermeneutics, many women have claimed the biblical affirmation of our being created "in the Image of God" both for the promotion of women's self-worth and self-esteem and to protest dehumanization by others. Granted, this seems to be wearing thin, but without it the whole edifice of human relations seems to crumble and fall. If one is in the image of God, then one is expected to practice the hospitality, compassion, and justice that characterize God. The Akan say, "All human beings are the children of God." What this calls for is mutuality in our relationships, seeking "one earth community," one household of the God of life.

NOTES

[1] Bernadette Mbuy-Beya, "African Spirituality: A Cry for Life," in *Spirituality of the Third World*, ed. K.C. Abraham and Bernadette Mbuy-Beya (Maryknoll, NY: Orbis Books, 1994), 65.

[2] Robert Sutherland Rattray, *Hausa Folklore, Customs, Proverbs*, vol. 2 (New York: Negro University Press, 1969), 258/30 and 256/18. "Rimi tsakar gida, ranan sara mutanen gida na kuka, na waje na murna," or "They pat the cow before they begin to milk her."

[3] Remark made by Lisa Meo in the working group on Cultural Violence at the International Dialogue of Women Theologians on Violence against Women, Dec. 7-12, 1995, San Jose, Costa Rica.

[4] Virginia Fabella and Mercy Amba Oduyoye, eds., *With Passion and Compassion: Third World Women Doing Theology,* Reflections from the Women's Commission of the Ecumenical Association of Third World Theologians (Maryknoll, NY: Orbis Books, 1988).

[5] Peter J. Paris, *The Spirituality of African Peoples: The Search for a Common Moral Discourse* (Minneapolis, MN: Fortress Press, 1995), 22.

[6] David Sweetman, *Women Leaders in African History* (London: Heinemann, 1984), esp. the stories of Yaa Asantewa of Ghana and Nehanda of Zimbabwe, 83-97.

[7] Florence Abena Dolphyne, *The Emancipation of Women: An African Perspective* (Accra: Ghana University Press, 1991), 26-27.

[8] Ibid., 34-35.

[9] From the repertoire of the Dwensie Singers of Accra, directed by Dinah Reindorf, a Ghanaian Methodist.

EPILOGUE

Mary C. Grey

In December 1994 the forty-five women theologians who met in Costa Rica were drawn by a shared concern and commitment to end global violence against women. The welcome by the Minister of Culture as he inaugurated the Feast of Christmas in the main square in San Jose epitomized some of the tensions within which we struggled. For Christian theology is our shared discipline and the Feast of Christmas offers a message of peace and goodwill to all. Yet, as has been made clear in the pages of this book, Christianity and Church teaching have in reality proclaimed, at best, an ambiguous message to women as to their human value and dignity, and, at worst, an ethic which constrains us to accept many forms of violence. And despite efforts to make peace in Bosnia, Israel/Palestine, and in Northern Ireland, the world continues to look very much the same.

WHAT DID WE LEARN IN OUR DIALOGUE?

It is important to ask, then, what we learned in our dialogue. We knew this was the beginning of a complex process, and that the task would be immense. We also knew that part of the learning experience was the journeying to be with each other (and for some women that was fraught with difficulty and even danger), the openness to the experience, the willingness to share stories, to embark on a different analysis, to celebrate rituals, to listen and to be changed by what we heard.

The first part of the learning was simply to take in *how much listening was needed!* And that it happened in this place, in this specific context was crucial. For we heard the stories of Costa Rican women themselves, so that the immediacy and urgency of our theme was made very real, and this urgency was reinforced by the visit to a police station staffed by women, where women gave testimony of violent attacks and received counselling. Quite starkly, we were aware that it was a matter of life and death. And it is always vital that theologians, even liberation theologians, and especially Euro-Americans, be made continually alert to the danger that their theology can slip into theory divorced from praxis.

Those of us who were theologians from the North learned, through this quality of listening, about *the deep and continual level of pain and suffering* experienced by our sisters from the southern hemisphere and the multiple interlocking oppressions responsible for many forms of violence against women. We heard the anger and bitterness at the ever-new forms of neo-colonialism which keep these oppressions in force. In fact, there was simply not enough time or emotion to give fitting reaction to the sheer volume of the vast cartographies of suffering that we heard. On the other hand, it was perhaps difficult for some of our sisters in the South to admit that women in the North also suffered from multiple forms of violence: domestic, economic and cultural. It seemed as if we had many pieces of a broken jigsaw, with hardly the time to begin to fit them together to construct a more acceptable and human whole.

Through the listening process, we learned *much about respecting otherness and diversity.* It was not merely about un-learning stereotypes about each other. It was more about learning each other's contextually specific language of truth, justice, and integrity. Words with meaning in one context could operate imperiously and with undertones of superiority in another. Violence against women assumed different meanings in different cultures, and it was not the task of outsiders to make superficial judgments. It became clear that sisterhood was something to be worked towards and not assumed. How could one use again a language of relationality, connectedness, reconciliation without taking into account the history of colonialism, oppression, and Western collusion in this?

Further, we learned that to divide women into categories of victim and oppressor was an oversimplification and falsifying of the truth, as the heartrending story of Chung Hyun Kyung and Hisako Kinukawa has shown. From all parts of the world came stories of the active agency of women in changing and transforming the many injustices in their lives. It was from this fundamental truth that a grounding hermeneutic for both a theology and spirituality of liberation arose: *If it's good for poor women, it's good for all* [96].

Finally, the lesson we learned which gave rise to most hope was the *sheer power of ritual* when we were crushed and disheartened by the realities of socio-economic analysis. The very act of articulating and celebrating our hopes or listening to those of others and being invited to be in solidarity with them was both an indication of a way forward and a heartwarming affirmation that, as theologians, our discipline and faith are both precious resources for the struggle.

Yet there was still one unanswered question. We encountered each other not only with the anticipation that we would analyze the specificities of the violence from which women, collectively, suffer but also with the hope that we would create together a spirituality as a resource for the struggle to overcome and change this. So, it is fitting in this epilogue to draw together some of the insights expressed in the dialogue, in both the official and unofficial exchanges, and to try to develop them further, embodying one more step in this immense task.

TOWARDS A SPIRITUALITY FOR LIFE

It is hardly a surprise that spirituality for life must be thoroughly countercultural. From the early days of feminist theological analysis, Mary Daly's expressive and accurate word "nekrophilic," or death-dealing, has been used to describe society. Just how death-dealing it is on a global scale has been evocatively described in this book. Susan Thistlethwaite, in her chapter on military violence, has shown how the "culture of doublespeak" inevitably brings a culture of death [123]. It follows, then, that the spirituality needed must be for life, for survival, for all that is "biophilic," life-giving, and life-loving.[1]

It also comes as no surprise for Christian theology to create once more a countercultural spirituality, since most of the great Christian spiritualities have expressed counter-cultural trends. The early monastic movement began as a flight to the desert, as a rebellion against the corruption of the cities. The twelfth-century saints, Francis and Dominic both founded their congregations with distinctive spiritualities in solidarity with the poor, in opposition to poverty and injustice in their contemporary Church and society. The medieval Beguines grouped together independent women who challenged the current norm that women should be either married or in convents.

However, this particular Spirituality for Life takes as norm not only *option for the poor* but *option for poor women.* Poor women are not seen only as victims of many forms of interlocking oppressions, in all their global diversity; these women are also seen as agents of transformation, their own and that of society. In a very real way, this builds on Gospel values, for Jesus himself took the image of the woman who, with yeast hidden in three measures of meal, leavened the whole, as an image of the Kin-dom of God (Luke 13:21). This biblical woman is a striking image for transformation.

The notion of resistance to the "culture of death" provided a second dimension of spirituality for life. "I resist, I struggle, I protest, therefore I am" was the grounding point of so many levels of praxis and strategies for survival. Resistance took many forms. In Hyun Kyung's powerful story of Soo-Bock, her very compliance with the soldiers was a strategy *of* resistance and *for* survival [137]. Resistance could be at the level of unjust legislation, the violence of authority, the humiliation of false stereotyping. But for us as Christian theologians a particularly vital task was identified, namely, to resist the damaging theology of suffering, submission, and expiation and the theologies of redemption and salvation which continue to underpin them. It was apparent that the work of undoing the damage of this strand in Christian theology has scarcely begun. It will always be a task for spirituality to ensure that there are safe spaces where women find courage and voice to tell the stories of suffering and abuse which they were told were essential, part and parcel, of being "woman" and "Christian."

A third dimension of a "spirituality for life" is remembering. This was clearest in the stories of cultural violence. In the testimonies of colonial oppression from Fiji, New Zealand, Brazil, Ireland, Africa, and many other countries, women showed how, through the collective memory of their people being wiped out, identity was similarly destroyed. The recovery of the lost memories is an essential part of building a spirituality for life. This is what Michel Foucault has called the "insurrection of the subjugated knowledges"[2] and Elisabeth Schüssler Fiorenza named as the dangerous memories of both oppression and freedom.[3] We *re-member ourselves into being and shared cultural identity.*

Elsa Tamez's chapter on "Cultural Violence" shows how this task involves exploring the myths and symbols through which a specific culture is shaped, but also asking questions as to the origins of the story, tracking it to a life situation, and asking whether an alternative truth is possible [12]. Tracking what seems to be an eternal myth to a culturally specific context with a deconstructive analysis can be a truly liberating event. What Elsa approached *mythologically* is tackled by other colleagues theologically in many contributions to this book. Re-membering biblical stories as a resource for survival and flourishing, in context-specific interpretations, is an activity in all our grassroots communities of liberation, a catalyst for transformative action. Re-membering foremothers and sisters who have been victims of the culture of death is one way of not surrendering them to the kyriarchal oppressors. They hold together our strength for the struggle. They are our stars of inspiration.

The fourth dimension of a spirituality for life was that it must be an embodied *spirituality.* The broken and violated bodies of women and girls, both rich and poor, were our starting point. This is a reality which has yet to be acknowledged, let alone mourned for or repented by the world as a whole. The healed bodies, the wholeness and well-being of women and children in their bodily realities, are where the praxis of this spirituality is grounded. As Reinhild Traitler points out in her contribution, *it is the reconstruction of the violated bodies in this world* which has to be our focus [77]. Thus, a whole new symbolism is brought to the act of eating, the act of sharing food, not normally imagined in the normal practice of Christian Eucharist.

Hyun Kyung had told us that Soo-Bock's decision to eat was her decision to survive [131]. Sharing food came to be a powerful symbol for us of resisting violence, and also of the enjoyment of food and bodily life. Jesus' promise to the disciples that their "joy may be complete" took on a more specific and vitalizing meaning (John 15:11). A new sacramental symbolism can blossom where the embodied well-being of poor women is held to be sacred and is celebrated as such by our ecclesial communities. The sacramental traditions, as Rosemary Ruether wrote, can be harnessed for our struggle within an ecofeminist spirituality of liberation [34].

Spirituality for life brings a real challenge to conventional notions of sisterhood *and* solidarity, which must form an integral part of spirituality if the Costa Rica dialogue is to have enduring meaning. The wide-ranging implications this brings for women from different contexts raises again the question of diversity and sensitivity to social location. For solidarity to be anything but an empty word, it must be effective and take multiple-embodied forms.

For both sisterhood and solidarity to be authentic notions involves, first, being honest about what level of relationship is possible and appropriate. The legacy of the past means that trust-relationships cannot be presumed, but have to be worked for. It also involves a long-term commitment to global networking around injustice issues. Through this networking is learned the kind of solidarity-in-action which the specific issue or group needs. For Euro-American women theologians this might mean a re-ordering of priorities, a re-learning of different agendas, in order to practice effective solidarity. Effective solidarity asks as well for commitment to change and transformation, which is really what a spirituality for life is aiming for. But change and transformation will involve us in different journeys of conversion. The task for theologians from the North is to become involved in the necessary praxis of reparation and restitution with regard to the post-colonial countries grieving their loss of land and still suffering new forms of neo-colonialism and marginal status. All of us, from South and North, are engaged with the theological/ethical task of articulating what precisely is involved with the many processes of reparation necessitated by the ever-new stories of violence inflicted on vulnerable categories of people and on the earth itself in *both our hemispheres,* and with discovering from the "treasures old and new" resources which will empower our healing (Mt. 13:52).

DARING TO DREAM

A counter-cultural spirituality, by definition, swims against the currents of a culture of death. How does it keep alive its hope? From where does it achieve its energy? How does it celebrate amidst brutality and despair? What we experienced in the liturgies at Costa Rica, and in the many expressions of friendship and hope, is the activity of dreaming and envisioning a changed future. *We dream therefore we are, together we will be; the entire earth will be transformed.* Stella Baltazar's essay dreams of a Jesus who embodies the feminine principle of Shakti from the Hindu tradition [64].

Ada María Isasi-Díaz spells out concretely what kinds of preferred futures will bring justice for Hispanic women in the United States [97]. This is within a re-imaging of the Kingdom of God as the *kin-dom of God,* in order to avoid hierarchical, imperialistic, and sexist overtones. This activity of envisioning the kin-dom of God as the kin-dom of transformed relationships is both a well-tried praxis of spirituality and simultaneously something completely new.[4] Christian faith has always known that the shalom of peace and justice which Jesus proclaimed cannot be achieved in history in all its fullness. Nor should it be confined to an otherworldly reality, devoid of its transforming potential for embodied existence. Dreaming dreams, and especially dreaming communal dreams, has not been a valued activity for Christians in the way that it has been for aboriginal people in Australia, New Zealand, and Indians in North America, for example. *Homo faber,* technological man, has managed to devalue and individualize dreamtime as idle fantasy. Imagination has become atrophied. We are given *Disneyland* instead of *Promised Land.*

What is new is that women are keeping dreams alive in the name of the human and non-human communities. And what is more, as we begin to live out of the dream of a changed future, we provide a catalyst for change in the very act. A recent example from England may give a clue. In the eighties, when the campaign to get rid of nuclear cruise missiles was at its height, women established the famous Peace Camps at the gates of Greenham Common. At Easter time, a vigil was held on Good Friday right through Easter Sunday morning. This became a focus for dreams and prayers for a different world. With the police behind and the soldiers in front, the Gospel Passion story of Jesus was read. There was a genuine sense of apocalypse.[5] The women, joined by men from peace groups, children, and grandparents, with their symbols of peace "embracing the base," were already living out of a changed world. And of course, the weapons left!

Daring to dream is of course already a prophetic stance. Keeping hope alive is a prophetic stance. Prophetic action, hoping, longing are of the essence of a countercultural spirituality. But to celebrate the sacred dimension of life when all hope of the just society seems lost and the enemy is at the gate, be this Bombay, Lagos, Caracas, Chicago, or London, is to proclaim that, in the end, as the mystics say, "All will be well." The God who drives to justice keeps open the invitation to the messianic feast on the holy mountain, where there will be no more grief and sorrow, only joy. *If we can celebrate, then God is . . .*

NOTES

[1] "Nekrophilic" is used throughout Daly's work, but as a description of society's violence against women, has its most powerful expression in *GynlEcology: The Metaethics of Radical Feminism* (Boston: Beacon Press, 1985).

[2] Michel Foucault, *PowerlKnowledge: Selected Interviews and Other Writings, 1972-1977*, trans. Colin Gordon et al. (New York: Pantheon, 1980), 81.

[3] Cf. *In Memory of Her: A Feminist Historical Reconstruction of Christian Origins* (New York: Crossroad, 1983).

[4] The notion of the kin-dom of right and just relations is a developed dimension within feminist theology. See Carter Heyward, *The Redemption of God* (Washington, DC: University of America Press, 1980); Mary Grey, *Redeeming the Dream: Feminism, Redemption, and Christianity* (London: SPCK, 1989).

[5] See Angela West, "The Greenham Vigil: A Woman's Theological Initiative for Peace," *New Blackfriars,* 67 (1986),125-147. She develops here the stance of "waiting at the gates of Greenham" as an apocalyptic stance.

FINAL STATEMENT OF THE "WOMEN AGAINST VIOLENCE" DIALOGUE

HISTORY

The International Dialogue of Women Theologians on Violence against Women brought together forty-five women from twenty-four countries in San Jose, Costa Rica, from December 7 to 12, 1994. The dialogue was called by the Women's Commission of the Ecumenical Association of Third World Theologians, formed in 1983 by the women members who took part in the Sixth Conference of EATWOT in Geneva in 1983.

This was not the first time women members had felt the need to identify themselves not only as liberation theologians but as women liberation theologians. The commission created in 1983 has its roots in an event which took place during the EATWOT General Assembly held in New Delhi in 1981. The specificity of women within the Association could not have come earlier. It was only at New Delhi that women felt numerically strong enough to make their voices heard and where they were therefore empowered to challenge the male members and to have women's perspectives become an integral part of EATWOT's agenda. The breaking of the silence around sexism at this gathering is now remembered as the "irruption within the irruption."

The Geneva Conference was a dialogue between "Third World and First World" theologians. Of the latter, some were women. The Geneva Conference was a significant milestone: not only did EATWOT women organize themselves into a commission; they also discovered and joined hands with women theologians in Europe and North America who were doing critical theology of liberation in a discussion of the possibility of identifying and working on commission concerns. EATWOT women initiated a process which would culminate in a dialogue after a period of separate studies.

Since then, the commission has been working towards having an international team to prepare for the international dialogue. The final choice of the theme was made by the women at the EATWOT General Assembly in Nairobi in 1992. In the course of the preparation, women theologians from the Pacific, Japan, Palestine, and South Africa were invited. The three years' preparatory process included national, regional, and intercontinental consultations on the theme of "Spirituality for Life: Women Struggling against Violence." This dialogue, which is the culmination of the process started in Geneva in 1983, is at the same time the beginning of a new phase in the global networking of women doing liberation theology.

We gathered with many hopes and expectations. We hoped for the development of mutual accountability in the face of market economy, militarism, racism, and sexism. We hoped to transcend the barriers of geography, language, and histories of exploitation to build a genuine solidarity. In this conference, we aimed to transform the theologies of liberation toward a greater recognition of the significant oppression suffered by women, especially violence against them, and to allow the spirituality of women resisting violence to move the theologies, churches, and societies toward ending violence against women, children, and men in all parts of the world.

PROCESS AND METHOD

As theologians, we recognize that the method we use for our theological process cannot be separated from the content. This is why our method for dealing with the issue of violence against women had to start with an attentive and careful listening to the voices of women who have survived many different forms of violence. We listened to our abused sisters in three ways. First, we had an immersion experience in San Jose, visiting three programs that work with women who have suffered different kinds of violence. Second, we listened to two Costa Rican women who witnessed to the great violence they have suffered physically, psychologically, and economically and how their psychic/spiritual resources have enabled each of them to survive and affirm life for herself and her children. Third, stories in the Regional Reports presented at our gathering gave additional testimony of how women in different parts of the world not only endure suffering but also prevail against such evil.

We are also aware of the importance of process in the doing of theology. Therefore, because of the importance of community and solidarity for us, our process included a long sharing about the work, challenges, and joys of each and every one of the participants. The process also included sharing the studies some of us had made of six areas of violence against women: domestic violence, militarism, health/violence against women's bodies, ecology and violence against nature, economic violence, and cultural violence. The presentations were discussed in small groups as well as in plenary sessions. Finally, a very important element of our process was the expression and celebration of our beliefs through innovative rituals rooted in the different cultures of the participants.

ANALYSIS OF CONTEXT

The content and process of theologizing can also not be removed from its context, and therefore theological reflection on violence against women necessitates an analysis of the context of this violence.

Women around the globe suffer violence in an on-going and systematic way. Violence against women and their children remains all-pervasive. It is found in all regions of the world. Violence cuts across social, racial, and class status lines, cultural differences, and religious denominations. We have seen in the last years an increase of violence against women not only in society but also in churches and religions. As the resistance of women against all forms of violence has increased, so also has increased death-dealing politics of right-wing religious movements. Such violence cannot be reduced to isolated incidents or simply individual experience. It is global and systemic. It must be seen in the context of the globalization of exploitation and domination in all areas of life. It is produced and sustained by the systemic death-dealing powers of racism, ethnic prejudice, heterosexism (as an ideology), class exploitation, colonialism, and patriarchy, which are inter-structured and multiply each other in women's lives.

We, who are committed to the struggle of resisting, changing, and transforming the structures of violence and domination, have come together from all the corners of the world to explore critically and to reflect theologically on the discourses of violence: cultural, domestic, economic, military, corporeal, ecological, and symbolic-spiritual. Starting with the sacredness and dignity of every woman, we have not only analyzed the structures of violence but also shared experiences and practices of empowerment in order to develop a spirituality for life that is sustained by the vision of justice, self-determination, and well-being for all of creation.

The lived experience of women around the world must be understood in the context of the present neo-liberal economic model which is being imposed worldwide as the normative project for all. After the so-called "collapse of socialist countries" the entire world is being monopolized by this model with its hegemonic messianic claims. In the name of globalization, the hegemonic powers of multinationals, uncontrolled financial institutions, worldwide mass media, and rich countries in the geo-political North (USA, Europe, Japan, etc.) go on to invade poorer regions in the South and poor minorities in wealthy countries. Recent developments of GATT (WTO), NAFTA, and EAGA can be viewed in this context. The predatory logic of neo-liberalism is reflected in the values and attitudes it carries, namely growing individualism, brutal competition, profit, greed, and the ideology of survival of the fittest. As a consequence of this dominant logic, there is an increase of inequalities and the exclusion of persons and entire social groups. Women around the world constitute such a social group in their own particular contexts and cultural traditions. Our theological discourses and practices provide an alternative analysis, vision, and praxis and anticipate the transformations we seek.

TOWARD A LIBERATING HERMENEUTICS

These theological hermeneutics are drawn from the work done by women committed to liberation around the world.

Hermeneutical Principle

The principle that emerged from our analysis is: Whatever is good and life-giving for marginalized and excluded women is good for all. We developed concrete ways to ascertain what is good and life-giving.

1. We must employ a socio-political-economic as well as a religio-cultural analysis from women's perspective in order to determine what is good and life-giving for women.

2. We need to take into consideration a religious-cultural analysis, which includes:

a. Critiques of cultures from within the cultures, from the perspective of women's daily realities.

b. Critiques of dominant cultures from the cultures of the dominated—both those excluded and exploited within the dominant cultures and those of other cultures—from the perspective of women's daily realities.

c. Analysis of women's resistance against demonization and scapegoating, which deems women responsible for evil in the world.

d. Analysis of women's struggles to keep the cultural memories that empower them and make it possible to maintain their self-identity.

e. Critical study of fundamentalist ideas that present a totalizing view of life and reality, often used to control and disempower women.

f. Recognition of the fact that there is not only one truth because the revelation of God happens in different ways in different cultures. Therefore we reject the dominant cultures' attempts to consider themselves to be the only ones that have received the truth and therefore must be its guardians.

Alternative Anthropological Discourse

We recognize that the androcentric conception of humanity both produces and is an outcome of the patriarchal and hierarchical organization of societies which objectifies women and their bodies. The violence—sexual, economic, sociocultural, and religious—endemic to this system that degrades and victimizes women is generally accepted as the norm.

Yet, the human being, as part of the cosmos, calls for inter-connectedness, equality, and the well-being of all in harmony. Such a community, then, is intrinsic to personhood, and life is continually renewed, just as it is in nature, moving towards greater fulfillment.

Alternative Theo-ethical Discourse

This alternative discourse promotes a changed theo-ethical discourse. We recognize, however, that the development of an alternative theo-ethical discourse requires several moments. We must deconstruct the theo-ethical language and practice that produce, sustain, and legitimize violence against women, and we must reconstruct liberating discourses of resistance and well-being. We dare not, however, allow ourselves to be only reactive; we must allow the work of women against violence to generate new theological categories and visions. Therefore:

1. Accountability and responsibility for all levels of complicity with oppressive systems should inform our praxis and our theologizing.

2. Involvement in liberative praxis to end violence against women should be considered both a precondition of theological work and its constant companion.

3. It is necessary to develop a theological discourse where embodiment is central and where the objectification of women's bodies is denounced and renounced.

4. Identification of women's bodies as the symbol of sinfulness has to be explicitly rejected.

5. Systemic violation of the whole earth and its creatures has to be denounced as evil and sinful.

6. We call for an end to an exclusively male language about God, which reflects the patriarchal and patri-kyriarchal (a system of domination by the father/lord/master/husband) structures of oppression and the violence of Christian biblical and church traditions. We must reconstruct our God-images, drawing not only from human images, female and male, but also from the whole of creation in all its richness and diversity.

7. We must deconstruct doctrines of God based on notions of power as domination and control, and we must reconstruct our doctrine of God as a communitarian model of participation and relationship. The power of God is the power to transform death-dealing forces into life-giving energies, to change fear of the other into honoring one another, and to move from greed to sharing.

8. We must deconstruct the symbol of the cross as it is used to glorify death and legitimate violence, including violence against women. The cross must be reconstructed as a symbol of unjust state violence. It must also be connected to life as the tree of life from which new life grows.

9. Resisting violence is a deeply spiritual work interwoven with the struggle for life. We must deconstruct theologies of the spirit that devalue physical life, especially life as symbolized in the bodies, and particularly in the sexuality, of women. Spirit/body dualism must be reconstructed toward a whole-life energy of resisting, renewing, sustaining, healing, and growing. Such a spirituality of and for life is continually being renewed not only through our experiences of work and struggle but also through those of prayer, contemplation, and communion in worship and action.

10. We reject theologies of resurrection that are focused on the denial of natural death. Because we affirm the kin-dom of God, the family of God, as a historical reality, the resurrection of the body is a present reality.

11. Our ethics needs to be constructed to recapture a sense of the common good/fullness of life for all.

   a. Given our hermeneutical principle, this construction needs to start with the everyday life of women who struggle against violence.

    b. We affirm that women's rights are human rights, economic as well as political, and the construction of an ethics of the common good/fullness of life must keep this principle at the center.

    c. The common good is not anthropocentric, however, but includes the whole of creation. Violence to humans and to nature are interconnected and not separate. We need to develop theological hermeneutics as well as the eco-social analyses to expand and identify these interconnections.

    12. We recognize that the perpetration of violence against women in and by religions, churches, and theologies is a very significant part of each of these discourses of violence. We see violence against women in religion and churches, and how it is theologically and symbolically perpetrated, as a crucial area for further discussion and critique.

A CALL TO ACTION

Violence against women thrives on silence. For this reason, action for transformation should include making women's voices heard. For this purpose, we recommend the publishing of a newsletter for women doing liberation theology, one that could document the violation or the defense of women's rights in the churches and in their daily life struggles. It could also serve as a venue for sharing stories of empowerment and resistance to violence.

We are committed to establish women's theological networks in all our regions and to have inter-regional exchanges of publications and other resources.

To guarantee the continuity of our work, we resolve to develop a global fund for women in theology with limited resources. It could provide opportunities for the theological education of women especially from the Third World. It could also facilitate networking among women theologians, strengthen South-South relations, and promote campaigns to counter violence against women in churches and society (agreed common-action day: November 25).

To promote the dignity of women, we shall embark on a campaign against trafficking of women. We will call the attention of our churches to their accountability on this issue.

To uphold the integrity of creation, we will oppose the attempts to patent life forms and the impositions of GATT (WTO) economies which are harmful to the environment.

We recommend that the EATWOT Women's Commission:

    1) widen the circle of EATWOT women to include other geographical areas with contexts similar to the current membership.

    2) continue the dialogue inaugurated in Costa Rica by sponsoring a similar encounter in four years.

ABOVE ALL, WE CALL FOR AN END TO VIOLENCE AGAINST WOMEN. *NO MAS VIOLENCIA CONTRA LAS MUJERES!*